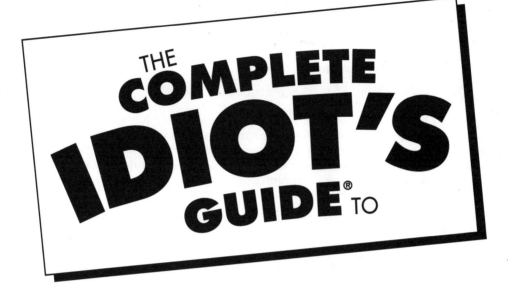

THE **COMPLETE IDIOT'S GUIDE**® TO

Buying and Selling Collectibles

Second Edition

by Laurie Rozakis

alpha books

Macmillan USA, Inc.
201 West 103rd Street
Indianapolis, IN 46290

A Pearson Education Company

This book is for Stephan, Joi, Samara, and Shelby Kravitz. "Make new friends, but keep the old; one is silver and the other gold." You are truly golden friends.

Copyright © 2000 by Laurie Rozakis

International Standard Book Number: 0-02-863836-0
Library of Congress Catalog Card Number: Available upon request.

02 01 00   8 7 6 5 4 3 2 1

Interpretation of the printing code: The rightmost number of the first series of numbers is the year of the book's printing; the rightmost number of the second series of numbers is the number of the book's printing. For example, a printing code of 00-1 shows that the first printing occurred in 2000.

Printed in the United States of America

0081-15760

Publisher
Marie Butler-Knight

Product Manager
Phil Kitchel

Managing Editor
Cari Luna

Acquisitions Editor
Randy Ladenheim-Gil

Development Editor
Amy Gordon

Production Editor
Christy Wagner

Copy Editor
Diana Francoeur

Illustrator
Jody P. Schaeffer

Cover Designers
Mike Freeland
Kevin Spear

Book Designers
Scott Cook and Amy Adams of DesignLab

Indexer
Tonya Heard

Layout/Proofreading
Darin Crone
Terri Edwards
Donna Martin

Contents at a Glance

Contents

ix

xiii

Foreword

The simple acts of accumulating and hoarding stuff no more makes one a collector than does having something "really old" make it a collectible.

Collectibles are defined not so much by how old they are but by how many people want them. And those who practice proper care and handling of their acquisitions are more likely to be collectors rather than just accumulators.

To oversimplify: All collectors are accumulators, though few accumulators are collectors.

Whether you think of yourself as a tenured collector, or merely among those curious folks wondering if they own something of value, this book will instruct and guide you.

In the collectibles marketplace, you will often hear: "The true value of an item is what one person will accept and another is willing to pay."

While true in a way, this hypothetical transaction omits some key elements. Imagine that the seller, due to ignorance or other variables, is asking only a fraction of what the item commonly brings. Of course this particular buyer is more than willing to pay the price asked, but this neither affects nor establishes "true value."

What happened here is that the buyer got a bargain. That's all.

Actual value is always based on scarcity and demand. An item can be 100 years old—thus qualifying as an antique—but if no one wants to own it, the actual value will be minimal. Just because something is old does not necessarily make it valuable.

Conversely, something of recent vintage can have exceptionally high value if it has become scarce and if there is already a demand for it.

When asked for some words of wisdom regarding what to buy that will later increase in value, some old-timers in the field are fond of saying "What will be valuable tomorrow is what you *don't* buy today."

While a tad cynical, there is an element of truth in that adage. What sells like crazy today will not likely be scarce tomorrow, and what does not sell now will most certainly be rare in time. The random element in this equation, as mentioned earlier, is that someone has to want it.

About 25 years ago, in one of our collectibles books, we coined the phrase "condition is everything." You will learn more about the importance of condition elsewhere in this book; however, the importance of keeping things in the best possible shape cannot be overstated.

For those fortunate enough to own well-preserved collectibles of value, they sooner or later are likely to consider selling. *The Complete Idiot's Guide to Buying and Selling Collectibles, Second Edition,* will be very helpful with that process.

You will learn the importance of properly appraising your collectibles—a task made easy for those with online access—as well as where the buyers are. It matters not what treasure or bargain is being offered if you are not plugged into the proper marketplace.

Fortunately, shopper publications exist for nearly every type of collectible. There is also an abundance of collector conventions and fan fairs. Also available are price guides (which may allow you to do your own appraising) with buyer-seller directories loaded with ads from dealers wanting to buy collections.

As important as any tool, though, is the Internet. The Net provides a cybermarket for nearly everything ever made. Whether you seek to build a collection, or dispose of one, there is a dot-com to accommodate you.

With this book as your companion, here's hoping you break tradition—and that what becomes valuable tomorrow is exactly what you buy today.

Jerry Osborne

An avid collector of pop culture since 1960, Jerry Osborne has authored 75 memorabilia price guides and reference books since 1975. Since 1986, Jerry has written the nationally syndicated newspaper feature "Mr. Music." He has founded and published several news and marketplace magazines for collectors, including the ever-popular *Discoveries*. Jerry's online aids include an appraisal service and a buy-sell collectibles site. Visit his home page for complete details: www.jerryosborne.com.

Introduction

In 1998 Mark McGwire's seventieth home-run ball sold for $3 million. The buyer? Comic book writer, artist, and baseball fan(atic) Todd McFarlane.

In 1999 a *Titanic* boarding pass went for $110,000. According to auctioneer Alan Gorsuch, it is the only known complete *Titanic* ticket. (The original owner, 19-year-old Anna Sofia Sjoblom, ended up safe and sound on lifeboat #16 with the pass still pinned to the inside of her coat.)

In 1996 the One True Card—a mint condition 1910 Honus Wager baseball card—was put up for auction. The card bears the undeniably homely image of a long-dead baseball player who was known to trade baseballs for buckets of beer. The card sold for $640,500. According to the best estimates, fewer than 40 of the Honus Wager cards exist, and only 10 of them are in collectible condition.

At the same auction ...

➤ Bill Bradley's New York Knicks jersey sold for $1,500; his gym shorts, for $2,200.
➤ A humidor made from a leather football and signed by Knute Rockne fetched $4,500.
➤ Babe Ruth's ink handprint went for $14,930.

A Shaker chest of drawers catch your eye? One collector anted up $99,000 for a lovely—and desirable—piece of Shaker furniture. Even a tiny Shaker box, less than three inches in diameter, changed hands for $12,000.

When it comes to collecting, there's no kidding around with children's toys. In 1999 a first-edition, hand-stitched Cabbage Patch Kid would set you back $8,000; and an original Barbie doll can cost $5,000. During the height of the Beanie Baby craze, one collector dropped $5,000 for six inches of fake fur and beans.

Noel Coward once said that the best souvenirs were memories. Fat lot he knew, we dedicated collectors jeer. It's pretty difficult to frame, catalog, or display a memory. The resale value is pretty weak, too. We like our souvenirs solid, something you can admire, fondle, and display. There's no denying that many collectors feel stirrings of avarice when a lovely object comes on the market.

If you've ever tried to find a parking spot at a flea market on a Saturday morning or ever been closed out of an online auction because the "room" is full, there's no doubt you've been bitten by the collecting bug. You search for affordable things of beauty and value. In a larger sense, however, you're also seeking a piece of the past. Beautiful objects from the past provide evocative memories of the rosy world of family memories and historic events. They connect us to our heritage and our world.

This book is designed to help the newcomer discover how to become a savvy collector. You'll learn which collectibles are hot—and which are not. I'll show you what's available in the major collecting fields and give you some brief historical background on the evolution of style and taste. Collecting beautiful objects is only part of the fun, however, so you'll also learn how to take care of your treasures and keep them beautiful and valuable for years to come.

In addition, you'll learn how to buy and sell desirables and collectibles on the Web, an exciting and important new marketplace. Along the way, you'll also learn how to distinguish between real collectibles and fakes, frauds, and just plain stupidity.

What You'll Learn in This Book

This book is divided into seven parts that take you through the process of becoming a confident collector. As you read, you'll see that collecting things involves much more than shopping and buying—that's the *easy* part! By the end of the book, you'll know how to create a collection that will bring you joy for life.

Part 1, "Why Is There a Boom in Collectibles?" first explores some recent finds and their prices. Then I'll survey the history of modern collecting so you can find out what makes a "thing" become a desirable or a collectible. In this part, you'll also discover whether you're a collector or an investor, learn how a collection is defined, and get the skinny on the hot collectibles.

Part 2, "Buying and Selling Like a Pro," helps you become a confident shopper. You'll learn how to determine a fair price for a collectible that you want to buy, and you'll find out how to bargain easily and effectively. Next is a lesson on how to appraise your collectibles. Get the inside scoop on the best markets for collectible sales, too. The final chapter in this part covers buying and selling through online auctions.

Part 3, "Paper Chase," first provides a detailed description of paper collectibles, including bookplates, postcards, theater memorabilia, and movie memorabilia. Then comes a chapter on collectible cards, including playing cards, Pokémon cards, and *Magic* cards. There's a chapter on comic books, too, as well as one on stamps and coins. Here, you'll discover the different types of postal stamps and stamplike things you may or may not want to collect, such as the new e-stamps. Find out how to start and maintain a paper money collection, too.

Part 4, "Feathering the Nest," starts off with a chapter on stuffed toys, focusing on Beanie Babies and teddy bears. Are Beanies still red-hot? Find out here! Then comes a chapter on other types of collectible children's toys, including dolls, dollhouses, miniatures, Disneyana, and mechanical toys. Puzzles are covered here too. The next chapter covers a wide range of home-centered collectibles and desirables, such as beer cans, bottles, pens, household implements, quilts, and records. Part 4 concludes with information on china and crystal, including earthenware, stoneware, bone china, porcelain, and ironstone.

Part 5, "Master of Arts: Photographs, Prints, and Paintings," explains how to get started collecting photographs, prints, lithographs, paintings, and drawings. The survey of different kinds of collectible drawings includes Fraktur, silhouettes, paper cutting, and caricatures.

Part 6, "All That Glitters Isn't Gold—but It's Probably Collectible," helps you learn about collecting antique jewelry, precious gemstones, gold, netsuke, and Native American jewelry. You will also acquaint yourself with silver, pewter, copper, brass, bronze, iron, and steel collectibles. There's also a brand-new section on one of today's hottest collectibles, costume jewelry.

Part 7, "Taking Care of Business," shows you how to catalog, display, store, clean, and insure your collection.

In Appendix A, I offer my predictions for future collectibles. That's where you'll learn which of today's items are likely to become tomorrow's desirables and collectibles. Appendix B has a bibliography in case you want to do some extra reading on specific collectibles.

More for Your Money!

In addition to all the explanations and teaching, this book offers valuable information to make it even easier for you to learn how to be a confident collector. Here's how to recognize these features:

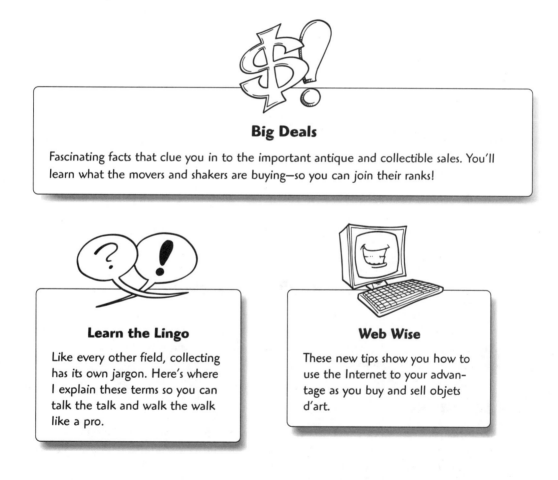

Big Deals

Fascinating facts that clue you in to the important antique and collectible sales. You'll learn what the movers and shakers are buying—so you can join their ranks!

Learn the Lingo

Like every other field, collecting has its own jargon. Here's where I explain these terms so you can talk the talk and walk the walk like a pro.

Web Wise

These new tips show you how to use the Internet to your advantage as you buy and sell objets d'art.

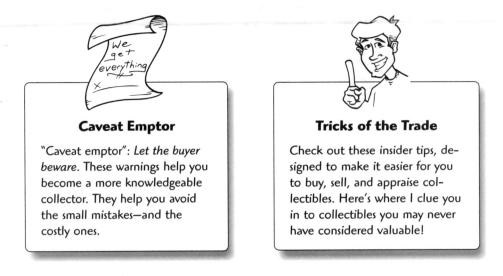

Caveat Emptor

"Caveat emptor": *Let the buyer beware*. These warnings help you become a more knowledgeable collector. They help you avoid the small mistakes—and the costly ones.

Tricks of the Trade

Check out these insider tips, designed to make it easier for you to buy, sell, and appraise collectibles. Here's where I clue you in to collectibles you may never have considered valuable!

Acknowledgments

As always, thanks to my wonderful husband and great kids. Your pride and support make it all possible. Dear hubby, thank you especially for your expert input on Chapter 11 and repeated fact checking. It's useful to have a famous comic book writer and landmark production executive living in the house. Thanks also to my dear son Charles for his section on *Magic* cards in Chapter 10 and our close friend Dennis Bengels for his invaluable suggestions for Chapter 8.

Thanks also to several people who brought in their prized collectibles for the cover photo: Kelly Cain, Susan Dunn, Phyllis Gault, Maureen McCarty, Joshua Rogers and Buffalo Gal Antique Mall, Eric and Shelia Schroeder, Sandra Schroeder, and Jenifer Willaert.

Special Thanks to the Technical Reviewer

The Complete Idiot's Guide to Buying and Selling Collectibles, Second Edition, was reviewed by an expert who double-checked the accuracy of what you'll learn here, to help us ensure that this book gives you everything you need to know about collectibles. Special thanks are extended to Dana Morykan.

Trademarks

All terms mentioned in this book that are known to be or are suspected of being trademarks or service marks have been appropriately capitalized. Alpha Books and Macmillan USA, Inc. cannot attest to the accuracy of this information. Use of a term in this book should not be regarded as affecting the validity of any trademark or service mark.

Part 1

Why Is There a Boom in Collectibles?

First collector: "Sonny, when I was just a little whippersnapper, you could pick up Shaker chairs from the trash heap."

Second collector: "And Beanie Babies were free with a McDonald's Happy Meal."

Recollections from the past are usually a bit distorted, but in this case most of the stories you hear about the good old days of collecting are true. There was a time—and not too long ago, either—when desirables and collectibles were as abundant as parking tickets. Alas, the past is no more.

Today, the mania to collect has reached such a fever pitch that some objects on eBay don't have time to get dusty before they're snapped up. Prices for many collectibles are rising higher than Don King's hair and faster than the national debt. Why? What has caused our national obsession with collecting? That's what you'll discover here in Part 1. So strap on your fanny pack, and let's get to work finding those bargain collectibles.

Chapter 1

It's Mine ... I Saw It First!— the Mania to Collect

In This Chapter

➤ The history of modern collecting

➤ Trash into treasure

➤ The collectibles craze

➤ Inside a collector's mind

Everyone collects something. Some people seek out celebrities' former possessions; others yearn for vintage costume jewelry, Pokemon cards, striking photographs, or first-edition books. Toys and beanbag plush are hotly sought-after collectibles; quilts and tools are sizzlin'. And who doesn't have a stamp or coin collector in the family? There are people who squirrel away gum wrappers; others have fine collections of beer cans, toothpicks, or hubcaps. If the object exists, someone somewhere desires it. And collects it. And loves that collection.

No one's immune to the collecting craze. Fed up with some underperforming mutual funds, a middle-aged insurance agent from New York invested her capital in Beanie Babies. She sank $12,000 in the plush toys and claims that her investment more than doubled when Ty announced they would no longer be producing any Beanies.

In this chapter, you will learn about the human desire to collect objects of beauty and value. You will discover that the urge to collect is as old as time itself—and as powerful. In addition, you will find out how modern collecting got started. This chapter will help you discover that you're not alone in your desire to collect whatever you collect: whether it be baseball bats, beer cans, or bracelets.

Big Deals

In 1874, Illinois farmer Joseph F. Glidden invented the first practical barbed wire. Greeted with rage, the prickly new invention inspired bitter feuds when land boundaries were disputed. However, a decade later, more than 120 million pounds of barbed wire were being sold annually. In 1957, Jesse S. James of Maywood, California, started a barbed wire collection. James meticulously catalogs and arranges his collection of antique barbed wire on 1½-by-3-foot panels, each containing 30 pieces of wire 18 inches long. James is not alone in his passion; barbed wire has become a sharp collectible.

You Bought a *What?*

The urge to collect is as ancient as the drive for food, clothing, and shelter. Historically, only the nobility, the highest-ranking members of the church, and the very wealthy had the time and the funds to patronize the arts. Artifacts of the past were high priced, scarce, and somewhat intimidating. Art auctions were held in imperial Rome, featuring war booty and elegant fakes.

In the 1400s, the great nobles of France and Italy followed Machiavelli's advice to princes to "also show his esteem for talent, actively encourage able men, and pay honor to eminent craftsmen." The great nobles' treasure troves manifested the glory of the state but were highly seasoned by the individual's personal taste and training.

Moving Uptown?

Prehistoric collectors took this biological imperative to the max; they believed they could transport their collections with them from this world to the next. We can determine the social status of the ancients by the items found in their tombs. Art objects, for example, were symbols of the deceased's important status. Art still signifies status and value today.

As a more affluent middle class began to emerge, they too were eager to acquire art and artifacts, if only to display evidence of their upward mobility. But it was not until the Industrial Revolution that the average Joe or Jane could even begin to think of satisfying their lust for collecting. For most people in the first half of the nineteenth century, life was too nasty, brutish, and short to allow for the luxury of amassing pretty things. Only members of the upper classes had the money and time to collect fine paintings, ancient coins, rare musical instruments, and the like.

Mass Wants Class

During the second half of the nineteenth century, the development of new types of machinery allowed goods to be mass produced. This drastically affected the lives of our forebears. Items that were previously created by hand through laborious effort could now be produced easily and quickly—and churned out by the tens of thousands. Factories sprang up in nearly all the large cities, ushering in a plethora of consumer goods. Couldn't get to the shop? Not to worry. Sears and Roebuck had a catalog that was heavy enough to break your foot. Didn't want to read all those pages? The traveling salesman would bring these new marvels right to your door and talk the money right out of your pocket.

Thanks to the Industrial Revolution, even the poorer classes could become collectors. Although they still couldn't ante up enough for an Old Master, diamond pendant, or walnut whatnot, they *could* now afford to collect such mass-produced paper items as cards, matchbooks, and bookmarks that were given away by the thousands. Marbles, tops, and small toys were almost as easy to procure and barter.

Naturally this situation distressed some fastidious collectors, whose acquisitions of rare and beautiful objets d'art were announced with pomp and circumstance. It remains a thorn in the side of a few high-minded antiques dealers who deplore the tendency of people to collect anything of lesser magnitude than fourteenth-century ivory diptychs. But the anguished cries of the antiques elite have been shouted down by the squeals of joy from the new members of the sport of millionaires and monarchs.

Web Wise

The World's Fair Collectors Society, Inc., is dedicated to preserving the history of world expositions—past, present, and the future. For more information contact Mike Pender, President, WFCS, P.O. Box 20806, Sarasota, FL 34276-3806; 941-923-2590; e-mail: wfcs@aol.com; Web site: members.aol.com/Bbgprod/ wfcs.html.

Tricks of the Trade

The selling of pop memorabilia, pioneered especially by Sotheby's auction house in London, has become big business—particularly if the item involves a personal association with such superstars as the Beatles and the King (Elvis, not B.B.). For example, Elvis's 1942 Martin D-18 guitar fetched $180,000 in 1991.

Take and Toss

Throughout the first half of the twentieth century, factories improved both the quality and quantity of their goods. Here are some of the goods that flooded the market:

➤ Comic books

➤ Inexpensive cameras

➤ Baseball cards

➤ Depression glass

➤ Records

➤ Radios

➤ Toys

➤ Costume jewelry

Big Deals

One of the world's most unusual collections belongs to Fay and Jimmy Rodolfos of Woburn, Massachusetts: They collect Dionne Quintuplet memorabilia. The quints were born on May 28, 1934, to Elzire and Oliva Dionne in rural Ontario, Canada. They were the first identical set of quints that had ever survived. Elzire was only 25 years old at the time and already had given birth to six children. She received no prenatal care with the quints until a week before their birth; the first three girls were delivered by midwives before the doctor arrived. The Rodolfos' collection includes "Famous Fives" dolls, postcards, scrapbooks, lamps, newspaper and magazine articles, photos, paper dolls, and much more.

The enormous quantity of available goods led to a change in the mass consciousness. Gone was Grandma's "a stitch in time saves nine" mentality. In its place was the belief in the value of replacement. With goods so inexpensive, why take the time and trouble to repair an item? Better to throw it out and get a new one.

The Collectibles Craze

You learned that people are driven to seek food, clothing, shelter—and pretty things. Until recently, most people were able to hold that last need in check. However, all that changed about a generation ago when people suddenly went gaga over collectibles.

The collectibles craze kicked in around the 1960s. Up until then, people believed that they could buy bigger and better every year. As long as technology continued to chug along, materials were available, and labor was cheap, we could have what we wanted when we wanted it.

A Lucky Few

But life began to change in the 1960s, and not just because the mini-skirt was invented. The price of many raw materials began to climb; labor followed soon after. Producers began to snip a little here and there. The design might be a little less detailed. Perhaps the fabric was not as thick. As inflation rose, Americans saw that their dollar wasn't stretching as far as it had just a few years before. The good old days of steady prices and improving quality slipped away in the wake of the Vietnam War and the increasing spiral of inflation.

Some people cued in to these changes earlier than others. A handful of these far-seeing folks went out and bought old models of selected items, recognizing their superior quality and design. These items usually cost very little, because most people still wanted new goods.

Web Wise

The National Cuff Link Society (NCLS) is a networking source for cuff link collectors and wearers. Membership includes a giant quarterly magazine, "The Link," free classified ads, shop discounts, price guidance, an annual convention, and sources for great cuff links. Their Web site is www.cufflink.com.

Inside a Collector's Mind

Goods from the past represent different things to different people. Collectors are motivated by some or all of these feelings:

➤ A desire to forge links to the past
➤ A love of nostalgia
➤ A belief that old items are better made
➤ A connection to childhood and simpler times
➤ A genuine admiration for the item
➤ A lust to make money

So, Should You Save That Wrapper?

How does something become valuable? While anything can become a desirable, collectible, or antique, certain objects undeniably become more valued than others. What makes some objects eagerly sought collectibles, while others languish on the back shelves? Why, for example, are pulp magazines from the 1920s more sought after than their far rarer counterparts from the turn of the century?

All items pass through the same three steps when they evolve from a functional item to a collectible:

1. **Item is a thing.** The item is valued for its function. Very few people, if any, collect it. The item has virtually no value as a collectible.

Caveat Emptor

The speed with which an item becomes a collectible determines how stable its value will be. In most cases, the more slowly an item becomes a collectible, the stronger the market will continue.

Tricks of the Trade

Blow torch collectors have established a group to promote and preserve the history of blow torches. Members are communicating, trading, and selling through their newsletter, *The Torch*. For a copy, send $2.50, or $10 for a year's membership. For information contact: Ron Carr, 3328 258th Ave. SE, Issaquah, WA 98029-9173.

2. **Interest builds.** The item attracts interest and collectors perk up. At this point, it is a *desirable*. (More on terms in Chapter 2, "The Brass Ring.") This creates a supply/demand situation that often drives prices up.

3. **Item is a collectible.** The item becomes valuable. Many people want to possess it for its appearance, not its function.

In addition to these characteristics, there are several other qualities that make an item into a collectible. Here's my Fab Five list:

1. Perceived beauty
2. Quantity
3. Price
4. Links to the present
5. Historical links

Let's look at each quality in detail.

Perceived Beauty

There is no doubt that beauty is in the eye of the beholder, especially when applied to collectibles. Nonetheless, a true collectible, like a beautiful person, has an appeal that is recognized by virtually everyone.

Even if the item doesn't strike your fancy for some reason, you can still recognize its appeal to others. There's a sexiness about the item that gives a familiar tingle. You can appreciate its craftsmanship, color, or shape; admire its glitter or gleam.

Collectors develop a feel for each item's appeal by viewing and handling a variety of the same objects. For example, if you are looking at stamps, see how you feel about the color, shape, and size of the design.

Quantity

Some collectibles become hot because there are enough of them to fire up a market. But if there are too many of them, the item would likely never become a collectible because everyone would have it. The market would be flooded by the item.

My husband, Bob Rozakis, is a recognized authority on comic books and comic art. He has been in the comic book business for nearly a quarter of a century. Every year, starry-eyed people come up to him at conventions and parties and say, "Gee, I'd have a copy of *Action #1* if my mother hadn't thrown it out when I went into the Army (left for college, got married, had a sex change operation, etc.)." My husband always responds, "If everyone had a copy of the comic, it would be too common to be a collectible. What makes that comic, and others like it, a hot collectible is that very few people have a copy of it."

As a result, people who hoard today's objects because they think they will become tomorrow's collectibles would be much better off spending their time cleaning out their closets. By their combined efforts, these people are working against each other. For an object to become a collectible, there must be enough of them to spark interest, but not enough to make them commonplace.

Learn the Lingo

Items of value are classified as **desirables, collectibles,** and **antiques.** I explain these terms in Chapter 3, "If Someone Makes It, Someone Else Collects It." Stay tuned.

Price

How much an item costs is a very important factor in whether or not it becomes a collectible. Nearly all desirables and collectibles start off being affordable by most people, thus creating a broad base of support. Within nearly all collectibles, however, a few items are more expensive, and finally the very fewest examples are most costly.

For instance, many stamp collectors are kids who start their collections by steaming canceled samples off envelopes. As they grow up, they buy the stamps they can afford, such as limited issues and first-day covers. If these collectors become sufficiently affluent, they can buy more and more expensive stamps to add to their collections. But if an item becomes too expensive, only the most wealthy collectors can afford to stay in the game.

Caveat Emptor

"Instant collectibles" were created to cash in on the collecting craze. They are aimed at the everyday person who believes he or she is investing in a legitimate collectible. Instant collectibles come in many forms; the most common are the "limited edition" plates, statues, figurines, ingots, and medals. Buy instant collectibles only if you like them as home decorations; they are unwise investments.

Links to the Present

Collectibles that have the greatest appeal usually have parallel items in the present. For example, there are antique toys and new toys, old portraits and new portraits.

Collectors like to collect items that are still being created in some form. This gives the present-day collection a vitality lacking in items that have merely historical interest.

Historical Links

Most collectibles stir powerful feelings about the past, a time we imagine as being kinder and gentler. For example, Beatles memorabilia brings back memories of the exciting 1960s; movie posters from the 1920s carry echoes of the silent films. The more a group of popular culture items captures the mood of the past, the more likely the items are to become collectibles, if they are not already valued.

The Least You Need to Know

➤ No matter what people admit in public, everyone collects something. And they feel very passionate about their collection.

➤ The Industrial Revolution enabled everyday people to satisfy their urge to collect pretty things.

➤ All items pass through the same three steps when they develop from a functional item to a collectible: (1) The item is a thing, (2) interest builds, (3) the item is a collectible.

➤ Objects become collectibles because of their perceived beauty, quantity, price, links to the present, and historical links.

The Brass Ring

Marilyn Monroe's famous "Happy Birthday" dress fetched $1,267,500 at a 1999 auction. Okay, so it *is* adorned with 6,000 rhinestones, and it did bewitch a president; but, still, $1,267,500 for a used dress? Yet, there are those who think this is a great deal: "We got the bargain of the century," claims buyer Peter Siegel, owner of a New York City memorabilia store. "We were prepared to go much higher," he added. From a collector's standpoint, he *did* walk away lucky. At the same auction …

➤ A diamond band that Marilyn Monroe received from Joe DiMaggio after their 1945 wedding sold for $772,500.

➤ Her traveling case and makeup went for $268,800.

➤ Even her temporary license brought big bucks—$145,600. Imagine what her permanent license would be worth to a serious collector!

The Guggenheims, Vanderbilts, and Astors collected art and homes. Queen Elizabeth of England has her horses; Princess Di went for baubles with hefty price tags. Baseball-great Reggie Jackson collects cars. Comedian Morey Amsterdam collected figurines of cellists. Robert Goulet collects frog tschotches, and Red Skelton collects clown statues. I'm every bit as happy with the plastic costume jewelry I pick up at a flea market for $2.00.

What conclusions can we draw from this amazing variety? If someone makes it, someone else will collect it. But there's more to collecting than the lust for acquisitions, as you will learn in this chapter.

I'll start by explaining just what a collection is—and is not. Then you can explore your own feelings about collecting by completing an easy worksheet. Next, we'll explore the spiritual, educational, emotional, and cultural satisfaction that collecting brings to the true believers. Finally, you'll learn some of the other advantages of being an educated collector.

What Is a Collection?

Everything and anything had a place in the great "collections" of the seventeenth century: porcelain, clocks, mermaids, Aztec headdresses, silk, cameos, jewels, scientific instruments, busts, statues, shells, medals, pistols, enamels, suits of armor, weapons, strange furniture. But a *collection* is more than a random accumulation of objects. That's the mess the Collier Brothers created with their piles of newspapers and trash. A collection, in contrast, is a methodical arrangement of objects of beauty and value. A collection has a plan, a governing principle (which may simply be to please the collector).

Learn the Lingo

A **collection** is a set of related objects that have value to their owner. The objects are arranged in a logical system or connected by a common theme. For example, the collection might be comprised of rooster objet d'art, in different forms. It might include rooster cookie jars, salt-and-pepper shakers, and pot holders, for example. Real roosters need not roost here, however.

Now that you know what a collection is, let's see why collecting has offered so much satisfaction to so many people through the ages and around the world.

The Rewards of Collecting

Why collect? You've learned that collecting is an innate drive. It prompted our ancestors Og and Grog to stash pretty bones in the back of their cave; it moved King Tut to make sure that his tomb was loaded with enough gold to sink an ocean liner. Throughout the ages, people have been moved to collect things that strike their fancy, so you're in good company. Take a closer look at your feelings about collecting by filling out the following "Collecting Inventory" worksheet.

Collecting Inventory

To see where you stand as a collector, complete this worksheet. Use your (collectible) Mount Blanc pen. If necessary, add some blank paper to provide more room for your answers.

1. List your current collections.

   ➤ _____
   ➤ _____
   ➤ _____
   ➤ _____
   ➤ _____

2. What are the best pieces you have in your collections? What makes them so special?

   ➤ _____
   ➤ _____
   ➤ _____
   ➤ _____
   ➤ _____

3. What are your strengths as a collector?

   ➤ _____
   ➤ _____
   ➤ _____
   ➤ _____
   ➤ _____

4. What are your weaknesses as a collector?

   ➤ _____
   ➤ _____
   ➤ _____
   ➤ _____
   ➤ _____

5. List the things you would collect if you had the time, money, or expertise.

   ➤ _____
   ➤ _____
   ➤ _____
   ➤ _____
   ➤ _____

continues

continued

6. List five reasons why you enjoy collecting.

➤ _____

➤ _____

➤ _____

➤ _____

➤ _____

Satisfaction Guaranteed

Collecting gives spiritual, educational, emotional, and cultural satisfaction. Because there's no limit to the items people can collect, there's something for everyone. Below are some of the primary advantages gained from collecting. Use these advantages as ammunition the next time your partner complains, "You're buying *more* inkstands? Don't we have enough by now to supply the whole danged U.S. Congress?" Your answer? See the following list:

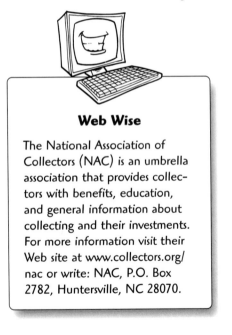

Web Wise

The National Association of Collectors (NAC) is an umbrella association that provides collectors with benefits, education, and general information about collecting and their investments. For more information visit their Web site at www.collectors.org/nac or write: NAC, P.O. Box 2782, Huntersville, NC 28070.

1. **Express yourself.** Today, we're often labeled by our jobs. I'm a professor and a writer; you may be a doctor, accountant, postal carrier, or bus driver. At parties, people say to me, "Oh, you're a teacher." Sometimes I'm labeled by my children's accomplishments or even by my husband's career. Like you, I'm rarely appreciated for myself. Collecting something that has meaning, something that you have selected, allows you to express yourself. Your collection shows the world that you are special. Many times our day-to-day jobs don't allow us to express our individuality. Collecting allows us to show our more creative side.

2. **Meet people.** Whether you're a new parent isolated by the demands of babykins, a recent divorcée or widow, or just an average Joe or Jane burdened by the demands of family and work, meeting people can be difficult. Sure, we grab some face-time with our coworkers at the water cooler and schmooze over our egg salad at lunch, but it's really hard to connect with the people who share our interests.

How often do you find yourself talking about work when you'd really rather be talking about the antique table you got at auction last Saturday or the perfume bottles you picked up at the little antique store in Saratoga? A collectibles show or convention is a great way to bring people with common interests together.

It's not surprising that many collectors have best friends who are also collectors. Some have even met their spouses over a convention table or at a flea market. And people who collect together tend to stay together—unless your partner gets to the item that you want first!

3. **Relieve stress.** No time to eat. No time to think. No time to breathe! Find yourself s-q-u-e-e-z-e-d in this box? You're not alone. Whether you're a corporate lawyer or a librarian, a homemaker or a hat maker, you're pulled in a dozen different directions every day. We live in a very stressful age, pressured to achieve and accomplish with nary a chance for winding down.

Collecting allows you the opportunity to relax and refresh your soul. I've seen highly placed business people, their faces lined with tension and their shoulders slumped with exhaustion, barking orders to equally harried subordinates as the job never seems to get done. But on the weekend, these same people, their faces alight with pleasure, are jovial and relaxed as they catalog their stamps, sort their coins, or hunt out an ivory statue to add to their collection. Less fattening than chocolate, less expensive than a Caribbean vacation, less sadistic than a Stairmaster, collecting allows you to unwind and enjoy life.

4. **Expand your knowledge.** Collectors learn fascinating facts about history, economics, math, social science, and art—to name just a few fields. Depending on your collecting interest, you might find out more about modern art, printing, or metalwork, for example.

If you're like the rest of us, you probably never got drafted to play major league football or tapped to sing on Broadway. Your still life of cereal-and-strawberries

Caveat Emptor

Don't throw out the baby with the bath water: The Web is a wild and wonderful place, but striking up a close professional relationship with a reputable collectibles store in your town is still an excellent way to get fabulous merchandise at fair prices. This topic is covered in detail in Chapter 4, "Shop 'Till You Drop."

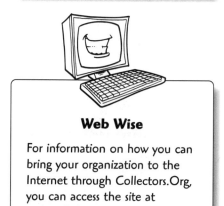

Web Wise

For information on how you can bring your organization to the Internet through Collectors.Org, you can access the site at www.info@collectors.org.

Tricks of the Trade

Often, dealers will buy a *lot* (a predetermined amount) of merchandise, in order to acquire those they want to resell. Savvy collectors look for items sold by dealers who are not specialists in that area.

Web Wise

As its name suggests, the International Swizzle Stick Collectors Association promotes swizzle stick collecting. The group holds conventions and issues a publication titled *Swizzle Stick News*. For more information, visit their Web site at www.theplant.com/issca.

isn't displayed in the Museum of Modern Art; you hung up your toe shoes a few years ago. But many successful collectors have attained a level of personal excellence in an area they, and others, find compelling. Such people are sought after for their knowledge and respected by others for what they know. Collecting gives you the opportunity to gain knowledge that you find interesting. It lets you be the head weenie at the roast.

5. **Have fun.** Most of us spend all day chained to a desk and all night sprawled in front of the TV. In between, we do endless loads of laundry, bankrupt ourselves at the supermarket, and make only marginally successful attempts to get fit. Collectibles get you up and out to spend time with people who have similar interests.

6. **Make money.** Finally, many collectors have learned that they can make a tidy piece of change through their collection. An experienced collector, for instance, can often find bargains from dealers. If you're willing to develop a keen eye, study hard, and do your homework, there's gold in them thar collectibles. See Chapters 24, "Inventory and Insure," and 25, "Spit and Polish," for detailed ways to make money buying and selling your collectibles.

Smarty-Pants

There's nothing stopping you from running out right now and buying all the pretty things you crave. (Okay, so there's the little matter of money, but that's why we have credit.)

Seriously, you know better. Credit line or not, you realize that your collection will bring more satisfaction (as well as profit, if you so desire) if it is put together gradually with care and understanding.

By learning as much as you can about collecting in general and your specialty in particular, you'll be able to ...

➤ Pay a fair price for pieces.

➤ Get pieces in good condition.

➤ Locate the exact pieces you need.

➤ Differentiate between the real thing and a fake or reproduction.

➤ Know how to take care of your collection.

➤ Create a collection of enduring value.

So take your time and work your way through this book carefully. The more you know, the better your collection will be. Rome wasn't built in a day ... but it's lasted for centuries. The same can be true for your collection, if you wish.

The Least You Need to Know

➤ A collection is a set of related objects that have value to their owner.

➤ Collecting gives spiritual, educational, emotional, and cultural satisfaction.

➤ Collecting objects you value allows you to express yourself, meet people, and relieve stress.

➤ Collecting is also a great way to expand your knowledge, have fun, and maybe even finance that sports car you've wanted since you were 18.

Chapter 3

If Someone Makes It, Someone Else Collects It

In This Chapter

➤ Discover if you're a collector or an investor—or a pack rat with an attitude

➤ Understand the difference among desirables, collectibles, and antiques

➤ Check out the law of supply and demand as it applies to collecting

➤ Get the inside skinny on the hot collectibles—find out which ones are sizzling now

Collecting beautiful and valuable objects has it all: a satisfying aesthetic experience, the possibility of economic gain, and pride of ownership. In addition, your collection makes an important statement about you and what you represent. Whether you are aware of it or not, your collection projects an image of how you perceive yourself and how you want others to perceive you.

This chapter focuses on *you* and collecting. First, you'll take a short, easy quiz to determine whether you have the heart and soul of a true collector. Then I'll show you how to figure out whether you prefer to collect or invest. As you will discover, this distinction makes a big difference in your approach to the collecting.

I'll give you a clear-cut definition of *desirables, collectibles,* and *antiques* so that you can tell how objects are classified. Then it's a quick class in Economics 101 so that you understand how the antique and collectibles markets operate. Finally, you find out which collectibles are *in*—and which ones are *out.*

Altogether, the information in this chapter will help empower you to stop amassing "stuff" and start collecting items of value and pleasure. I'll give you the tools you need

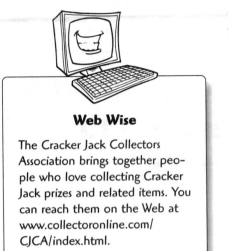

to realize that you *can* be a successful collector—that you can enjoy collecting as a pastime, hobby, or career.

If It Walks Like a Duck ...

You can tell a zebra by its stripes, a duck by its quack. Psychologists claim to be able to tell a collector just as easily by similarly clear-cut signs. No less-august figures than psychiatrist Sigmund Freud and naturalist Charles Darwin believed that collecting was instinctive. Psychologists, in contrast, have argued that collecting is a culturally stimulated experience, like the urge to crunch your abs or eat something squishy that you can't pronounce. But, hey, we don't remember who *those* psychologists were. At any rate, take the Collector Quiz in this chapter to see if you've got the mentality of a collector.

Sharpen your (1939 World's Fair) pencil. Then take this quiz to see whether you have the authentic collector mentality.

Collector Quiz

Yes	No	
❑	❑	As a child, you hoarded treasures in your special treasure box. This was usually an old cigar box or candy container, but a shoe box with a lid would do in a pinch.
❑	❑	As you grew up, you replaced all those cat's-eye marbles and baseball cards with more expensive and meaningful memorabilia.
❑	❑	You would still have your baseball cards if your mother (sister, aunt, father, etc.) had not thrown them out when she (he) cleaned out the attic (garage, closet, basement, etc.). You remind your mother (etc.) of this transgression at least once a year—normally at a major family gathering.
❑	❑	Certain objects give you great pleasure because of their beauty and value.
❑	❑	If you had more money, you would collect more expensive and beautiful objects.
❑	❑	You feel that possessing something beautiful is an exhilarating experience, a real rush.
❑	❑	You believe that your collection or collections say something about you, your values, and beliefs.

Yes	No	
❑	❑	You agree that a person's collection reveals his or her cultural, social, and economic status.
❑	❑	You have lusted after someone else's collection or any part thereof.
❑	❑	When you see toys you played with as a child for sale at garage sales, you get so excited that you buy them.

Bonus Questions:

❑	❑	At least once in your life, you spent too much for an object because you believed that it would appreciate in value. Or just because you really liked it. A lot.
❑	❑	You lose track of time when you stare at your treasures. Hours can pass this way.
❑	❑	You have been known to fondle the objects you collect.
❑	❑	Your heart goes pitter-patter when you are near one of your beloved possessions.
❑	❑	You dream about finding the rarest item associated with your hobby—an Action #1 comic, for example.
❑	❑	You would never consider selling your collection unless your family was starving and the rent was six months overdue—and then you'd still stop and think it over.

Score:

1–2 yes answers	You have been known to drive past a flea market without kicking yourself the next morning.
3–4 yes answers	You can pass up the pot holder shaped like a turkey but not the bargain-priced toys from Mickey Dee's.
5–6 yes answers	No antique store is safe when you're loose.
7–8 yes answers	You've been bitten by the "collecting bug"; hide your charge card.
9–10 yes answers Yes to all the bonus questions	You're the real thing, bunkie: Collector Americanus. Either you can write this book, or you should add it to your book collection.

Are You a *Collector* or an *Investor?*

Each of us hopes that our family heirlooms and flea market finds will turn out to be worth a fortune. But a collector isn't in it solely for the bucks. Study the following lists to see whether you can tell the difference between a collector and an investor. Which descriptions cling to you like a wet (collectible) T-shirt?

Collectors ...

➤ Save a collectible because they like the item.

➤ Consider items in the collection as children to be cherished.

➤ Are interested in buying, selling, trading—and possessing.

➤ Are passionately in love with the items they collect.

➤ Get pleasure from their collection that cannot be reckoned in terms of money.

Investors ...

➤ Buy the item only because they want to resell it at a profit.

➤ Consider items in the collection to be merchandise.

➤ Are interested in buying, selling, and trading.

➤ Are excited over the thought of making a profit from the item, not possessing it.

➤ Are business people, first and foremost.

Tricks of the Trade

Consider becoming a collector, but adopt and use the best traits of a dealer. Learn to use a dealer's methods to get what you want for your collection. Buy what you can, keep the best for yourself, and resell the rest. That way, you can have your cake and display it, too.

This is no time to sit on the fence, kiddo. You can't be a wuss with *me* because collectors and investors often work at cross-purposes. After all, a collector wants to own the finest pieces, but these are the very pieces that a dealer needs to turn a profit. Therefore, you have to stand your ground now. What will it be? Collector or investor? Not deciding before you start buying will make it impossible for you to collect with a pure heart or invest with a sharp mind.

Put down your (antique jade) worry beads and dry your tears. I'll let you off the hook a little. Today, it is very hard to be a pure collector. The finest pieces in just about any collection usually cost some serious money. As a result, you are going to have to learn to wheel and deal to build a respectable collection. That's why you bought this book, right?

Three's Company: Desirables, Collectibles, and Antiques

I wish people would ask: "Can I give you a vacation home in Aspen?" or "How *did* you get to be so gorgeous?" but instead they always ask me these three questions:

1. What is a *desirable?*

2. What is a *collectible?*

3. What is an *antique?*

And sometimes I even get this: When do desirables and collectibles become antiques?

No need for you to be in suspense, so let's answer these questions right now.

Desirables

A *desirable* is an object that people covet but whose future value is unknown. For example, desirables include the following things:

➤ Beanie Babies

➤ Danbury Mint objects

➤ Pokemon cards

➤ Premium toy rings

➤ *Star Wars* figures

➤ Transformers (plastic toys)

Learn the Lingo

A **desirable** is a collected object whose value is uncertain. Desirables include Coca-Cola beanbag toys, *Magic* cards, and GI Joe figures, for example.

Collectibles

The word *collectible* has been defined as often as the terms "Liberal" and "Conservative"—and just as erroneously. Here's a definition you can use: "A *collectible* is an item that was originally made to serve a utilitarian purpose but has since transcended its original function through intense collector interest." Generally, collectibles date from 1950 to the present.

Occasionally, a collectible may not have any true quality, or its quality may be completely beside the point. The point of these collectibles is association, rather than intrinsic merit. The powder brush that Anne Boleyn used on the morning of her execution and the string of pearls that Marie Antoinette wore before her head was parted from her body both have a value of their own as ivory and pearl, but this value is nowhere as important as their association. The same is true of the black leather jacket that John Lennon wore in 1962 (sold for a staggering $47,900 at a recent auction) or Jimi Hendrix's black felt hat (which went for a more respectable $24,000).

Learn the Lingo

A **collectible** is a coveted item made in the last 50 years. Collectibles include original Barbie dolls, comic books, and 1960s-era plastic costume jewelry, for instance.

Antiques

"You have to be an antique to appreciate them."

—Fay Madigan Lange

An *antique* is also an object that people collect because it is beautiful, rare, unique, or any combination of these attributes. But an antique is different from a collectible in one major way: An antique must be at least 100 years old. We have the U.S. Customs service to thank for this distinction; leave it to the government to set us straight. But according to this definition, no consideration is given to quality, style, craftsmanship, or any other aspect. According to law, a collectible becomes an antique simply when Willard Scott can celebrate its 100th birthday. But most dealers and collectors consider 75 to 100 years an acceptable range in which to rank a "collectible" as an "antique."

Even with the best efforts of the government, *antique* is not a precise term. In the beginning of the nineteenth century, the English painter Thomas Rowlandson is rumored to have made this point while a chamber pot was being auctioned off: "What am I to bid for tomorrow's antique?" Right or wrong, the word "antique" has a more snobbish appeal than "collectible," and this often translates to a higher price.

And There's More

Just to make it more confusing, there are other collectible terms as well as the theory that old equals valuable. Here's some guidance to keep you on track.

"Collectible Art"

Collectible art is an all-purpose term that includes the visual, decorative, and functional arts. A true collectible encompasses the creations of old masters and rare antiques to almost anything that required skill and talent to create. For example, a toaster is a functional object whose purpose is to turn bread a crispy brown. A painting, in contrast, serves only to embellish a home or office. Neither the toaster nor the painting becomes a collectible, however, unless enough people decide to regard it as one.

The Good, Bad, and Really Bad

To some people, antique = quality = value. As a result, they not only lust after true objects of value but also seek out anything "old" or "collectible." The primary requirement is age, and not even a whole lot of that. As a result, the market has become clogged with good, bad, and really bad. The only characteristic all this stuff has in common is age—it was all produced in the past. The equation? Antique = old.

Going by this yardstick, everything will become an antique if we wait long enough: a magnificent painting, a rusty flyswatter, and even aged Aunt Alice. Following this reasoning to its logical conclusion, the number of "antiques" is virtually unlimited, but the amount of *collectible* art is quite limited.

Sometimes it is easy to tell the difference, but more often it is not, especially for newcomers to the field of collecting. By the end of this book, you will learn that age does not equal value. In many years, a fine work of art will become a rare treasure; in an equal number of years, a piece of trash becomes an old piece of trash, whether we call it an antique or not.

Big Deals

Sid Sackson has the largest and most extensive private collection of board games in the world. His collection totals about 50,000 games and complete reproductions of equipment and rules. His collection fills several rooms in his home. Sackson also has a library of more than 1,000 game books in 13 languages and over 2,000 magazines on games.

Voodoo Economics and Collectibles

Age is one of the sieves that separates the wheat from the chaff, or, in our case, the true desirables and collectibles from the merely old stuff. The value of an object is determined in large part according to the law of *supply and demand.*

A diminished supply of anything—gasoline, houses, or diamonds—raises the demand for it and the price. The increased price, however, will often decrease the demand, resulting in an astonished, "You expect me to pay *what* for this old picture?" Once again, this lowers the price.

Despite what economists would have us believe, these checks and balances work well with guns and butter, but not with collectibles. With collectibles, the rise in price alone can spark enough interest to increase demand and further spike the price. The spiral can continue indefinitely, as long as the supply remains finite. In terms of collectibles, here's how supply and demand works:

➤ **Demand.** The demand for any desirable or collectible is first created by its beauty and later by its performance on the market.

➤ **Supply.** The supply is determined by the creator and should balance with the anticipated demand.

➤ **Supply/demand ratio.** This is the most crucial factor in the collector market. The demand for an object must exceed its supply to tickle our collector bone. Therefore, the desirability of any desirable or collectible is linked to its supply/demand ratio. Without that challenge and excitement, there's no thrill of the hunt. And so there's no hunter.

What's Hot—and What's Not

To become a major player as a collectible, an item must cause enough people to look at it with admiration. Like sneakers, restaurants, movie stars, and ice cream flavors, some objects are more in demand than others. Which objects will become desirables or collectibles? We all know that beautiful furniture, carpets and rugs, coins, stamps, and fine art are sought after. So are fine books, porcelain, exquisite jewelry, textiles, and prints.

Caveat Emptor

A thing of beauty is a joy forever—or until it breaks, chips, scratches, peels, or flakes.

But what about the desirables and collectibles that aren't so well known to the newcomer to Collection World? Here's the inside scoop, a list of the hottest collectibles on the market today. These items are *steady* but only if they're vintage, one-of-a-kind, out-of-print, or rare:

But first, a disclaimer: The items in the following list are hot right now, as I'm writing this book, but always remember that trends come and go. I'm not promising that when you buy this book—which could be a year after I wrote it—these things are still sizzling. So caveat emptor—let the buyer beware.

➤ Advertising items
➤ Advertising trade cards
➤ Animation art
➤ Antique clothing
➤ Antique tools
➤ Ashtrays
➤ Autographs
➤ Banks (antique metal toys)
➤ Barbed wire
➤ Barbershop items
➤ Baseball cards
➤ Beanie Babies

➤ Beatles memorabilia
➤ Beer cans
➤ Bicycles
➤ Bottle caps
➤ Bottles
➤ Boy Scout memorabilia
➤ Cameras (old and well made)
➤ Christmas ornaments
➤ Clocks
➤ Clothing buttons (antique)
➤ Coca-Cola memorabilia
➤ Coin-operated machines

- ➤ Comic art
- ➤ Comic books
- ➤ Corkscrews
- ➤ Country store items
- ➤ Dinnerware
- ➤ Dolls
- ➤ Elvis Presley memorabilia
- ➤ Fast-food toys
- ➤ Fishing lures
- ➤ Folk art
- ➤ Gemstones
- ➤ Glassware
- ➤ Hat pins
- ➤ Hollywood memorabilia
- ➤ Items associated with magic
- ➤ Jazz memorabilia
- ➤ Keys (old)
- ➤ Kitchen implements
- ➤ License plates
- ➤ Light bulbs (early)
- ➤ Locks (antique)
- ➤ Marbles (old)
- ➤ Matchbooks
- ➤ Menus
- ➤ Military items
- ➤ Minerals
- ➤ Model railroad items
- ➤ Movie memorabilia
- ➤ Music boxes
- ➤ Musical instruments
- ➤ Native American art
- ➤ Newspapers (old)
- ➤ Norman Rockwell items
- ➤ Olympic pins and other memorabilia
- ➤ Paper money
- ➤ Paperweights
- ➤ Perfume bottles
- ➤ Phonecards
- ➤ Pinups
- ➤ Plates
- ➤ Playing cards
- ➤ Plush toys (e.g., Meanies, Bammers, Planet Plush)
- ➤ Political items
- ➤ Postcards
- ➤ Posters
- ➤ Postmarks on envelopes and postcards
- ➤ Pottery (art pottery)
- ➤ Pulp magazines
- ➤ Quilts (old, handmade)
- ➤ Railroad memorabilia/model trains and the full-sized ones, too
- ➤ Rock and roll memorabilia
- ➤ Royal Doulton china items
- ➤ Rubber stamps (old)
- ➤ Schoolhouse items
- ➤ Sea shells (unique)
- ➤ Sheet music
- ➤ Silver items
- ➤ Soda cans (vintage)
- ➤ Sports memorabilia
- ➤ Stock certificates
- ➤ Stoneware
- ➤ Teddy bears
- ➤ Telephones
- ➤ Temperance memorabilia
- ➤ Theater items
- ➤ Thimbles

➤ Tobacco items

➤ Tools

➤ Toys

➤ Trading cards

➤ U.S. Civil War items

➤ Walt Disney items

➤ Wine

The Least You Need to Know

➤ Be a collector, but use the best traits of a dealer.

➤ Buy what you can, keep the best for yourself, and resell the rest.

➤ A desirable is a collected object whose value is uncertain, such as beanbag toys and Disney figures.

➤ A collectible is an item that was originally made to serve a utilitarian purpose but has since transcended its original function through intense collector interest.

➤ An antique is a collectible that is at least 75 to 100 years old.

➤ The law of supply and demand applies to collectibles only so far. With collectibles, the rise in price alone can spark enough interest to increase demand and further spike the price.

Part 2

Buying and Selling Like a Pro

All the world's a fair to collector Peter Stathes. That's because he treasures memorabilia from the World's Fair of 1964 to 1965. His collection boasts admission tickets, bumper stickers, a Unisphere coin bank, matchbooks, ashtrays, souvenir gift boxes, and even World's Fair lollipops. How has Stathes gathered all these treasures? He knows how to buy and sell collectibles with assurance.

In Part 2, you'll learn my Rules for Acquisition and how to shop at every possible venue: auctions, flea markets, swap meets, mail order, stores, and yard sales, and through the Web. I'll teach you how to bargain like a pro, too. By the end of this part, you'll be ready to join the Buying and Selling Big Leagues—whether you're strapping on that fanny pack or booting up your computer!

Shop 'Till You Drop

In This Chapter

➤ Assess your shopping skill

➤ Learn the Rules of Acquisition

➤ Shop at auctions and antique shops

➤ Hunt through flea markets and mail order

➤ Collect while you vacation

The California gold mines are kaput, pirate loot lies buried under the briny depths, and the stock market is in a swoon. Nonetheless, more treasure hunting goes on today than ever before.

Today, fortune hunters search under porches of old houses, in dust-clogged attics, and at antique stores. They haunt flea markets and swap meets, charity bazaars and house-wreckers' lots. They're the first at auctions, whether county or city. Some even have an antiques dealer on retainer. The current collecting boom has made superstars out of everyday stuff and some not-so-everyday stuff: jail padlocks, railroad spikes, first-edition books, and stamps.

In this chapter, you will get the lowdown on shopping for collectibles. You'll learn the ins and outs of buying the objects you desire for your collection. We'll start at the very beginning, with the Rules of Acquisition. It's a jungle out there, kiddo. I wouldn't send you out without arming you with sufficient knowledge.

Next, I'll take you on a tour through Collectible Country. We will visit great places to buy desirables and collectibles. On our tour, you will learn the advantages and disadvantages of shopping in each venue. Along the way, you'll get great tips that will help you shop like a pro. So put on your walking shoes and let's get started.

Big Deals

R. S. "Dick" Kemp of New Hampshire collects trucks. Big trucks. He has over 100 old trucks (mostly Mack) that date back as far as 1916. Kemp began his collection in 1952 with a 1930 Bulldog Mack that he bought for $50. Only 63 Mack trucks were built in 1947, and Kemp owns two of them. Kemp learned to drive a truck when he was 14 years old and was driving a big rig for a living by the time he was 16. If trucks tickle your fancy, Kemp displays his collection in "Kemp's Mack Truck Museum."

Tricks of the Trade

The American Political Items Collectors (APIC) is a national group that furthers the collection, preservation, and study of Ameri-can political memorabilia. APIC sponsors one six-week paid internship at the Smithsonian Institution in Washing-ton, D.C., each summer. For information on the internship program and an application, contact APIC at their Web site, www.collectors. org/ apic.

The Rules of Acquisition

Buying is easy. Spending money is as simple as opening your wallet or whipping out a credit card (with a flourish) and chanting the familiar mantra, "Charge it, fella." But buying wisely is hard. Remember: Shoppers are made, not born. In this section, you'll discover ways to create a collection of beauty and value without mortgaging the ranch or selling your firstborn. (Unless your firstborn is an adolescent; then be my guest.)

Are You a Super Shopper?

Test your SQ—Shopper's Quotient—with this easy True/False quiz.

Test Your SQ (Shopper's Quotient)

True	False	
____	____	It's better to buy first and think later. Otherwise, the bargain might get away, and you could miss a once-in-a-lifetime deal.
____	____	Even if you hate an item, it's a good idea to buy it to round out your collection or to hold for later resale.
____	____	Start by buying big; this is no time to be a wuss.
____	____	It's a waste of time to make friends with the owners of local antique shops; they usually don't know enough to help with specialty items.
____	____	The condition of an item should *not* be a crucial factor in your decision to buy it.
____	____	The best buys are usually found in unexpected places: barns, flea markets, and swap meets.
____	____	People rarely get good deals in antique shops.
____	____	Collectibles have fixed values.
____	____	Don't rely on yourself; you must seek out experts to verify your feelings.
____	____	Try not to ask questions. It will just make you look foolish and lessen your chance of getting a good deal.

Answers

Every statement is false. If you scored 100 percent, I'd trust you with my AmEx any day.

However, if you answered ...

6–9 false	You've been mall-crawling, haven't you?
3–5 false	Warning: Untrained shopper. Shop only at your own risk.
1–2 false	Don't buy a thing until you read the Top Ten Rules of Acquisition.

In the Know

Whether you're a novice or an expert, you can benefit from studying my Top Ten Rules of Acquisition. And here they are:

1. **Buy only what you can appreciate, enjoy, and live with.** This is the #1 rule of collecting. Consider making it into a sampler or having it tattooed around your navel. If you don't like the object (and I mean really *don't like* it), don't buy it. Remember: You could end up with a cast iron gargoyle leering at you from the mantel or an insufferably cute shepherdess statue turning your stomach. And no one will take it off your hands.

2. **To start, play it safe.** When you're starting out, it's not the time to take a walk on the wild side. Enter slowly; the water can be really cold. Begin by looking for "blue-chip" items—collectibles that have recognized value. As you gain knowledge and confidence, you will become less conservative.

3. **Buy things in good (or great) condition.** Not all beautiful things are created equal; some may come with defects. Most concealed defects will have very little effect on the collectible's aesthetic value, but they can have a tremendous effect upon its market prospects. A $10 difference in the cost of a collectible can result in a $1,000 difference in its value and resale price.

4. **Develop a critical attitude.** You have smart brains; after all, you wouldn't be a collector if you didn't. Now is the time to think for yourself. It doesn't hurt to be a little cynical. Be suspicious of excessive claims made about an object. Comments like "One of a kind," "Worth a fortune," and "You'll never get a bargain like this again" should set off alarms.

Caveat Emptor

If something seems too good to be true, it very likely is. This is especially true when it comes to collectibles.

5. **Remember that a collectible is worth only what someone will pay for it.** "You'll make a bundle on this item!" "A real treasure—certain to zoom in value." "You can't lose money on this baby." Ever hear these phrases? If you're lucky, the speaker was easy to recognize by his greasy handlebar mustache and sinister laugh. More likely, the speaker was a sweet little old lady with apple cheeks, the owner of an ador-able antique store tucked into a country inn. It's all the same—you were targeted. Remember: No matter what someone tells you, no matter what value may be listed in a book, a collectible is worth only what someone will pay for it. See Rule #1.

6. **Buy the best you can afford.** Remember the advice your mama gave you (or should have): It's just as easy to fall in love with a rich mate as a poor mate. Mama was on to something here. Listen up, collectors: It's just as easy to swoon over a collectible with good prospects as it is over one with lousy prospects. No

argument here; just a question: "How can I tell which collectible will soar in value and which will sink faster than a gangster with cement overshoes?" That's covered in Chapter 5, "Hey, Big Spender."

7. **Cozy up to a dealer.** The probability of finding an antique shop in your neighborhood that has exactly what you want all the time is about as likely as the check being in the mail. However, it's always a good idea to investigate all local resources thoroughly and completely. You may not find what you want every time, but a reputable dealer can help you locate items that you want or need to round out your collection. Knowledgeable dealers make excellent resources, too, especially regarding appraisals and authentication.

8. **Ask questions.** You can tell that the gewgaw on the shelf is pretty; you think it must be valuable because it's carrying a hefty price tag. But what makes it so valuable? Don't be afraid to ask. Ask the salesperson what makes it worth collecting and why. Keep asking until you get an answer that makes sense to you. An inquiring mind makes you seem more intelligent, not less.

9. **Location, location, location.** The three rules of real estate apply to collecting as well. People cherish the myth that gold can be found in dross; the messier and more rundown the store, we think, the more likely we are to find the bargain of the century. Specialty stores have cottoned to this mind set years ago; some shop owners intentionally display items in disarray. They throw heaps of sweaters or shoes on a table, knowing that most customers will assume that heaps of messy items translate to a great deal. Never assume.

Don't think that a very elegant store has nothing to offer or that a poorly lit barn will offer untold treasures. Often, just the opposite is true: solid deals can be made in an elegant antique store, but the barn may be packed with dreck. Ma and Pa Kettle wised up years ago; it's likely that by the time *you* get to the barn, they've sold all the good stuff to the fancy antique store down the road.

Tricks of the Trade

Smart collectors very often have their dealers set aside special pieces for them. The dealers give their special customers first crack at the item. This is another advantage to establishing a professional relationship with a dealer.

Caveat Emptor

Never buy any desirable, collectible, or antique that you don't fully understand. If you can't "see" what makes something so special, back off. If you don't understand why it's so expensive, run; don't walk. Wait until you do understand. Then you can buy. This holds true for stinky French cheese, co-op apartments, and exercise machines as well.

Big Deals

How much does a piece of Camelot cost? Jackie O's pearls—the fake ones, yet—were auctioned amid much hoopla for $211,500. And how about the $772,500 paid for a set of JFK's golf clubs, complete with badly tattered golf bag?

Caveat Emptor

Evaluate all Web sources very carefully. Remember that anyone can post a Web page and include any information he or she wants. There's no guarantee the person even has the advertised item available for sale.

10. **Do your homework.** You'll find plenty of information in this book, and there are reams and reams more available. Study the major publications such as *Antiques* and *Maloney's Antiques and Collectibles Resource Directory*. You can get these in many libraries. Also look for local magazines such as *Arts Weekly* (Connecticut), *Maine Antique Digest* (Maine), and *The Antiques Trader Weekly* (St. Louis, Missouri). Publications such as these are often free at collectibles shows and auctions. Also check out the book *Garage Sale and Flea Market Annual: Cashing in on Today's Lucrative Collectibles Market* (Collector Book). It has current values on today's collectibles and tomorrow's antiques.

Don't forget to browse the Web for information. At different Web sites, you'll find listings for swap meets, flea markets, auctions, private sales, and estate sales. The Web is also a great way to stay current on prices, especially eBay and other online auction houses.

Your source is valid if …

➤ It is recent and timely. Values and prices can change very quickly in the antiques and collectibles market.

➤ It can be verified in at least two other published sources.

➤ The publication has been around long enough to be considered reliable.

➤ It is respected by others in the field.

➤ It is published by a reputable publisher.

➤ The author has no obvious ax to grind.

➤ It make sense. If the author's claims seem outlandish, they probably are. Trust your gut.

Deal of a Lifetime

A reporter once asked the legendary bank robber Willy Sutton why he kept breaking into banks. "That's where the money is," Sutton is reported to have answered. Why do collectors frequent flea markets, antique stores, and swap meets? Let me count the ways:

➤ A sheaf of official records that Ben Franklin kept while he was Postmaster General was found in the binding of an old book. The binder had put the official records there to stiffen the binding.

➤ In 1968 the last printed copy of the *Declaration of Independence* in private hands was found in the basement of a Philadelphia bookshop, where it had been hidden for over half a century. Take a deep breath at this one: it was sold for nearly a half million dollars.

➤ One of the world's rarest stamps, a Hawaiian "missionary," was found under a chunk of peeling wallpaper.

I know you're drooling, so I'll stop now. Here's the truth: The find of a lifetime is just that—a one-shot deal. It's a myth we cherish, like "I'll lose ten pounds in time for my reunion." The truth? Most fine collectibles are purchased at reputable establishments by dealers and collectors who have done their homework. So don't pass up a chance to snoop under the porch or peel the wallpaper from the walls of a crumbling mansion, but spend most of your time shopping at the sources outlined next.

Don't Scratch Your Nose! Shopping at Auctions

You can find a lot of ... um ... neat stuff at auctions, as the following list shows. Which of these five unusual "steals" appeals to you?

➤ **George Washington's laundry bill.** A laundry bill dated 1787 and signed by George Washington and two of his colonels sold for $1,100 at an auction. According to the document, Mary Firth got the job of washing the General's unmentionables as long as she bought her own soap.

➤ **Swedenborg's skull.** The skull of Swedish philosopher Emanuel Swedenborg sold at Sotheby Parke Bernet, London, March 6, 1977, for $2,850. The buyer wanted to reunite the skull with its skeleton in Uppsala, Sweden.

➤ **Smile!** The earliest known photograph of a photographer taking a picture was auctioned at Christie's, London, in 1977. It sold for $9,860.

➤ **Outhouse.** In 1974 a one-seater, nineteenth-century oak outhouse sold at a New England auction. The going price for the best seat around the house? $140. The lucky buyer wanted to dismantle it and use the pieces to make picture frames.

37

➤ **Bat an eyelash.** At a 1979 private auction in Beverly Hills, Judy Garland's false eyelashes sold for $125.

Source: Wallace, Irving. The Book of Lists. *New York: William Morrow, 1980.*

Big Deals

In 1890 a company in Liverpool, England, sold 180,000 mummified Egyptian cats from a burial ground near Beni Hasaan for 3.15 shillings per ton. The mo- ral of the story? Don't be so quick to throw out that dead cat.

Caveat Emptor

Important auction lots are often illustrated. This can be misleading, however, since the seller usually pays for the photographs in an auction catalog to increase chances for a good sale. As a result, these photos often show the items in the best possible light. Problems with the items may not show up clearly ... or at all.

Read the Auction Catalog

Auction catalogs usually come out a few weeks before the auction. Here's how to read these documents effectively:

➤ First skim the pages. Then go back and focus on those items that you want.

➤ Be sure to read the small print, especially the sections called "Conditions of Sale" or "Standard Notices."

➤ Check for a glossary and a key to abbreviations and terms. Read them all. Important buzzwords include AF ("as found") and "Not subject to return."

➤ Be alert for boldface or capitalized entries; they are usually important pieces.

➤ Think carefully about the wording of each description.

If the auction house doesn't publish a catalog, be sure to get a copy of the terms, especially if they aren't posted. Ask the auctioneer before the sale begins.

Pay careful attention to how an item is described in an auction catalog. Break the house auction code with this cheat sheet:

Term	Meaning
The picture is attributed to Van Gogh.	The picture is a real Vincent creation, as far as the auction house knows.
The picture is labeled "Van Gogh."	The picture is probably a copy.
The picture is "in the style" of Van Gogh.	The picture could be a fake.

Read the Reference Literature

Get your hands on any books or articles mentioned in the auction catalog. See if the items you want have been the subject of controversy. This should set off a flashing red light and maybe even a siren or two. Remember: It is highly unlikely that you are going to get a bargain without doing some heavy homework.

Get Price Estimates

Sales rooms usually print a list of *price estimates,* which are a range of prices that they expect each lot to bring. If there are no written price estimates, get a verbal one. But since a significant length of time can elapse between the writing and the printing dates, prices may be wildly out of date. Counter this by checking several different sources, including dealers and friends bitten by the "Collecting Bug."

Mark the Items You Want—and What You'll Pay for Each

Next to each item you want, write down how much you are willing to spend for it. The best lots are often left to the end. As a result, you can often get good deals as people run out of money.

Auctions are dramatic and exciting. It is easy to get carried away and spend more than you intended. Marking your top price—and sticking to it—can help you prevent overspending. Save your catalogs. Since they are marked with the estimates, the prices achieved, your estimates, and your purchase prices, they become valuable reference documents.

Tricks of the Trade

Sometimes, the lots immediately before and after important lots will get less attention than they merit because of the buildup and letdown for the Big Event. You can take advantage of such distractions and momentary lapses in concentration to get a great deal.

View the Items

Never buy anything you have not viewed. Never. Then take this rule one step further and be sure to inspect the lots that interest you. I recommend that you check out everything else as well; you ne-ver know what will turn up. I could tell you tales that would make your mouth water and your knees shake, but I'm too nice to torture you with auction envy.

Learn the Lingo

A **reserve** is the price below which the vendor will not sell an item at an auction.

Tricks of the Trade

Be sure you know the likely pattern of the price jumps by which the bidding will advance. By finding that out, you'll know how much you're bidding at each step. The auctioneer may move in jumps of $2.50 (going from $5.00 to $7.50 to $10.00, for example), $5.00, or $10 to $25. Most auctioneers will not deviate from their preset jumps. Thus, if the auctioneer is asking for a raise of $5 from $90 to $95 and you bid $91, you may be out of luck because your bid won't be acknowledged.

Don't be intimidated: Try to handle all the items you're interested in, looking for cracks, repairs, and other problems. For example, it is often easier to find a repair to a porcelain bowl with your finger than with your eye. Ask for what you want to see. Keep asking until you get it. After all, you're shopping for *your* collection.

Reserves

A *reserve* is the price below which the vendor will not sell an item. You want to know the reserve so you know the lowest possible bid. Some auction houses disclose the reserve price. In these instances, it will be printed or posted.

Bidding

Making a good bid is not the sole province of the experienced and well-dressed. Anyone can bid well at an auction with a little practice. There are affordable prices at even the most prestigious auctions. In spite of the tale about the man with the itchy nose ending up with the Ming vase, only in the movies do auctions encourage subtle Cary Grant eyebrow-arching bids.

In real auctions, the normal practice is to make it absolutely clear to the auctioneer that you are bidding. You don't need semaphore, though. Raising your hand, holding up your catalog, or nodding will work just fine. Besides, although you are legally liable to pay for a lot that is knocked down to you, you will rarely be asked to ante up if you made a genuine error.

Buying Retail

Collectible and antique shops are probably the best places to seriously study the varying qualities of collectibles and antiques. Unless you were voted class klutz, shop owners allow you to wander freely and examine the pieces that interest you. You don't even have to put on your Gucci loafers to browse. But even more important, antique shops are learning grounds where you can ask questions. Don't be afraid to ask the key question, "Can you tell me more about this piece?"

A Flea in Your Ear

It's Saturday morning in the Poconos. The digital clock on the car dashboard reads 6:00. There's nary a creature stirring ... except smart shoppers headed to the yard sales, house sales, and flea market/swap meets. These canny shoppers have been up for a while now, and they're armed. They wear fanny packs crammed with dollar bills. Some shoppers have as much as $1,000 in cash. They carry self-stick labels with their names on them to reserve choice items. They have water bottles, fruit, and sun hats. Days before, they have scoured the ads and mapped out their routes. They shop by area to cover the most places in the least amount of time. As the seconds click by, they are eager to get moving. Better get out of their way. They are fierce.

Web Wise

Today's Flea Markets is a quarterly magazine that provides information on the flea market industry. For more information on the National Flea Market Association, visit their Web site at www.unitedine.com.

If the early bird catches the worm, the early yard-sale shopper catches the best collectibles. Every yard sale/flea market maven has a story about the Tiffany studio lamp that he or she bought for 50¢ and resold for $500. The ads say the sales start at 10:00, but these shoppers feign ignorance and beat the crowds by hours. Some of these "shoppers" at yard sales are professionals—especially the ones who camp at the door by 5:30 A.M. They scoop up the best stuff for resale at their own shops at a much higher price. The best defense is a good offense: Get to the yard sale at 5:00 A.M. Or pay a little more and buy the item in their stores.

Tricks of the Trade

Attend flea markets late in the afternoon to get great prices on leftovers. Of course, you'll have to want leftovers.

Don't believe me? Advertise a yard sale for 9:00 A.M., but be ready to see your first customers by 6:00. When you let down the ropes, the shoppers will dive into your goods like teenagers to a pile of hamburgers. Dashing from treasure to treasure, they put stickers on the items they want.

Follow these steps to get the best deals at these sources for collectibles:

➤ Shop in the most affluent areas. Unscrupulous sellers have been known to truck in merchandise from other areas, but logic decrees that you are most likely to get the best collectibles in the best locations.

➤ Plan your route the night before. Map it out, and make sure you know how to get to each place. Take the ad with you.

➤ Get up early. Obscenely early. Then get going. If the sale looks really good, people even sleep overnight outside, waiting for the sale to open. Really.

➤ Eat breakfast, even if you hate breakfast. You will need the energy for the fray. Fistfights have erupted over much-desired objects.

➤ Look for items that don't fit a dealer's specialty. The dealer will likely be anxious to get rid of it for a song. But remember: Don't buy it unless you want it.

➤ Check all used appliances before you buy them. Plug them in and make sure they work.

➤ If you're comfortable with bargaining, do so now.

Mail-Order Bride

Consumer Affairs and the Better Business Bureau (BBB) handle complaints against a wide variety of businesses. The BBB recently issued a study of complaints against mail-order companies. Their findings? Most complaints were registered against mail-order companies that provide only a box-office number. Complaints were fewer against firms that gave a street address, and fewest still against those companies that added a phone number.

Assessing a mail-order firm is difficult because you obviously can't visit the premises. You can't meet the staff and check out the shop. However, there are many instances when you must shop by mail order because the items are not available any other way or you have no access to the shops.

Use the "Mail-Order Buying Checklist" before you order a collectible by mail. It will help you determine whe-ther the catalog dealer is reputable.

Caveat Emptor

Don't count on bad weather keeping crowds at bay. Some of the largest crowds turn out in foul weather.

Mail-Order Buying Checklist

❑   The mail-order company has been in business for several years.

❑   The store has a solid reputation in the trade.

❑   Your friends and fellow collectors have good things to say about the company.

❑   The company makes reasonable claims rather than outrageous ones.

❑   Prices are within accepted limits—neither too low nor too high.

❑   The company projects a professional image.

❑ Any consumer complaints lodged against the business have been resolved to the consumer's satisfaction.

❑ The mail-order company offers solid guarantees against problems and damages.

❑ There is a fair return policy.

❑ You can reach a real person with real authority on the telephone.

Order Me Another Margarita, Dahling ... and Then Let's Hit the Shops

My friend Tom is a part-time antiques dealer in Hawaii, specializing in ivory. He times his vacations to New York to coincide with the big city antique shows in the autumn.

Rita buys and sells antique jewelry. She melds business with pleasure by shopping at every store, yard sale, and auction she comes across during her vacations.

What both Rita and Tom, along with scores of other collectors, have discovered is the pleasure of planning a vacation around shopping for a collection. I highly recommend this approach because it offers numerous advantages:

➤ The chance of snagging a really remarkable addition to your collection

➤ The delights of a vacation

➤ Possible tax breaks

➤ Finding unusual additions to your collection

The Least You Need to Know

➤ Buy only what you can appreciate, enjoy, and live with.

➤ Ask questions to learn what you need to know.

➤ Buy things in the best condition you can afford.

➤ Develop a critical attitude toward each item.

➤ Remember that a collectible is worth only what someone will pay for it—no matter what anyone promises.

Chapter 5

Hey, Big Spender

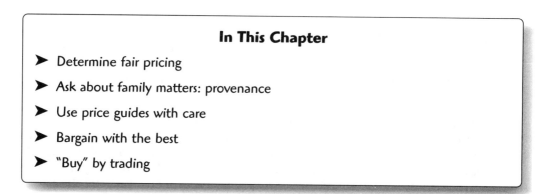

In This Chapter

➤ Determine fair pricing

➤ Ask about family matters: provenance

➤ Use price guides with care

➤ Bargain with the best

➤ "Buy" by trading

Have you ever bought a desirable, collectible, or antique and come away thinking that you paid too much and should have done better? Or, have you wanted to buy a decorated jug at a yard sale but didn't know how much to offer? Do fancy antique shops intimidate you? Relax. This chapter will help you buy with confidence.

In the previous chapter, you learned about places to shop for collectibles. In this chapter, you'll learn specific techniques for becoming a powerful buyer. First, I'll teach you how to tell whether the offering price is fair. You'll learn the importance of provenance and price guides. I'll show you how to bargain like a pro, too.

How Much Is That Doggie (Statue) in the Window?

Although the legal definition of an *antique* still requires that the object be a hundred years old or older, more and more people are considering collectibles as "young" as 30

Caveat Emptor

Much of the worry about the prices of desirables, collectibles, and antiques exists because people aren't aware that this is a unique business. And it *is* a business, although some collectors view it more as a divine quest.

or 40 years old to be antiques. This expanded definition has come about partly because of the great increase in the prices of "real" antiques.

As a result of this rise in prices, certain kinds of antiques are out of reach for the average collector. For instance, silver, pewter, and eighteenth-century furniture are largely closed to newcomers—even those with relatively deep pockets. Almost no good examples exist outside museums and large private collections, and when a piece is offered for sale, its price is in the stratosphere. This is why intelligent people, people like you, have turned your interest to new, younger collectibles. But this presents its own problems, especially with regard to pricing.

It's unlikely that you'll be able to afford a genuine eighteenth-century highboy, but at least you'll know what it costs. The reverse is true of the newer collectibles and antiques. If you've been diligent about saving your pennies, you probably *will* be able to buy many of these hot collectibles, but it's unlikely that you will be able to easily determine their price. The prices asked for newer collectibles can vary not only from state to state and from city to city, but often from shop to shop within the same community as well.

Antiques dealers, flea market vendors, and auctioneers are business people. They buy and sell, just like other business people. But their work is different from other retail establishments in one crucial area: When they sell an item, they can't reorder. They may not be able to get another comparable piece for weeks, months, years, if ever. And the price is not fixed; the dealer may have to pay more or less for the same object over the years. As a matter of fact, there are no fixed prices at all. The dealer is free to ask what the market will bear.

Provenance—a Collectible's Family Tree

"Well," the seller declared with utter conviction, "my cuckoo clock is undoubtedly priceless because Prince Albert once wound its stem." I moved away *fast*. I didn't want to be the one to break the news that even if the Artist Formerly Known As Prince wound her cuckoo clock, it likely wasn't worth a bundle.

Many times I have been told that an item is valuable because it is associated with someone famous. I call this the "George Washington slept here" syndrome. First of all, unless the Father of Our Country had sleeping sickness, he couldn't have slept everywhere he was spotted dozing. Second, who cares? The ultimate determinant of value is quality, not prior ownership.

Such background or origin information is called *provenance*. Provenance does not necessarily equate with value or profit. Every collectible has a provenance. It may begin with you, or it may go back several generations in your family. The only time you can cash in on provenance is when these two conditions are met:

➤ The prior owner was very important.

➤ There's clear-cut documentation to back up the claim of provenance.

But even when the provenance is established, the value of the piece must ultimately rest on its own merit—in other words, how good the piece is. Many people have overbid at celebrity auctions, only to wake up the next day with the equivalent of a collector's hangover when they gaze sorrowfully at a load of junk. "I got carried away," is a frequent refrain. They suddenly realize that the items won't hold their value any longer than a soap bubble its shape.

Guiding Light?

So how *do* dealers set prices on the objects we lust after? Do they just pull them out of thin air? Although it may seem that pricing is as capricious as Spring, those in the know rely on more than the laws of supply and demand when it comes to inflicting sticker shock. Although the dealer's purchase price is a factor in determining an item's resale price, dealers often use *price guides,* authoritative books that list the prices of various objects. Prices are determined by the usual suspects: age, condition, rarity, and so on.

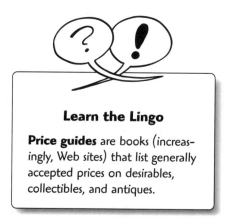

Just about every object worth collecting has been ranked in its own price guide. To make your life easier, I list many well-regarded price guides in Appendix B, "Further Reading." Price guides will solve all your buying problems, right? Not so fast, fellow collector. Here are some points to consider when you use price guides.

➤ Price guides represent prices recently achieved at auction and asked for in shops and advertised in the periodicals devoted to collectibles. Therefore they provide only guidelines.

➤ Price guides are not dealers' price lists, although some dealers base their prices on the values listed.

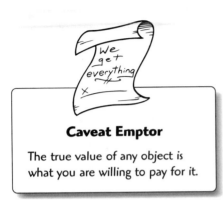

Caveat Emptor

The true value of any object is what you are willing to pay for it.

➤ Price guides generally show what *collectors*—not *dealers*—are willing to pay. Collectors usually want certain objects far more than dealers do and so are willing to pay more. Remember this when we turn to selling collectibles in Chapter 6, "Buy, Buy."

➤ Pay very close attention to the "condition" column. An object in mint (perfect) condition will fetch far more than one ranked as "fair" or "poor."

➤ As a result, don't accept any prices cited in a guidebook as gospel; use them as just a guide. That's why they're called price *guidebooks*.

So, Can You Knock Off a Few Bucks?

Some people are delighted at the opportunity to shave a little off the top; others recoil in horror at the thought of asking for a better price. Here's the number one rule of bargaining: No matter how good a deal you might get by bargaining, it's not worth it if you or the seller feels uncomfortable. Go with your personal style. Bargain if you feel comfortable with it. Don't bargain if it makes you queasy. Otherwise, the item might feel tainted, no matter how much you saved. Then the pleasure is gone.

That said, let's talk about the right way to bargain. First, avoid the lame tactic, "I spent all my money on donuts, so could you charge me less for this vase?" or the déclassé, "My husband will kill me if I spend more than $5 on this." Nix a derogatory comment, "What a piece of trash. I'll give you a buck to take it off your hands." Deep-six this demand, "You have to give me a better price." No one likes to be ordered around.

Bargain Basement

The key to bargaining is to make the seller feel like he or she has the upper hand. Never insult, demean, or hector as you bargain. Here are my Top Three Best Bargaining Lines:

1. "What's the best you can do on this?"

2. "Can you do a little better on this item?"

3. "Would you take (name a price) for this?"

This approach shows the seller that there may be some difficulty involved, given the state of the economy, the mortgage on the shop, the price of his teenager's sneakers, and so on. The seller is then in the position of doing you a favor. The seller appreciates your effort, so you're likely to get a better deal.

Big Deals

In 1982 a famous movie producer paid more than $50,000 at auction for the balsa wood sled named "Rosebud" that was used as a prop in Orson Welles's movie *Citizen Kane*.

Horse Trading

Now, how can you bargain comfortably and easily? Adapt these suggestions to your personal style.

➤ **Know your prices.** Before you can bargain, you have to know what something is worth. It's not unusual for items to be overpriced. I once saw a clock tagged $50 at a flea market. I knew it was worth $30. Knowing its accepted value made it reasonable for me to offer $20 to $25. Other times, collectibles may be priced accurately. I recently saw a newspaper ad for Depression glass priced at $125— a fair price. In that case, $100 would be a respectable counteroffer.

➤ **Be reasonable.** As you saw in the previous examples, you should make fair offers. If the item is in mint or excellent condition, you can bargain within a range of 5 to 25 percent. If the item is in poor condition, you can offer as much as 75 to 90 percent less. How can you determine how much to try to knock off the price? Read on.

➤ **Be sensible.** If you want the item badly, buy the item. Don't play games if you don't want to sour the deal. But if you don't want the item enough to pay more than a specific price, stick to your guns. Don't insult the seller by offering too little, but don't pay too much for something you really don't want.

➤ **Time your purchases.** At flea markets, house sales, swap meets, and the like, you'll be able to bargain much more easily at the end of the day than at the beginning. Everyone starts a sale optimistically, but by the end of a hot, buggy afternoon, even the most professional

Caveat Emptor

A price tag is not a contract. A seller never has an obligation to sell you anything.

seller is muttering, "You mean I have to pack up all this stuff and put it in the truck?" Rather than having to cart everything back to the house/truck/store, most dealers will bargain freely as they are getting ready to leave. However, be aware that you are getting last crack at the merchandise; so if you want an item badly, buy it when you see it first thing in the morning.

➤ **Buy more than one item.** Sellers want to sell. The more you buy, the more money they make. This is a key leverage point in bargaining. Here's how you can make this fact work for you.

Let's say you see three perfume bottles you want.

1. Start with the one you want the most. Ask the seller, "What's the best you can do on this?"

2. If he or she sticks to the asking price of $25, suggest that you might be interested in Perfume Bottle #2, if the price is right. It's marked $15.

3. Offer $35 for the two bottles.

4. Now indicate that you want Bottle #3, too. It's marked $12.50. What can he do on that? He might say that you can have all three bottles for $45.

5. Make an offer of $40.

The seller expected to sell one item and receive $25. Now he or she can sell three items and get $40. If the seller agrees, you will have gotten the first bottle for its full price of $25, the second bottle for $5 less than its marked price, and the third bottle for $7.50 less. If the seller doesn't agree, you have the option of still purchasing only the first bottle, or as many as you want, for the stated price.

Tricks of the Trade

When you go hunting collectibles, carry enough cash. Also, sort and separate your bills into denominations and place the bucks in a safe place on your person.

➤ **Use cash.** Almost all casual purchases of collectibles are done with cash, even in shops. Many (if not most) well-established shops take credit cards, but be aware that they are charged a percentage by the credit company for this customer service. In many cases, it's a piece of cake to get a 5 percent discount simply by paying with cash rather than plastic.

➤ **Don't bargain over pennies.** It never fails. At every garage sale/yard sale/flea market, I see a shopper pick up an item with a 50¢ sticker and say, "Will you take a quarter?" Get a life. The seller feels demeaned; the buyer needs a smack on the side of the head with a polo mallet. Bargain when it counts, not for nickels and dimes.

Even-Steven: Trading

One of the best ways to "buy" antiques and collectibles is to trade for them. Say that you have a pair of brass and iron fireplace tongs made in the early 1800s. They are valued at about $200. You don't need them because you have a similar pair in better condition. One day you are in a local antique shop and you see a fine-quality brass merchant's scale, made in the mid-1800s. It would be perfect for your collection, and it's valued at $200. Voilà! A fair trade is born.

Keep trading in mind the next time you're a little cash poor but inventory-rich.

The Least You Need to Know

➤ For desirables, collectibles, and antiques, there are no fixed prices at all. The dealer is free to ask what the market will bear.

➤ Provenance is the source or origin of a collectible. A piece's provenance tells who owned the piece at one time.

➤ Use price guides as just that—guides to prices. Everything is carved in sand, not granite.

➤ Be reasonable, sensible, and considerate when you bargain.

Chapter 6

Buy, Buy

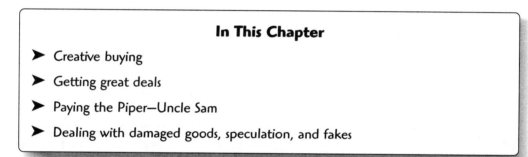

In This Chapter

➤ Creative buying

➤ Getting great deals

➤ Paying the Piper—Uncle Sam

➤ Dealing with damaged goods, speculation, and fakes

Ready, set, buy! You're almost there, partner. In the previous chapter, you learned specific techniques for becoming a powerful buyer. In this chapter, I'll give you more ideas for trading, one of the best ways to "buy" the pretty things we all covet. Then I'll discuss some of the most important problems with buying desirables, collectibles, and antiques—especially how to avoid getting stuck with damaged goods and fakes. You'll also learn how to make money buying and selling collectibles.

Buy High, Sell Low

When asked his advice for making a killing on Wall Street, the wealthy financier hooked his fingers in his vest pocket and drawled, "Buy low, sell high." Simple, no? Then why have so many investors found themselves in the reverse position of buying high, selling low, and losing their shirts?

Most people who begin collecting like to believe they can get their money back should they need to sell their collection. For those who buy collectibles intelligently, there is a

Caveat Emptor

Unlike death and taxes, turning a profit in the collectibles market is not a sure thing. Making money in collectibles is first cousin to making money in the stock market. You can win big—but you can lose big.

Tricks of the Trade

We all tart up a little for company. Extend this to the collectibles you're buying. Almost all dealers use some kind of showcase or stand to display their goods. Everyone looks at the goods, not realizing how much the display contributes to the whole effect. Consider buying the display as much as the goods. It's a great way to get some fine-looking display cabinets, stands, and the like.

good chance they will come out ahead. I know a comics collector who sold his childhood collection of comics at a tidy profit. He used the money to fund his college education. Smart cookie, if you ask me.

Not everyone is so savvy, however. But once you've read this book, you'll be ahead of the game, too.

Buying for Big Bucks: Top Five Hints for Hitting the Collectibles Jackpot

For those of you who are interested in buying antiques and collectibles for profit, I make the following suggestions:

1. **Inflation is good for collectibles.** During an inflationary cycle, people are more apt to buy collectibles at the current price level because they are afraid that the items will cost much more in the future. Conversely, deflation is bad for collectibles. During a deflationary period, people like to keep their money on hand to take advantage of bargains. Historically, collectibles do not sell well during these times.

2. **Always buy the best items in the best condition.** Good cooks know the secret: Start with the freshest, finest ingredients, and it's almost impossible to mess up. How bad could the brownies be if you used imported Dutch chocolate and rich creamery butter? The reverse is also true. Even the most talented cook can't salvage a dish made with rancid oil or spoiled fish. Remember: With collectibles, the law of supply and demand sets the price. The best pieces in the best shape will always be the ones collectors lust after most fiercely. In addition, since wealthy collectors usually go after the best pieces, the best stuff is likely to hold its value better should the economy suffer a downturn. When other collectors have resorted to eating pork and beans and selling their collections, wealthy collectors can afford to grill filet mignon and hold on to their collectibles until the market rises. Average and poor-quality merchandise is hard to unload during the best of times; it can become an albatross hanging around your neck during a recession.

3. **Go for collectibles that are linked to the present.** Items that are still produced in some form, such as coins, stamps, and furniture, have more appeal than items that are obsolete. There is certainly a market for armor, straight razors, and 45 RPM records, but the market for books, paintings, and glass is bigger and better. A living collection continues to bring collectors to the fold; a dead collection attracts far fewer people.

4. **Shun "instant collectibles."** Buy those plates, thimbles, cookie jars, and whatnots if you like them as household decorations; don't buy them as investments. They hold their value about as well as a snowball holds its shape in August.

5. **Buy with your head, not your heart.** If you love it, buy it for pleasure—but not for investment. The item that appeals to you might be the least valuable item in the genre. That's okay, unless you're interested in resale. If you want to make money from your collection, learn as much as you can before you buy, and buy items that will hold their value or increase.

All in the Family: Uncle Sam

Assume that tomorrow you buy a stamp that you've been drooling over for years. This makes you a collector. You finance it by selling an autographed letter. This makes you a dealer. In passing, you gaze lovingly at your other investment-grade stamps. You know they will pay for your child's college education. So you're an investor. Collector, dealer, investor: you'll very likely wear all three hats. No one cares which hat you wear when.

Actually, you and I don't care, but our uncle does. Our dear Uncle Sam—and his kinfolk at the Internal Revenue Service—has his eye on you.

As far as the government is concerned, all collectors fit into one of two groups: You either intend to make money from your collection or you don't. If you make money, the government wants its cut. If you don't make money, the government wishes you well. But Uncle is not without mercy. If you intend to make money but actually suffer a loss, the government will share in that loss to some degree. This is only true if you are selling collectibles as a business. Consult your accountant for specific guidelines that apply to your tax situation.

But for many collectors, the picture is not so rosy. People who buy things for investments, even when they don't especially like them, often get slapped upside their heads when prices plummet. Sometimes they can't even recoup their initial investments. People who do not learn the ropes may find themselves *on* the ropes. Avoid heartache by following these guidelines for buying collectibles:

➤ **Start small.** Stick with inexpensive collectibles that give you pleasure. This way you are not spending a lot, so you don't have to worry about losing a lot.

➤ **Learn, learn, learn.** Pay attention to what everyone says. Then sift through the information to see what makes the most sense. Double-check it in several sources.

➤ **Keep careful records.** That way, if you do have to sell, you can square things with Uncle Sam easily. I recommend that you use a separate checking account or charge card to purchase antiques and collectibles. Record your cash purchases in a ledger.

Big Deals

When Frank Horwath of Illinois was just a kid, he began collecting nails. His father was a carpenter, and young Frank was often called upon to sort the nails. Today, Frank has more than 15,000 varieties of nails, including hand-forged, cast, and machine-made samples. All the nails are documented and mounted on display boards. It is probably the most complete nail collection in the world. Among his treasures is a nail from the Dome of the Rock, the oldest existing Islamic shrine; a nail from the home of William Ellery, one of the signers of the Declaration of Independence; and a collection of nails from most of the state capitol buildings.

Trouble in River City

Like true love and super premium ice cream, every passion has its downside. With love, it's the reality of bills and children; with ice cream, it's those darned calories. When you buy antiques and collectibles, you face equally upsetting dangers:

➤ Damaged goods

➤ Fakes and forgeries

➤ Speculation

Let's take a look at each of these risks.

Damage Control

Take a moment to skim the collectible ads in any newspaper or magazine. I'll bet my collection of antique pins that you'll find one that says, "We buy broken Hummels and other porcelain." Look a little further down the page. Can you find the ad that declares, "We sell repaired Hummels and other porcelain"? Substitute any reparable collectible for "Hummel" and "porcelain," and you'll find this ad all over the world.

What do you do if you discover something odd on a collectible? How can you tell whether it's a defect or merely an imperfection having no real consequence? If it is your lucky day, maybe the imperfection is even something that adds to the value of the collectible. The problem with damaged goods is that you really can't tell whether the damage is significant, at least not without help. Here are some solutions:

➤ **Talk to the dealer.** Most dealers can be trusted; after all, their reputations are at stake. That's why many serious collectors use the same dealers over and over. They develop trusting relationships.

➤ **Research the item.** If you have any doubts at all about the item, you need to research it in greater detail. Check pictures in reference texts and price guides; talk to other collectors.

➤ **Get a professional appraisal.** If the collectible is especially valuable, call in an expert to do an appraisal.

The final decision can only be yours. If you are unhappy with what you have discovered, don't buy the object.

In addition, many pieces come damaged. Repairs can definitely affect the price of the item. The specific reduction will vary greatly, though, depending not only on the extent of the damage but on how the buyer perceives the damage. Here are some examples:

➤ **Glass.** Damage can destroy the value of a glass piece. Many dealers will not even handle cracked or chipped glass.

➤ **Ephemera.** Even slight damage can be almost impossible to repair and will therefore sharply affect the cost (and value) of the piece.

➤ **Pottery.** Damaged stoneware and other pottery, in contrast, is usually easier to repair and thus the price is not significantly affected.

➤ **Furniture.** The price of antique furniture is also not greatly affected by slight damage that's been well repaired.

As a rule of thumb, you can count on getting a piece for about 50 percent less than the asking price if there is noticeable damage.

But the amount that a collector is willing to pay for a damaged piece depends on how badly the collector wants the particular piece. Damaged one-of-a-kind or very rare pieces usually fly off the shelf because buyers know they are not likely to get an undamaged one. On the other hand, damaged mass-market items

Caveat Emptor

In 1979 a promoter placed an ad in *Barron's* magazine called "Collecting as an Investment." It resembled an editorial that compared a new "limited edition" plate with plates that had risen greatly in value. Although the article was clearly identified as a paid advertisement, it was widely distributed to "limited edition" collectors as "an article that appeared in *Barron's,* and reprinted with permission." It worked. The plates zoomed out of the warehouse, but resale value was zilch. Beware: Fake editorials are still planted in several collectibles and antiques publications.

Tricks of the Trade

Cracks and chips in an antique stoneware jug (one more than 100 years old) are considered serious only if they pierce the designs. Otherwise, the value won't be seriously affected.

will languish in dusty corners, because collectors know that a better piece will undoubtedly come onto the market soon. What does all this mean? To start with, it means that in some instances, you can bargain to get a better deal.

"Need, Speed, Greed"—What About Fakes?

What are your chances of coming across a fake antique or collectible? Higher than you think—much higher. For example, in the decade and a half that Thomas Hoving was with the Metropolitan Museum of Art, he examined 50,000 works of art in all fields. He claims that *fully 40 percent* were either phonies or so badly restored or misattributed that they were just the same as forgeries. Since then, Hoving is sure that the percentage has risen. What few professionals are willing to admit is that the art and antique world is permeated with fakery.

Galloping Gimmes

One reason there are so many fakes around today is due to greed. Everyone wants to get rich quick. When the collectibles and antiques market exploded in the seventies and eighties, fakes flourished. The young instant millionaires and billionaires bought art and antiques for investment or as a sign of prestige and social superiority. Originals were not plentiful enough, and fakes filled the gaps. And despite the general crash of the art market, fakes continue to flourish.

For example, about 25 years ago, an unscrupulous art dealer "invented" an Egyptian tomb hidden under tarps in the desert. He used the "tomb" to unload piles of second-rate Egyptian antiquities to rich and gullible people. John and Yoko Ono Lennon, interested art collectors, were not as stupid as most; they insisted on traveling to Egypt to see "their" tomb. In a panic, the dealer had the Lennons' tarot card reader call them in Cairo and warn them that a dangerous man in Egypt would harm them and they should return to New York at once, which they did. Of course, the tarot card reader was in on the scam. The Lennons avoided buying the fakes.

Squeeze the Goods

One of the best ways to detect fakes is to examine or handle as many as possible of the objects you want to collect. By doing this, you'll learn the look or the feel of the real thing. It is also important to read as much as you can about the collectibles you want. Finding this information is not as difficult as you may think, and I hope this will become more apparent as you read on in this book.

Use the "Is It Real? Checklist" guidelines as you examine each article.

Tricks of the Trade

A fake will often look richer and more appealing than the original. It may look slightly older, too.

Is It Real? Checklist

❑ Look at the article closely and jot down your first impression. First impressions are almost always right.

❑ Examine the object in as much detail as possible. Take your time and scrutinize every inch of the object. Use a magnifying glass.

❑ Describe the condition of the piece, noting every bump and scrape.

❑ If possible, ask what the item was used for. Remember that, until recently, most objects that we now collect served a purpose.

❑ Determine whether the condition of the piece supports the way it was used. If not, what appears incongruous?

❑ Does the item show wear where it would logically appear, for example, the table ring on a plate or the footrest on a highchair?

❑ Describe the style of the work. Is there one single style or many different ones?

❑ Figure out whether the date given for the work matches the date of its style.

❑ Gather as much documentation as you can. Remember that such documents are very easy to fake.

❑ Ask about the existence of provenance. Can it can be proven.

❑ If the work is extremely valuable, you may want to submit it for sophisticated professional analysis. Some of the tests available include carbon 14 dating, thermoluminescence, ultraviolet, x-ray, and autoradiography (which evaluates particular pigments).

❑ Check out any rumors in the marketplaces about what the object really is and where it really comes from.

After you have completed the guidelines, list all your doubts and track down every one. If you cannot explain each one to your satisfaction, keep looking—before you buy.

Caveat Emptor

Ironically, if nothing at all is known about the fake antique or collectible, it is often taken more seriously, since people believe that great works of art will be found in the most unlikely spots.

Speculation

One time or another, most collectors get swept away by exceptional market prospects. Like gamblers on a roll, we wager just a little bit more than we planned to. A dash of speculation adds a zest to collecting, but heavy speculation is a very different kettle of (collectible) fish.

The logic seems unshakable: "If one of an item is good, ten must be better." Nope. There's no way to corner the market in any event, so why buy more of the identical item? And if dealers seem unwilling to sell, the speculator becomes even more determined. Heavy speculation is risky business. Manufacturers and dealers survive. The big losers are always the speculators themselves.

The Least You Need to Know

➤ Never assume that you'll recoup what you paid for an item.

➤ Inflation is good for collectibles.

➤ Always buy the best items in the best condition, especially collectibles that are linked to the present. Shun "instant collectibles."

➤ Buy something because you like it, not for speculation. And keep careful records for the tax man.

➤ Damages affect the value of collectibles to different extents, depending on the type of damage and the item itself.

➤ Beware of fakes; there are more of them for sale than you think.

Chapter 7

Treasures and Turnips: Selling Your Collectibles

In This Chapter

➤ Reality check: Get a handle on selling collectibles

➤ Pricing and appraising collectibles

➤ Tool time

➤ Secrets to selling success

➤ Selling at yard sales, shows, and auctions

If your luck as a collector has held so far, you may already be experiencing a problem common to most of your collector compatriots: Your purchases are threatening to overrun your home. The garage is full, the attic floor is sagging, the trunk of the car is bulging, and you suspect that a few extra children may be hiding under the boxes in the living room. And there's a great art auction today, a promising garage sale on Saturday, and who could miss the annual swap meet on Tuesday? You're in over your head.

It's time to sell a few things, bunky. Take a deep breath, stop kicking the floor, and get ready to part with some of your purchases.

In this chapter, you'll first learn how to price your collectibles. I'll give you step-by-step instructions for figuring out how to appraise your objets d'art. To make it even easier, I've provided helpful worksheets and displays. Then, I'll list the best markets for selling your collectibles. I also promise to share your pain at parting with some of your collection.

This Little Piggy Went to Market

Cocky seller at an auction: "This vase is priceless."

Eternal optimist at stamp show: "I know I'll get a bundle for my stamps."

Beautiful dreamer at a rare book show: "I'll be able to retire on the money I get for my first edition of *Green Eggs and Ham.*"

Web Wise

Joining professional organizations is a great way to keep up with current prices. The Train Collectors Association, for example, can be reached on the Web at www.traincollectors.org. The U.S. Historical Society (which issues historically inspired collectibles, such as sculptures, miniatures, plates, and dolls) is on the Web at www.ushsdolls.com.

Some of these hopeful souls may hit the collectibles jackpot, but most will be disappointed. In Part 1, "Why Is There a Boom in Collectibles?" you learned the cardinal rule of selling collectibles: *A collectible is worth only what someone will pay for it.* No matter what the guidebook says, what the auctioneer promises, what the shop owner claims—the market is a fickle thing.

For example, some desperate parents paid $250 to $325 for the "highly collectible" Tickle Me Elmo during the 1996 shortage. Today, Elmo and his tickle are back on the shelves—selling for about $30. And who can predict the future? Some baseball cards have done well for their owners. For example, a second-year Mickey Mantle card produced by Topps Card Company now trades for $15,000 to $20,000. On the other hand, most items associated with former Cincinnati player Pete Rose attract few buyers. Who knew Mickey would have staying power but Pete wouldn't?

How can you sell your collectibles with confidence? Read on to find out.

Pennies from Heaven: Pricing Collectibles

Price an item by learning the five W's:

1. What is it?
2. When was it made?
3. Where was it made?
4. Who made it?
5. Why is it worth its value?

Here's how to make this method work for you.

Tools of the Trade

First of all, you shouldn't sell anything until you know what it is worth. You must begin by getting an *appraisal*—a knowledgeable estimate of an object's value. You can do this yourself or hire an appraiser. If your items are very valuable, you will of course wish to seek out professional appraisers.

But if hiring a professional appraiser will cost you more than the value of the object, it's time to learn how to do an appraisal yourself. And even if your objects are extremely valuable, you want to have an idea of their worth before you hire an appraiser.

Appraisers would like you to think they use specialized equipment to appraise different objects. They actually use inexpensive, everyday tools—nothing you can't get at your local hardware store. Here are three of the most useful tools to have on hand when you judge the value of a collectible: a black light, calipers, and a price guide. Let's look at each tool in detail:

Learn the Lingo

An **appraisal** is a written or oral estimate of the value of a collectible.

➤ **A black light.** Professionals use a black light to find damage and identify fakes. The black light (which is actually violet or purple) "sees" through the surface to reveal cracks, changes in texture, glue, blotches of paint, and other irregularities. As a result, a black light is especially useful to analyze glass, find damage in porcelain, discern repairs to furniture and sculpture, and reveal overpainting of pictures.

Using a black light takes practice; you must know what you're looking for before you use it. A black light works best in a completely dark room.

Caveat Emptor

Black lights are pricey, and you may not want to invest the money in one. You can make your own black light by buying a black light bulb from a hardware store or novelty shop and screwing it temporarily into a lamp. But read the directions carefully before you start because a black light can be dangerous to your eyes.

➤ **Calipers.** You can buy this handy tool in a hardware shop. Because early furniture was often made from unseasoned wood, the finished product dried out and shrank. Experts examine furniture with a calipers to find irregular shapes in finials, legs, and spindles. A trained eye can usually spot such irregularities quickly and easily, but beginners find calipers useful.

To use the calipers, tighten them until they barely touch the wood. (Caution: If you screw them too tightly, you may mar the wood.) Then gently rotate the calipers. If the calipers become tight and drag, or if you see a space between the instrument and the wood, then you have an irregular shape and an older piece of furniture. On the other hand, if the calipers measure a perfectly round piece, the furniture is modern.

Tricks of the Trade

You can also use a scale to weigh small objects such as silver flatware. Any well-calibrated scale, such as one used by chefs to weigh amounts of ingredients, will be fine for most objects.

➤ **Price guides.** There are standard, authoritative price guides for every type of collectible, from baseball cards to Barbies, comics to coins, silver to sculpture. These are clearly labeled: The one for Disneyana, for example, is called *Tomart's Disneyana Catalog and Price Guide.* You can often get the guide you need from the library. It's important to get the most recent guide, however, to keep up with selling and pricing trends in your field. This will tell you what's hot—and what's not.

Appraise Like a Pro

When you appraise an item, you name it, describe it, and assign it a monetary value. Professional appraisers give weight and authenticity to their appraisals by presenting their judgments in written form on letterhead stationery. You can appraise an item by preparing a chart like the following one. It's an appraisal of some comic books that recently sold at auction.

Appraisal Chart—Comic Books

Article	Description	Appraised Value
Captain America #1	VF condition	$36,000
Human Torch #2	GD condition	$2,000
Slam Bang #1	VF condition	$1,000
More Fun #53	FN condition	$30,000
All Flash #1	VF condition	$11,000
Description Code		
MT	Mint condition	Near perfect in every way
NM	Near mint condition	Minor imperfections
VF	Very fine condition	Small creases in spine
FN	Fine condition	Above-average copy
VG	Very good condition	Average used comic book
GD	Good condition	Small pieces may be missing
FR	Fair condition	Centerfold may be missing

Appraisal Chart

Article	Description	Appraised Value
Michael Jackson's glove	White, rhinestone-covered	$27,900
Prince outfit	*Purple Rain* stage costume	$18,600
Teddy bear	Rod-jointed Steiff apricot plush, ca. 1904	$11,770
Teddy bear	Red plush Steiff once owned by Princess Xenia of Russia, ca. 1906–1909	$12,100

When you appraise collectibles for sale, start by separating the items into two piles: the items you know about and the items you don't know about. Appraise the items you know about first. Then tackle the unfamiliar ones. They will need some research and time.

This Little Piggy Sold Roast Beef: Know the Market

A desirable, collectible, or antique is usually sold in very much the same place and manner in which it was purchased. For example, if a rare vase bought at an exclusive antique shop is offered for sale, it will likely be placed at a similar gallery. An old plate bought at a flea market often ends up being sold at a flea market. Collectibles such as stamps and coins that were purchased at retail establishments will usually be resold at stores when their owners want to trade up or raise cash. Desirables purchased through collector trade publications will attract the most attention (and best prices) when offered for resale through these same publications. Of course there are delicious exceptions, but they are too rare to bet the ranch on. Therefore, by considering the source of your collectible, you should have a better idea of where and how it will be sold.

Viva La Difference?

Beginning collectors usually buy from whatever source strikes their fancy—a display in a store window, a flea market, a thrift shop, and so on. The source really makes very little difference as long as

Caveat Emptor

Don't be discouraged when you first start appraising. You *can* learn to judge quality. Once you begin to examine pieces closely and make comparisons, you will find that you will develop a sixth sense for distinguishing the wheat from the chaff.

Tricks of the Trade

To restore or not to restore—that is the question. Here is the answer: If it is clean, if it works, and if it looks good, don't restore it. Keep the price down, sell it, and sell it fast.

Web Wise

In Chapter 8, "CyberShopping: Buying and Selling Online," you'll learn all about selling on the Web.

you are pleased with your purchase and intend to enjoy it. It does make a big difference, however, if you are looking to sell your collectible or antique.

There are also regional differences in taste that affect pricing. Victorian furniture, for example, is much more in demand in California than it is in Florida. Regional tastes and preferences have a strong influence on the demand for specific collectibles.

The Secret to Selling Success

Here it is: Buy low, sell high—and sell fast. Although prices in the antiques and collectibles markets seldom jump as wildly as the Dow Jones, desirables, collectibles, and antiques, unlike stocks, are not easy to store. A thousand shares of Coca-Cola stock can fit in your pocket; an antique console or cabinet might crowd a small room. And while you can usually liquidate a thousand shares of stock with a telephone call, the same cannot be said of a piece of furniture, a pile of comics, or a series of prints. So sell your unwanted desirables, antiques, and collectibles fast to keep your cash available for the next deal that comes along.

There are many places to buy desirables, antiques, and collectibles. Fortunately, there are just as many places to sell them. Each place has its strengths and weaknesses, and successful sellers use nearly all these venues, depending on what they are selling and when. So let's take a look at some of the best places to sell your prized possessions.

Selling Privately

If you have relatively few items for sale, opening a shop or hitting the show circuit is premature. Put an inexpensive classified ad in the newspaper to attract private customers. You can keep the names, addresses, and telephone numbers of especially good customers to use as you build a client list. This way, the next time you have some items for sale, you can contact these people first—if they haven't already called you 17 times to see whether you have anything new.

Let Their Fingers Do the Walking: Advertising

Start by finding out which newspapers are the most widely read in your area. Study their ads carefully, compare rates, and make your choice. When you write your ad, use boldface type to emphasize the item being sold, stress the positive aspects of the piece, and include the price. This serves to screen out all but the most serious buyers. Here's an ad you can use as a model:

> **ANTIQUE SETTEE.** Circa 1860. Hand-carved walnut. Original finish and upholstery. $500. Call 555-1234 after 5 P.M.

Show and Tell

As a courtesy to your family, let them know when someone is coming to see the items you have for sale. Then Grandma can get off the treadmill, and your brother-in-law won't walk in the room in his skivvies. I recommend that you place the items you have for sale in a separate room, such as a garage. It is uncomfortable for everyone to transact business amid the breakfast dishes.

Money Business

You have stated your price, now let the buyer make an offer. Why? The offer may be more than you intended to settle for. Perhaps you are ready to take as little as $350 for the settee you advertised at $500. The buyer may offer $450. Look momentarily upset, and then snap it up and reel it in.

But if the buyer's offer is too low, explain with your best company manners that you have too much invested in the piece to let it go for that little. You may also want to groan a little for effect, scratch your head, and look pained. A soft chuckle may also work. Then continue the discussion until a mutually agreeable price can be established. If not, move on to the next buyer.

When you finalize the sale, give a receipt. Indicate the amount, the date, and an exact description of the piece. Mark it "All sales final" and shake hands. I favor cash over checks.

Tricks of the Trade

Make sure that any furniture you have for sale is clean and empty. No one wants to open a drawer and find an old cheese sandwich, Junior's jock strap, or the dog's bone. If this does happen, under no circumstances should you squeal, "Oh! *That's* where it went!"

Caveat Emptor

Always get payment in full. You're selling an object, not establishing a relationship.

Selling at Yard Sales

GIGANTIC FAMILY YARD SALE! Yard and garage sales are other good ways to weed items from your collection. Organizing a multifamily sale is not much more difficult than setting up your own event, and it's worth the effort because it can attract hundreds of additional people and thousands of additional dollars.

Neither Rain Nor Shine …

While sitting over a cup a' java with the neighbors, pick a time for the sale. Don't limit an event of this magnitude to just one day; try to run it over Saturday and Sunday. Avoid scheduling the sale the same time as big local attractions such as country fairs, high school commencement, traditional travel holidays, and highly publicized trials. Also be on the lookout for major street repairs, which could make it hard for even the most determined customers to reach the sale. Pick the location; it should be the house that is easiest to reach and owned by the most good-natured neighbor.

Of course you can hold a yard sale all on your own. But there is profit in numbers …

Alert the Media

Place ads in the newspaper; tack signs and flyers to everything that doesn't move. Here's an effective ad that you can use as a model:

> **GIGANTIC FAMILY YARD SALE!**
> OVER 25 HOUSEHOLDS!
> 62 Sunset Avenue
>
> Saturday and Sunday
> June 1 and 2
> 9 A.M. – 4 P.M.

Make big, bold signs. The wording should be large enough to read as you're driving by. My area has tag sales all the time in warm weather, and it drives me nuts when the sellers write in pen in itty-bitty print, or print it on their computer in 12-point font. I can only see it if I walk up to it and read it. As a result, many sales have lost my business (and I've been known to go to seven sales in one day). My favorite for signs? I've found that fluorescent orange and yellow paper with big black lettering works great.

Tricks and Tips

I offer these hints as a veteran of many garage and yard sales:

➤ **Clearly mark every item with the price.**

➤ **Put away any items that are not for sale.** People will buy *anything*.

➤ **Arrange items by types.** For example, put all the tools in one area, all the clothing in another, and all the books in a third.

➤ **Be ready for the early birds.** As you have already learned in Chapter 4, "Shop 'Till You Drop," the Super Shoppers will be ringing your doorbell at 6 A.M. Make a lot of coffee.

➤ **Have plenty of people to help.** Watch for items that "walk away" and people who look less than honest.

➤ **Have plenty of change on hand and keep a close eye on the change box.**

➤ **Be strapped for cash.** Unless someone is assigned to permanently sit by the change box, wear a carpenter's-type pocketed apron or a zip-type fanny bag around your waist.

➤ **Count all money carefully,** both the amount tendered and the amount returned in change. A small calculator is useful for the busy or math-impaired (like me!).

➤ **Paper or plastic?** Be sure to have old newspapers and bags ready for wrapping up the sales. Novice buyers and walk-ins won't be prepared with their own wrapping and bags.

➤ **Have fun.** Let the kids have their own mini-sale of toys and lemonade; have plenty of junk food on hand to add a festive mood to the day.

Tricks of the Trade

A few days before the sale, mark the route clearly so that Wrong-Way Corrigans don't get lost. And the day after the sale, be sure to remove all the signs so that myopic stragglers don't end up on your doorstep for weeks to come.

Selling to Dealers

Dealers who have a shop or participate in many road shows are often short on inventory. As you gain a reputation as a knowledgeable collector, dealers will become interested in your collection. You can save yourself and the dealer miles, hours, and dollars by taking pictures of pieces that you have for sale. If you're mailing photographs and information to dealers and want your materials returned, indicate that on your cover letter and enclose a stamped self-addressed envelope.

Web Wise

You can also scan pictures of your collectibles and e-mail them to dealers. Many savvy private collectors/dealers have established their own Web pages, where they post items for sale. It's easier to do than you might think, so why not give it a try?

Consider taking the idea of selling to dealers one step further and look for specific items that you know certain dealers want. When you make a great find, wash, sort, and label each piece before you present it to the dealer. Make the items as attractive and easy to view as possible—just as a dealer would do.

Do your homework so that you can be straightforward about the price that you want.

It's Showtime! Selling at Collectibles Shows and Flea Markets

If you have enough merchandise and time, you may want to dip a toe into the waters of swap meets/collectibles shows/flea markets. Flea markets are far more casual than collectibles shows; they also tend to attract fewer Daddy Warbucks types. Save your quality items—furniture, glassware, fragile books, and the like—for a major indoors antique show. This will prevent the great unwashed from pawing over your valuables. Either event, however, will give you a greater opportunity to sell a wide range of items.

How can you tell when it's showtime?

➤ Do you have the physical stamina? We're talking some serious heavy lifting.

➤ Do you have the inventory? You can't sell it if you don't have it.

Study the shows before deciding where to exhibit. Match your goods to the spirit of the show. Avoid the temptation to bring everything you have. Instead, select those pieces that will draw attention to your booth, will complement each other, and will transform a browser into a buyer.

Hey, Check It Out!

Use these suggestions to attract buyers to your booth:

➤ **Avoid clutter.** Give each piece enough space so it can be noticed. Let people see three sides of the bookcase, not just the front.

➤ **Make it easy to shop.** Wide, open paths make it easy for people to reach your booth, especially the physically challenged shopper. Place the larger pieces along the back of the booth, middle-sized pieces in the middle, and low pieces as an island in the middle. As shoppers approach the booth, they are naturally drawn in one end of the booth and out the other.

➤ **Highlight one special piece.** This is your draw, the piece that makes 'em come and look. You may not sell the vase with the $1,000 price tag, but if nearly everyone comes to admire it, you *will* get a chance to sell something else.

➤ **Provide plenty of light.** Dark booths are unappealing and vaguely sinister. They make it appear as though you are hiding flaws and damages in the merchandise. Light makes everything seem more valuable.

➤ **Clean your merchandise.** A sparkling piece of glassware or a polished tabletop is much more appealing than a dusty and dirty one. An added bonus: Potential buyers can see there are no hidden flaws or damage and will appreciate the loving care their purchase received by its previous owner.

➤ **Price and describe each item.** Make it easy for browsers to know what they are handling. The price tag tells them how much it costs, but the description tells them why it's worth the price.

➤ **Dress for success.** Don't look like a schlump. Dress neatly and well. Look alert and happy. This is not the time to schmooze with friends. You're working, so work. If you want to be treated like a professional, you have to look and act the part.

➤ **Keep your booth clean.** No food or drink. This greatly lessens the chance of accidents and damage.

Selling at Auctions

One forty-seven going once. Do I hear one forty-eight? One forty-eight? Won't someone give me one forty-eight? I've got one forty-eight. Now one forty-nine. Do I hear one forty-nine? Come on, folks, we know this chest is worth two hundred if it's worth a nickel. One forty-nine is a steal. Do I hear one forty-nine? One forty-eight going once. You're going to kick yourself in the morning. One forty-eight going twice. SOLD!

That simple word "sold" leaves one person elated, several people frustrated, a bunch of people uncertain, and the rest of the audience eager for the auctioneer to move on to the next item. Nothing in the collectibles business is as unpredictable as an auction, and few places offer such odd deals. Dealers pull out what's left of their hair trying to figure out why a table identical to one priced at $300 in a shop sells at an auction for $500, yet an auction held the following week, for an identical table, brings only $200.

So what makes the difference? *You.* Auctions bring together a wildly diverse group of collectors, buyers, investors, sellers, and mere onlookers. This lends auctions their excitement and unpredictability. Although you will probably not have enough merchandise to hold your own auction, you can take even a few pieces to a local auctioneer for sale.

Types of Auctions

Any collectible and antique can appear on the auction block. Here are a few of the most common types of auctions:

➤ **Household auctions.** Sometimes referred to as an "estate auction," perhaps the most common type.

➤ **Farm auctions.** Dominated by machinery and tools but may also include old furniture and household items.

➤ **Antiques auctions.** Held indoors often in elegant surroundings.

Caveat Emptor

Never attend an auction without doing your homework first. You could get stung badly.

➤ **Consignment auctions.** Held on a regular basis, such as the second and fourth Sunday of every month. The auctioneer assembles a collection of antiques and household goods to be auctioned off to the highest bidder.

The Price Is Right?

Most auctioneers will give you a brief verbal valuation of an object without charging a fee. If you appear to be a serious vendor with some important antiques and collectibles, a valuer will often travel short distances, free, to appraise your collection. In nearly all cases, you will be charged for out-of-town visits. Some valuers ask to see photographs of the items you will be offering for sale before they will comment on value.

Timing Is Everything

How quickly can a lot be offered for auction? This is a key point. Since furniture auctions are held frequently, furniture is easily placed for general sale. But special items, such as comics or dolls, may be retained for a collector's sale. This allows the auction house enough time to gather a large enough selection of these items and to contact collectors worldwide. What does this mean to you as the seller? You could wait months until the items you want to sell come under the hammer.

Fees

Check the fees beforehand so there are no unpleasant surprises. I recommend that you visit the auction house in person and get everything in writing. Here are some of the fees you might be charged:

➤ Minimum charges per lot.

➤ Fees if a lot fails to reach its reserve. The auctioneer who received your items for sale will want to agree on a reserve quickly. Don't allow yourself to be pressured. It may be possible to wait to see what interest your goods spark. This will help you set a more realistic reserve than if you make a quick decision.

➤ Cataloging fees.

➤ Fees for illustrations.

➤ Insurance charges.

➤ Sales commission.

Talk the Talk and Walk the Walk

You can't walk the walk if you don't talk the talk. Here are some terms you should know to be a real auction maven:

➤ **Buyer's pool (or buyer's ring).** This is a conspiracy used by a group of buyers, generally big-time dealers, to hold down the bidding on key items in order to increase the profits. Here's how it works: A group of dealers who would normally be bidding against each other agree before the auction which one will "buy" each item and what the top limit will be. When that item comes up, the other dealers in the group do not bid, thereby clearing the path for the designated buyer. Afterward, they divvy up the spoils. This can hurt you as a seller because it can drive prices down on items that you have on the block. It's also illegal.

Learn the Lingo

A **reserve** is the price below which the vendor will not sell an item. An auctioneer cannot reveal the reserve, but you may be able to get the information from someone in the salesroom.

➤ **Call-ups.** A person can request that a particular piece be put up for sale as soon as possible. The auctioneer pauses every so often in the bidding and asks for "call-ups." This allows buyers to get what they want, pack up their tents, and move on to other auctions—or go home to gloat over their purchases. As a seller, "call-ups" tell you what's hot and what's not.

➤ **Choice.** This means that the final bidder has the choice of all the items sold in a lot. It also means that the bidder will have the choice of taking any number of them, from one to all. Thus, if six glasses were sold "choice," the buyer could take one, some, or all. If any remain, they are often offered to the second-highest bidder at the hammer price. If they remain unsold, they are auctioned again—usually at a greatly reduced price.

Obviously this is not as good for the seller—and that's you in this chapter.

➤ **Consignments.** To help spice up what would otherwise be a dull sale, auctioneers will often take pieces on *consignment*. These great pieces usually come from well-known collectors who are disposing of parts of their collection or from dealers who had items left over from other sales. As a seller, you can offer any item you want on consignment as well.

➤ **Jumping bids.** This is a psychological move used by bidders to discourage other bidders from staying in the game. Let's say the bids are progressing at $5 jumps and the price is currently $200. A bidder wants to knock out the opposition and so "jumps the bid" to $225. This is nice for the seller; it lets you know you have an eager-beaver buyer.

➤ **So much apiece, take all.** This is most commonly used with sets of antiques where you will bid on just one of them, but your final purchase price will be the last bid times the number of items. For example, if a set of four glasses is up for bid and the auctioneer announces at the beginning they will be sold "so much apiece, winner take all," and someone bids for one glass at $10, the final price will be $10 × 4 = $40. This is great for you as a seller, because you will be able to sell more sets of merchandise.

The Least You Need to Know

➤ Start selling items from your collection when the dog disappears under the boxes—and your dog is a Great Dane.

➤ With some simple household tools and reference materials, you can appraise most collectibles yourself.

➤ If possible, know where the article came from before you try to sell it.

➤ The secret to selling success is to buy low, sell high—and sell fast. This frees your cash for other purchases.

Chapter 8

CyberShopping: Buying and Selling Online

In This Chapter

➤ The Internet explosion

➤ Overview of online auction sites

➤ Three kinds of online auction sites

➤ Buying collectibles online

➤ Selling collectibles online

The familiar advertising slogan "Let your fingers do the walking" has taken on a whole new meaning since the Internet explosion. No matter what you collect—china to chairs, teddy bears to trains, and furniture to figurines—you'll find it for sale on the Web.

Because of the growing popularity of these sites, chances are very good that you'll be letting *your* fingers walk (or your mouse click) through cyberspace to buy and sell collectibles. As a result, you need to know how to operate in this exciting new environment. That's what this chapter is all about.

First, we'll survey some of the most popular online sites for collectibles. Then I'll explain the differences among these sites, providing examples of each one. Finally, I'll show you how to buy and sell your collectibles at online auction sites.

Going, Going, Gone!

Today, I found the following items for sale on a top online auction site:

Framed Abbott Graves Watercolor Painting

Four-Foot Cast Brass Eagle with Outstretched Wings

Rare Stoneware Face Vessel—Georgia circa 1900

Jacobean Bed

Chippendale Secretary Desk—circa 1780

Bronze Statue of a Polar Bear by C. Bertran

Black Hawk Horse Weathervane

William S. Aylward Marine Oil Painting

Three Little Pigs Hooked Rug

Dorflinger Brilliant Cut Crystal Compote

Fine Set of Paint-Decorated Chairs

Maritime Ships Painting on Board

Early Nineteenth-Century Needlework of a Girl Mourning

Large Clipper Ship Weathervane

This is only the tip of the iceberg. Increasingly, collectors use online sites to buy and sell items in thousands of categories, including antiques, artwork, Beanie Babies, books, computers, coins, collectibles, dolls, electronics, ephemera, glass, jewelry, gemstones, magazines, photography, pottery, porcelain, sports memorabilia, stamps, and toys.

Business is booming online, with new cyberstores and auction sites popping up weekly. Don't take my word for it; following are the one-month average sales figures for the top 10 Web sites. Some of these sites offer only collectibles, and others offer products that will surely become collectibles—someday!

Web Site	Number of Total Sales
1. www.amazon.com (Amazon)	11.3 million
2. www.ebay.com (eBay)	10.0 million
3. www.aol.com/shopping (America Online)	9.4 million
4. www.bluemountain.com (Blue Mountain Arts)	9.2 million
5. www.bn.com (Barnes & Noble)	4.4 million
6. www.cnet.com (CNET, software download service)	4.2 million
7. www.cdnow.com (CD NOW)	4.2 million
8. www.mypoints.com (MyPoints)	3.6 million
9. www.freeshop.com (FreeShop)	3.2 million
10. www.valupage.com (ValuPage)	3.0 million

These sites can be divided into three distinct types of online shopping sites:

➤ Online auction sites

➤ Companies with Web sites

➤ Hybrid sites

Let's look at each type of online auction site in greater detail.

Online Auction Sites

In 1995, when he was 28 years old, Pierre Omidyar started eBay to help his girlfriend, a Pez collector having difficulty locating the dispensers she wanted. What started out as a small group of Pez collectors has turned into a veritable gold mine. As of this book's publication date, eBay is the world's largest online auction site.

Big Deals

In addition to being the world's first person-to-person online trading community, eBay is the world's biggest one. In the first quarter of 1998 alone, eBay individuals sold $100 million worth of merchandise; by the fourth quarter, sales were $307 million. Whatever you need, odds are you'll find it at eBay: There are over 2,000 categories and more than 2.5 million auctions a day.

Like similar online auction sites, eBay serves as a middleman. The company brings together buyer and seller. There's no office, no warehouse, no gallery: These online auctions exist only in cyberspace. Currently, there are more than 350 Internet auction sites. Here are some of the most popular ones, arranged in alphabetical order:

➤ Amazon Auctions

➤ antiqnet.com (antique networking)

➤ Antique Photo (antique and historic photographs and related literature)

➤ Auction Universe (people-to-people online auction)

➤ Auctions MSN.com

➤ Bidshack.com

➤ Boxlot.com (antiques, collectibles, jewelry, coins, stamps, dolls, glass, postcards, ephemera, toys, trading cards, and more)

➤ Coin Universe

➤ Collect This

➤ eBay.com

➤ ehammer.com

➤ Excite Auctions at classifieds2000.com (collectibles, audio/video equipment, and musical instruments)

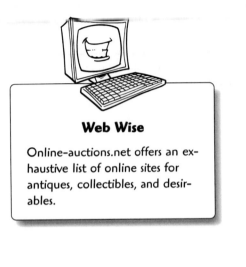

Web Wise

Online-auctions.net offers an exhaustive list of online sites for antiques, collectibles, and desirables.

➤ Haggle Online

➤ icollector.com (premium-quality lots from auction houses and dealers worldwide)

➤ Numismatics Online (coins)

➤ Quixell Ltd. (British)

➤ Sandafayre (postage stamp auctions with a range of philatelic items; single stamps, postal history, essays, proofs, postcards, collections, forgeries, revenue items, albums)

➤ tias.com (the Internet Antiques Shop)

➤ Universal Studio's Online Auction (live, interactive auctions specializing in celebrity memorabilia and collectibles)

➤ Up4Sale.com

➤ Utrade.com (person-to-person auction)

➤ Yahoo! Auctions (toys, sports memorabilia, etc.)

Companies with Web Sites

Increasingly, well-known antique stores and auction houses have established Web sites to attract additional customers. These companies include famous auction houses for fine arts and antiques such as Christie's and Doyle's.

Unlike the previous type of online auction sites, these firms conduct the majority of their business through real storefronts. They often publish print catalogs and have live auctions. You remember the kind: Real people sit together in the same room at the same time. But in addition, these businesses maintain a Web presence.

Hybrid Sites

Then we have composite sites that focus on online sales but do maintain warehouses around the country where sellers can deposit goods, if they wish. Buyers can then travel to these warehouses to examine the goods in person. An example of such a site is ehammer.com.

Brave New World

It's easy to buy collectibles from an online store. You simply "shop" for your goods by looking at pictures of each item on your computer screen. Then you select a method of payment, usually a credit card. For more on payment methods, see the "Top Ten Tips for *Buying* Collectibles Online," found later in this chapter.

But shopping through an online auction is a horse of a different color. All auction sites operate differently; so before you bid, know the site's rules, its warranties (if any), and exactly whom you're doing business with. For example, individuals hawk their own collectibles on eBay. The company leaves it to the buyers and sellers to handle the entire transaction and work out any problems. On occasion, eBay has banned a vendor from the service for unscrupulous behavior, but, in general, you're on your own.

The eBay site promotes honesty with its public message feature. Buyers can post comments about any seller, and sellers can post comments about customers. This feature can be used only if the buyer's or seller's e-mail address is listed on an auction page. Be aware, though, that the threat of public disclosure is no safeguard against getting fleeced (a buyer or a seller can change e-mail addresses). Furthermore, sellers fear it's too easy for a good reputation to be smeared by one disgruntled customer.

Basically, here's how an online auction works. Sellers post an ad on an auction site such as eBay, Onsale, or Auction Universe, describing the item they have for sale. Buyers respond by bidding on the item they wish to buy. Each item has indicated times specifying when its auction will start and when it will end. When the auction is over, the highest bidder wins. There are some significant variations, however, so stay tuned.

Tricks of the Trade

Some sites work in conjunction with companies like TradeSafe, which holds an escrow account for the interested parties to make sure everything is on the up-and-up.

Caveat Emptor

Online auctions can be addictive. From diamond rings to used coffins (I kid you not), the variety of available products seems limitless. The potential of getting that ultimate bargain, that ultimate high, is the carrot of the moment.

Caution: Cyber Con Ahead

The eBay auction site was founded on the belief that people are honest and trustworthy. Most are; some aren't.

The Internet Fraud Watch cites Web auctions as the number one Internet fraud. Online auction houses that serve as middlemen—such as ebay.com—say upfront that they don't guarantee the articles being offered for sale. They also don't guarantee that winning buyers will pay what they bid. This means you can get bitten on both ends, buying as well as selling. So how can you protect yourself? Try these ideas.

Top Ten Tips for **Buying** *Collectibles Online*

1. **Check the site.** We all know the stock prospectus mantra: "Past performance is no guarantee of future earnings." It holds true for online auction sites as well. Just because the site has a great reputation doesn't mean that you won't get burned. That's because you're not trading with *the site;* you're trading with *an individual* who is using the site.

   That said, you're still better off shopping at a reputable online auction site than at a shady one. Look for an online auction forum that's been established for a while, one that has policies for dealing with problems. Then, if a problem arises with a purchase, you have a clearly defined path to resolution.

   For example, every eBay user is covered by insurance free of charge under the terms of their program. If you paid for an item and never received it (or if you received the item, but it's less than what you expected), eBay will reimburse buyers up to $200, minus a $25 deductible.

Learn the Lingo

Snipers are people who close you out by bidding on an item moments before the auction closes.

Learn the Lingo

FAQs are "Frequently Asked Questions," an online tour through a Web site.

2. **Look before you leap.** Make sure you clearly understand the bidding procedures and policies *before* you place a bid. The temptation to jump right into the auction is powerful. Resist. Yes, a one-of-a-kind Ming vase may slip through your fingers while you're trying to get the lay of the land. On the other hand, by waiting to buy until you know how to bid, you'll avoid upsetting and expensive mistakes.

   Spend some time at the online auction site before you buy. For example, you'll learn to watch for *snipers,* people who bid on an item the moment before the auction closes. A sniper can outbid you by as little as a buck. Even if you're online, you may not have time to offer a counter bid. To prevent this problem, the better sites have a five-minute delay, extending the bidding time.

   A great place to start familiarizing yourself with a site is with its *FAQs* (Frequently Asked Questions). These lists usually give an overview of an online auction site.

3. **Shop a lot.** You may think you're getting something unique from the online auction—and you may be. But it's also possible that the item is

offered for sale on another online auction site for less money. So shop around; after all, there are more than 100 auction sites devoted to antiques, collectibles, and desirables.

In addition, you'd be surprised how often you can get the collectible you want from an online store rather than from an online auction. Remember: When you buy from a store, you get a warranty and a better return policy.

4. **Don't forget fees.** Some auction sites are free; others charge a percentage. For example, there's no charge to browse, bid on, or buy items at eBay, but you do pay fees to list and sell items.

    Nail down site fees as well as shipping and handling costs before you bid. You may discover that a seemingly "great buy" may not be so great by the time you add on shipping and handling.

5. **Check "auctions ending today" for best buys.** At the end of every day, check the "Auctions Ending Today" page to see what items are selling for. This not only will help you track the cost of items you collect, but can also help you decide whether you want to branch off into other collectibles.

6. **Use logic.** If the price is too good to be true, it probably is. There are two reasons for this: The item isn't what you think it is, or the item has a shady past.

    My friend Dennis Bengels, an expert on on-line auctions, shared his considerable expertise on these issues. Dennis told me about some books that were advertised as first editions. They were indeed first editions—book club first editions—and so they were worth far less than trade first editions.

Tricks of the Trade

Make sure the item's condition is clearly spelled out before you bid on it.

Caveat Emptor

An ounce of prevention: Ask that all items be insured when they're shipped.

Dennis also told me hair-raising tales of items that are listed at online auctions far below market price because they "fell off the back of a truck." You don't want to buy stolen goods.

7. **The name game.** Get the name of the person selling the item. That way, if something goes wrong, you have a starting point for resolving the issue. Remember that the online person you are dealing with can be anyone, based anywhere. Since it's easy to fake an e-mail address, make sure you know whom you are dealing with before you give out your address and any other personal information.

8. **Create a paper trail.** It's easy to lose track of a purchase if you make several trades in a short time. You might also forget the exact price you agreed to pay, or the date by which the item should arrive. So every time you complete a transaction, keep the following documents: a copy of your bid confirmation, correspondence with the seller, and a copy of the check (if you paid by check).

9. **Card it.** Pay with a credit card, if possible. That way, if you have a dispute with a seller, you haven't parted with any cash. By law, credit card companies must stand behind faulty merchandise or transactions paid for with their cards.

10. **Keep your cool.** Online auctions are exciting; there's no denying that. As with any whiz-bang environment, it's easy to get carried away ... way away. Although bidding often starts at an enticing $5, bids can rise quickly to the item's market value. And sellers may specify a *reserve price*, an undisclosed bottom line that bids must reach before the seller is willing to sell.

Decide how much you're willing to pay for an item, and stick to it. And buy only items you want. An item is only a bargain if you want or need it.

Top Ten Tips for Selling *Collectibles Online*

Now let's look at the other side of the transaction: selling collectibles at online auction sites. Try the following ten tips to make sure your sale goes well.

Tricks of the Trade

Price your item "off-dollar," at $19.99 rather than $20.00, for example.

1. **Make a match.** Sell your item on the right site. Just because you like one specific online auction site better than another one doesn't mean that it's the best place to sell your item. To find the best online auction site for your items, start by frequenting newsgroups and perusing mailing lists devoted to that particular collectible. Find out where members and well-known collectors sell their goods online.

   Also decide how much to charge for your item or items. Try www.biddersedge.com, a free service that lets you search two dozen sites to get the past high, low, and average selling price of any item that was ever auctioned online.

2. **Choose the auction method.** In addition to choosing the best site, choose the best auction method for your item. Most sites offer two choices: *Yankee Auctions* or *Dutch Auctions*.

   ➤ *Yankee Auctions* have open bidding, with the item going to the highest bidder. This is the more popular format. Use it when you are selling one item or a group of items to one high bidder.

➤ *Dutch Auctions* determine the price by the lowest of the winning bids. Use a Dutch Auction format when you have many copies of the same item to sell. For example, if you have 10 identical Beanie Babies to sell, the 10 highest bidders are all winners. If the highest bid is $100 and the tenth highest bid is $80, the top ten bidders pay $80 each.

No matter which auction method you select, you'll be given a Web page for each item that you want to auction. You'll have to provide the *category* in which you want your item listed, a *description* of the item, a one-sentence *summary* of the item, the *opening price* to start the bidding, and your *shipping terms* and accepted *method of payment*.

3. **Look before you leap.** This is the same rule that applies to buyers: Make sure you clearly understand the procedures and policies *before* you offer an item for sale. This is especially true if you're used to one site but are offering your item for sale on another.

4. **Set a reserve price.** A *reserve price* is the lowest price a seller is willing to take for an item. It protects you as the seller. When you set a reserve price, you don't have to sell if the market value turns out to be lower than you had hoped. Usually, you establish the reserve price when you list an item. The reserve price must be higher than the minimum bid price, and it is always kept a secret from buyers.

For example, you can start the opening bid at $2, with a reserve price of $24.99. You don't have to sell the item unless someone bids $24.99 or more.

5. **Set seller's fees.** Sellers, too, have to know the fee structure. Sites usually charge a posting fee or listing fee, ranging from 25¢ to a few dollars. This fee depends on the cost of the item. For example, an item that you want to auction for less than $9.99 would likely have a posting fee of 25¢. One that you list for more than $50, however, would carry a fee of $2.

There's also a *completion fee* or *gavel charge* of 5 percent or lower. This is the fee you pay if your item is sold. For example, an item sold for $25 or less would have a 5 percent fee,

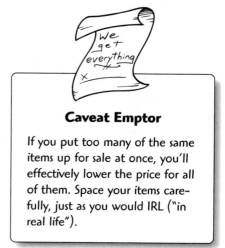

Learn the Lingo

A **reserve price** is the lowest price a seller is willing to take for an item.

Caveat Emptor

If you put too many of the same items up for sale at once, you'll effectively lower the price for all of them. Space your items carefully, just as you would IRL ("in real life").

while one that sold for $1,000 might have a fee of 1.25 percent. Usually the higher the selling price, the lower the fee percentage because the auction company still receives a high return: 5 percent of $25 = $1.25 return; 1¼ percent of $1,000 – $12.50 return.

6. **Set buyer's fees.** Shipping and handling aren't free. You don't want to cheat yourself or the buyer, so find out the standard online shipping and handling costs for items similar to those you have for sale. You can do this by checking online at several different sites. Set your fees accordingly.

Web Wise

If you want to post a digital photo and don't have or are unfamiliar with scanning equipment, you can get online tutorials at www.pongo.com/howto and www.pages.ebay.com/aw/phototut-index.html.

Tricks of the Trade

If you can't process credit cards, ask for a money order rather than a personal check when you sell an item online. That way, you know the check will clear.

7. **Be honest.** Describe your item fairly and fully. Don't worry that your honesty will scare off some potential buyers. After the auction, your honest description will save you the annoyance of returned items and demands for refunds.

If possible, include a digital photo. Buyers are much more likely to bid on an item they can see. If you do post a digital photo, crop any distracting background items and avoid fussy colors or music. Fancy colors and music often take so long to upload that buyers may lose patience and move on to the next item.

Answer any e-mail inquiries promptly. As with any kind of business, your strongest asset is your reputation. Because of the Internet's unique structure, news travels fast. If you cheat someone, it will spread faster than a computer virus.

8. **Get cash on the barrel.** Insist on prepayment for both the collectible and the shipping/handling. If you haven't been paid within a reasonable amount of time, sell the item to the next highest bidder. To me, a "reasonable amount of time" is about two weeks.

9. **Protect yourself.** To be fair to the buyer, ship the item promptly, but never before the check clears (if you accepted a personal check). Be sure to package the item properly to avoid damage in transit.

10. **Use the medium.** Take advantage of the unique nature of the Internet to make the transaction go smoothly. Notify the winner via e-mail, and ask the winner to verify that he or she will indeed be buying the item. Send an e-mail when you receive

payment, too. Finally, e-mail the seller when you ship the item so that he or she knows when to expect it. Follow up with an e-mail to make sure that the item has indeed arrived.

If your item doesn't sell, don't despair. You can always re-list it. Many online auction sites will let you re-list a second time for free. To increase your chances for success, try listing the item in a different category. For example, if no one bid on the item in *Military Memorabilia*, try *Antiques—Civil War*.

Big Deals

For the first time, the U.S. Mint has announced revenue derived from its Internet sales of numismatic products: The total since April 1, 1999, is nearly $7 million. "We've been surprised and delighted by how quickly our customers have adapted to ordering over the Web," Mint Director Philip N. Diehl said. "Cumulative Internet revenues have doubled nearly every month since we started taking orders in April." To learn more about the Mint's online offerings, visit its Web site at www.usmint.gov.

The Least You Need to Know

➤ Business is booming on Web auction sites for collectibles, and new sites pop up weekly.

➤ Online auction sites, companies with Web sites, and hybrid sites offer different services.

➤ When you buy online, check the site. Make sure you clearly understand the bidding procedures and policies *before* you place a bid, and shop around for the best deal. Also, factor in fees and verify the source of each item. Keep good records, pay by credit card, and don't get carried away by the excitement of the medium.

➤ When you sell online, offer your item on the right site, choose the most suitable auction method, and make sure you clearly understand the deal.

➤ Set a reserve price and explore fees. Describe your item fairly and fully, insist on prepayment, and establish a paper trail.

Part 3
Paper Chase

The postcard read like any one of millions of notes that college students send to their kinfolk back home: "My tests are over and I'm just starting the second term," scribbled the 19-year-old Georgetown University freshman to his grandmother.

But two things made this postcard special enough that the auctioneer thought it would fetch more than a few dollars. First, there was a photograph on the front, identifying the small town of Hope, Arkansas, as the home of the world's largest watermelon. Second, there was the identity of the card's author, who signed his message "Bill." Above his home address, he had scribbled "Wm. J. Clinton."

What was the top bid for this postcard? Over $4,000. As the fate of this postcard shows, certain ephemeral objects can have tremendous value. Comic books, stamps, baseball cards—it's all here. In Part 3, you'll learn how to sift the wheat from the chaff. There are bargains waiting for the plucking. On your mark, get set, go!

Chapter 9

Pulp (Non)Fiction

> **In This Chapter**
>
> ➤ Becoming a paper maven
>
> ➤ Collecting bookplates and postcards
>
> ➤ Stargazing at theater and movie memorabilia
>
> ➤ Striking it big with matchbooks

In this chapter, you will learn about *ephemera*—what it is and what are the most desirable collections. First, I'll teach you what you need to know about paper to help you buy the best items in the best condition. Next, you'll learn about bookplates and postcards. I'll even take you backstage to get the insider's info about theater and movie memorabilia. Finally, we'll strike up an acquaintance with matchbook covers.

Ephemera—Here Today, Gone Tomorrow

What is *ephemera?* Is it a dance craze, a floor cleaner, or an artificial fat? Sorry; it's none of the above. Ephemera is printed or handwritten, is two-dimensional, and is made to be discarded. (No, that does not define your ex.) A devoted ephemerist conveniently ignores the fact that many examples of ephemeras, such as modern baseball cards, were created to be discarded, not collected.

As this definition suggests, ephemera is usually paper, although handkerchiefs and badges are also considered fair game by ephemera collectors. Here's a list of the most commonly collected ephemeras:

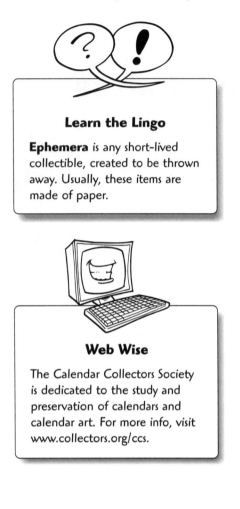

Learn the Lingo

Ephemera is any short-lived collectible, created to be thrown away. Usually, these items are made of paper.

Web Wise

The Calendar Collectors Society is dedicated to the study and preservation of calendars and calendar art. For more info, visit www.collectors.org/ccs.

➤ Betting slips
➤ Bookmarks
➤ Bookplates
➤ Calendars
➤ Calling cards
➤ Death warrants
➤ Draft cards
➤ Greeting cards
➤ Grocery stamps
➤ Letterheads
➤ Letters
➤ Lottery tickets
➤ Magazines
➤ Menus
➤ Mourning cards
➤ Newspapers
➤ Postcards
➤ Programs—theater, sporting event, circus
➤ Ration cards
➤ Sheet music
➤ Tickets
➤ Timetables
➤ Valentines
➤ Wanted posters

Ephemera can be divided into three categories: *fleeting, semidurable,* and *everlasting.* Here's the breakdown:

Type of Ephemera	Examples
Fleeting	Lottery tickets, valentines
Semidurable	Postcards, maps
Everlasting	Commemoratives, stock certificates

The Paper Chase

"Better living through chemistry" was the mantra for scores of sixties love children and for those of us who groove on that tangy diet cola afterburn. Chemicals have brought us such great inventions as plastic storage containers that burp and tomatoes that bounce. But chemicals have been a nasty thing for paper. Before chemicals were introduced into the papermaking process, paper could exist for hundreds of years without turning brown and crumbly. Brown and crumbly is wonderful on a pie crust, but it signals the beginning of the end for paper. You can find books from the 1600s with snowy-white pages, whereas many books from the 1940s are as brittle as a jilted lover.

One of the most important criteria for assessing paper collectibles is the condition of preservation. Avoid brittle paper as you would other twentieth-century scourges: cellulite, gas guzzlers, and buying retail. Once paper has become brittle, nothing can be done to save it. Eventually it will become dust. Light browning, however, is not a death sentence for paper products. Effective first-aid is available for lightly toasted paper.

Back from the Dead

Paper conservation has become as much an art as California freeway driving. It's amazing what these paper wizards can do. Using everyday chemicals like benzene, professional restorers can take a book apart and bathe each page until the decomposing chemicals have vanished like ring around the tub. Tape marks can be vanquished; stains blown away. Of course, this type of restoration carries a significant price tag. Be sure the collectible is worth the expense before you commission a professional restorer.

And kiddies, don't try this at home. Paper restoration is a skill that requires special training. No matter what someone says about spraying mildewed books with Lysol, recoloring faded pages with felt-tipped markers, or slapping some flour-and-water paste over rips, resist the urge. Similarly, don't soak anything but yourself in warm water to remove stains. It's a no-go on playing with water-damaged books and book presses, irons, or other painful-looking tools. If you feel the urge to play with paper, go to a diner and color the place mat.

Caveat Emptor

Besides browning, check paper collectibles for rips, tears, creases, stray marks, and soiling. All of these damages drive the price and value south faster than college kids heading to Florida for spring break.

Cut and Paste

Some ephemera collectors don't mind owning a repaired paper item. Certain collectors even seek out damaged paper ephemera for the pleasure of restoring and repairing it. I wish these people well, but I tell you that damaged or repaired paper items should be sold as such.

Tricks of the Trade

Normally, the cost of a colectible paper item drops by half when it is damaged.

Your best defense is a good offense. Examine each prospective buy inch-by-inch. Do this carefully and thoroughly. Then you can judge the item's condition for yourself.

Bookplates

The day after books were invented, friends and neighbors started borrowing them—and forgetting to return them.

What to do? Our ancestors came up with the concept of *bookplates* to remind the borrower of the book's original home. It's more subtle and elegant than putting a homing device or heavy chain on a book.

Learn the Lingo

A **bookplate** is a small rectangle of paper that book owners paste in the book to show ownership. Bookplates can be custom made or ordered from stock.

A bookplate is a small rectangle of paper that book owners paste on the endpaper or the first page of the book to show that they own it. The custom of using bookplates began in Europe in the seventeenth century, when only the upper crust owned books. The early plates were much more than an ID, however. Bookplates allowed the owners to ...

➤ Express their family status.

➤ Show their individuality.

➤ Flaunt their wealth.

These papers were often engraved on copper, silver, or wooden plates. Some were even hand drawn by such noted artists as Albrecht Dürer and his buddies.

The Bookplates Are Coming, the Bookplates Are Coming!

The first bookplates traveled across the pond to the colonies with their Dutch and English owners. Nathaniel Hurd was the earliest American bookplate engraver; examples of his work date back to 1748. Other artists, including Paul Revere, produced bookplates for America's newly hatched nouveau riche.

In the late 1800s, photomechanical ways to reproduce images were developed. As a result, book ownership was no longer restricted to the wealthy, and many regular folk began buying books and bookplates. The availability of mass-produced bookplates didn't prevent the wealthy and distinguished from commissioning their own hand-produced bookplates, however.

Top Notch

The plates that bring the highest prices are those drawn by sixteenth-century artists like Albrecht Dürer and those once owned by *Time* magazine cover boys such as JFK. Among the most popular photomechanically reproduced bookplates are those drawn by popular late-nineteenth- and twentieth-century artists like Maxfield Parrish, Rockwell Kent, and Arthur Rackham. Pretty bookplates also sell at a brisk pace.

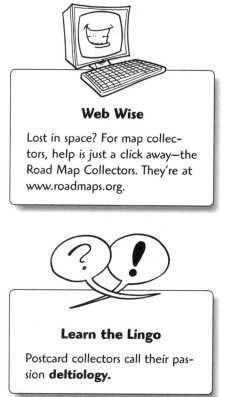

Web Wise

Lost in space? For map collectors, help is just a click away—the Road Map Collectors. They're at www.roadmaps.org.

Learn the Lingo

Postcard collectors call their passion **deltiology.**

Wish You Were Here: Postcards

Quick! What's "*deltiology*"? Stumped? It's what postcard aficionados call their special variety of collecting. And *you* thought it was something piggy.

The first postcards appeared in the 1870s as advertisements. Souvenir view cards came into being in the United States in 1898.

Before you go hunting for postcards, decide on one or two subjects that interest you. Search out a collectors' club in your region. You can get leads by asking at antique shows and shops where postcards are sold. Postcard conventions provide an excellent source for collecting possibilities for what's hot and what's not. You can also get the inside skinny on pricing and trading.

As with other paper collectibles, condition is crucial. Postcards must be mint to be valuable. That's not to say you can't have a lot of fun amassing a pile of dog-eared postcards, but if you want to be a collector and not a pack rat, go for cards in the best possible shape. To protect your collection, mount your postcards on acid-free paper in albums or protect them with glycine coverings and file them in boxes.

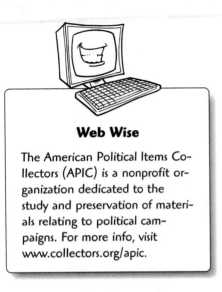

Web Wise

The American Political Items Collectors (APIC) is a nonprofit organization dedicated to the
study and preservation of materials relating to political cam-
paigns. For more info, visit
www.collectors.org/apic.

Poster Girl

Posters in general are hot collectibles. What to buy? First and foremost, the artist's name determines the value of a poster. The ranking poster boy is French painter Toulouse-Lautrec, who created 31 posters from 1891 to 1900. In a recent auction, *Le Moulin Rouge,* advertising a cabaret, went for $220,000.

Savvy art lovers try to snap up today's posters as they appear, with an eye to tomorrow's trends. Commemorative posters are popular. For example, abstract expressionist Robert Motherwell created a poster for the Mostly Mozart festival in 1991. The poster sold for $100. Motherwell died later that year, and five years later the same poster was worth $1,000.

Poster collecting offers something for everyone's taste. For example, car posters (those cheap decorating mainstays of bachelor apartments) are worth a bundle if they date from the early 1900s. "Keep in mind that these were not originally produced to be saved and collected," says Jack Rennert, founder of Poster Auctions International, which recently set up the auction of rare vintage car posters. "They were meant to last three weeks, at best, on city walls. They were printed on cheap paper. This is very ephemeral art." The prices, however, are anything but cheap. A 1919 Peugeot poster by René Vincent, for instance, fetches from $10,000 to $12,000.

Follow these guidelines when you shop for collectible posters:

1. Reissued posters are not worth nearly as much as the originals. To identify reissues, look for a small *R* or *r* on the bottom margin.

2. Avoid posters that appear to have had their lower margins sliced off.

3. Check for telltale signs of pinholes and creases—they're signs of a repro that was made from a damaged original.

The Play's the Thing: Theater Memorabilia

Shakespeare declared that "the play's the thing," but for collectors of theater memorabilia, it's often the playbill—not the play. Dedicated collectors of theater memorabilia hunt down every scrap of paper linked to their favorite performer, playwright, or play. Sought-after items include the following:

➤ Cigarette cards depicting actors, costume designs, scenery

➤ Photographs

➤ Programs

➤ Props

➤ Posters
➤ Reviews from newspapers and magazines
➤ Scripts
➤ Tickets

Sign on the Dotted Line

For serious collectors of theater ephemera, autographs are often the crème de la crème. They are treasured partly because they are rare. Like other paper collectibles, many did not survive; in addition, some theater personalities refused to grant them. George Bernard Shaw, for example, would not give autographs; other stars have been known to demand a donation to their favorite charity or even a personal fee in exchange for their John Hancock.

Stagestruck

Designs for stage sets and costumes are also in great demand by collectors. In part, their appeal arises from the fame of those who tried their hand at stage design: Picasso and Braque, for example, both drew stage sets. Drawings linked to famous performers or artists are the most highly prized. If you're looking for drawings, shun pristine sketches. Go for drawings marked up with notes to costume and prop departments.

Get with the Program

Programs are another important collectible in theater memorabilia. The first programs, issued in the 1850s, were small playbills or posters. Some were pasted in the lobby; others were sold to theatergoers, as is still the practice in England.

Web Wise

The Universal Autograph Collectors Club offers information for anyone interested in collecting autographs of famous personalities. Their Web site is www.uacc.org.

Tricks of the Trade

It's very hard to find programs that headline the Broadway superstars of the past. With some luck, however, you may be able to find a past biggie listed at the bottom of the cast list, before he or she made the marquee.

The programs that have many theater buffs panting are those distributed on Opening Night (also called "First Night"). It's the cachet of being the first performance. Programs can also include autographed pictures of the actors and reviews—a two-fer! When you consider the many actors who played the vaudeville circuit and kept scrapbooks, you can see what possibilities present themselves to resourceful collectors.

95

With theater programs, it's age as well as condition. Modern playbills fetch very little, if anything. I tried to donate my huge pile of programs dating from the 1970s through the 1990s to the Lincoln Center for the Performing Arts Library. They weren't interested because they already had far too many playbills from this era. Now, playbills from the 1920s ... that's a different matter to a collector!

Movie Memorabilia

The field of entertainment collectibles is enormous, including everything from tickets, posters, and scripts to costumes, props, and the films themselves. For example ...

➤ About a decade ago, Herman J. Mankiewicz's scripts for *Citizen Kane* and *The American* sold at auction for $231,000.

➤ A 1932 Universal poster for *The Old Dark House,* starring Boris Karloff, went for $48,400 in 1991.

➤ Judy Garland's ruby slippers from *The Wizard of Oz* walked away for $165,000 at a recent Christie's auction.

So much to collect. So little time. Let me help you. Here's a list of the most desirable movie collectibles.

Cels for Sale

Cels are hand-painted scenes that are shot in sequence to make up a cartoon film. Cels are painted on *celluloid,* hence their name. My mother, a skilled artist, painted some of the earliest cels. Wearing thin white cotton gloves to prevent smears on the celluloid, she carefully filled in figures with tempera paints (today acrylics are used).

Learn the Lingo

Cels are hand-painted scenes of a cartoon.

As a young child, I remember pawing through stacks of old cels on rainy afternoons. I also remember helping my mother throw them all out when we moved from New Jersey to New York. In 1991 just one of the 150,000 color cels from *Snow White* (1937) sold for $209,000; two years earlier, a single black-and-white cel showing Donald Duck in the cartoon *Orphan's Benefit* (1935) fetched $286,000. Ah, had I saved just a handful of those old cels!

Posters for a Price

You learned earlier in this chapter that posters in general are a very sought-after collectible. Movie posters are especially popular.

In the era of silent films, movie companies often hired the finest commercial and graphic artists to design their posters. Visual appeal was vitally important in a period without radio or television ads. The movie poster, long a pariah, has become a hot collectible. The biggest stars get the biggest prices: For example, a poster of Humphrey Bogart in *Casablanca* is valued in the thousands. Use these four guidelines when you search for posters:

1. **Age.** Many old posters disintegrated; others were destroyed in wartime paper drives. A noble end for the paper, perhaps, but a calamity for collectors.

2. **Visual appeal.** Beauty is in the eye of the beholder, but visually appealing posters can be judged as you would any other work of art. They blend color, light, shading, and form to create a stunning whole.

3. **Marquee madness.** Posters featuring films that have become part of the American psyche, such as *Gone with the Wind, The Wizard of Oz, Citizen Kane,* and *King Kong,* are the hottest. There is a small but growing market for posters of cult classics such as *Night of the Living Dead,* a low-budget Philly shock flick.

4. **Stars.** Big names bring 'em out. Look for posters featuring such head turners as Clark Gable, Cary Grant, Greta Garbo, Katherine Hepburn, Valentino, Marilyn Monroe, Humphrey Bogart, and Lauren Bacall.

> **Tricks of the Trade**
>
> Some lucky collectors find vintage posters in old movie theaters. Even though most of the large movie theaters in the big cities have already been ransacked, caches are still to be found in shuttered moviehouses in less-traveled regions. If you do get lucky, remember that rips and tears are inevitable; but try to avoid posters that are brittle and missing pieces.

Which posters will be worth the most? The ones that combine all four factors. Find Bogie on a poster (in excellent condition) of *The Maltese Falcon* and you're talking some serious money. Okay, so the poster costs more than the popcorn. At least it's not fattening.

Loose Paper with a Link

Dedicated movie memorabilia collectors are a broad-minded lot: They'll collect Dixie cup lids, sugar packets, and scripts, as well as autographs, stills, and magazines. What makes a seemingly innocent sugar packet a hot item? Its *association* and *visual appeal*. Let's start with association.

Collectors want items linked to famous stars and films. A script for *The African Queen* is worth a bundle more than one for *Amazon Babes at the Bowl-a-Rama* ... though *Amazon Babes* did have its moments.

Second, collectibles are sexy. There's a certain frisson of excitement that a desirable collectible sends off. How can you pick up the vibes? Haunt the collectible shows to find out which pieces turn collectors on. Look at the paper items to see which ones are flying off the floor and which ones are wallflowers at the dance.

A Striking Example of Collectibles: Matchbooks

"Got a match?" Not anymore. Since war was declared on tobacco, and disposable lighters became so affordable, matchbooks have been about as welcome as a pitbull with an impacted molar. Twenty years ago, there were about 20 matchbook makers in America. Today? Only three matchbook companies remain. But even these three companies can't sustain their business on matchbooks alone, so they all also produce buttons, plastic mugs, and T-shirts.

Web Wise

For more information on the American Matchcover Collecting Club, visit their Web site at www.matchcovers.com.

The sorry state of the matchbook industry has not deterred serious matchbook collectors. The American Matchcover Collecting Club's (AMCC) members feel a burning urge to save beautiful examples of the genre. The AMCC promotes the preservation, collection, education, and availability of pre-1965 collectible matchcovers through its national collecting club.

One matchbook from World War II, for example, has a picture of Hitler. Each match is shaped like a bomb; the striker is Hitler's backside. The sentence reads: "Strike at the seat of trouble." The matchbook sells for about $75, making this a most affordable collectible. But other matchbooks can sell in the thousands of dollars, satisfying the high-end market as well.

The Least You Need to Know

➤ Ephemeras are paper items meant to be discarded. As a result, ephemera is the only collectible that can offer you something for nothing.

➤ Paper falls apart. Don't try to fix it yourself.

➤ Buy all paper collectibles—cards, posters, scripts, and so on—in the best possible condition.

➤ Bookplates and postcards are popular collectibles.

➤ Theater and movie ephemeras are extremely desirable collectibles.

➤ You won't strike it rich with matchbook covers, but they may strike your fancy.

Chapter 10

Card-Carrying Collectors

In This Chapter

➤ Baseball cards

➤ Sports cards

➤ Playing cards

➤ *Magic* cards

➤ Pokémon cards

Before the turn of the century, baseball cards came in packets of tobacco and cigarettes, mere giveaways intended to stiffen the spines of wimpy cigarette packages and entice unwary consumers to sell their souls to Mr. Butts. Today these old baseball cards are worth their weight in gold—almost as much as some of the players.

As you've no doubt guessed by now, this chapter starts off with a play-by-play on collecting baseball cards. You'll delve into the history of baseball cards and learn how to build a collection. Not into America's pastime? Don't worry; there's a lot of information about other collectible sports cards, too.

Then we'll explore how to collect traditional playing cards. Whether you prefer royal intrigue or airline freebies, there's plenty to learn.

The chapter concludes with sections on the newest collectible cards: *Magic* cards and Pokémon cards. So sit back, put up your feet, and let's shuffle some cards together.

Take Me out to the Ball Game: Baseball Cards

Collectors are a passionate lot. They defend their choices with great brio—whether their treasures are budget Elvis-on-velvet or rare cabinets inlaid with mother-of-pearl. Some people love Elvis-on-velvet, and others hate it; but no one dislikes baseball cards. These sweet little cards are as quintessentially American as belly-bomb burgers and spandex pants.

When I say "baseball cards," what comes to mind? Nearly everyone envisions a four-color cardboard card, 2½ inches by 3½ inches. There's a picture of the player on one side, and his stats appear on the flip side. But baseball cards were not always in this form.

Tricks of the Trade

For additional information on collecting baseball cards, check out a standard reference guide on the subject, such as *Collecting Baseball Cards: How to Buy Them, Store Them, Trade Them, and Keep Track of Their Value as Investments*, by Donn Pearlman.

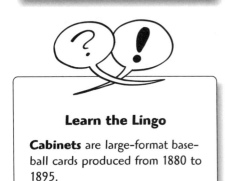

Learn the Lingo

Cabinets are large-format baseball cards produced from 1880 to 1895.

Up to Bat: The Beginning of Baseball Cards

The first baseball cards were issued around 1886 by New York–based Goodwin and Company, a tobacco corporation, as incentives for buying their products during an era of intense competition. Mounted on heavy cardboard, these cards were about a third the size of today's baseball cards. One side featured a black-and-white photo of a player; the other side listed other available cards. The promotion worked well, so other cigarette companies quickly stepped onto the field.

From 1880 to 1895, the tobacco companies churned out many different baseball cards. Most were small, as described above, but some firms offered larger cards called *cabinets*. By the end of the 1890s, the American Tobacco Company so dominated the industry that the lack of competition made offering these cards unnecessary.

As a result, very few cards were produced during the next 15 years. Fortunately for collectors, in 1909 the "golden age" of baseball cards started.

First Base: The Golden Era #1

The first golden age of baseball cards saw the issuing of the most distinctive, innovative, and valuable cards to date. Now candy makers joined the league. The cards of this era were characterized by fine artwork, brilliant color, and creative formats such as *double* and *triple folders*. Most collectors consider these the most gorgeous baseball cards ever produced. (Yes, they fetch a hefty price.)

In 1915 the tobacco companies stopped including cards with cigarette boxes. The candy makers, however, continued producing and distributing the cards until the 1920s. The golden age, therefore, lasted from 1909 to the late 1920s. World War I put the kibosh on this shining period. It also marked the permanent departure of the tobacco industry from the baseball card business.

Time out on the Field: A Lull in the Action

The end of the 1920s was a relatively quiet period for baseball cards, characterized by cards of questionable quality. The tobacco companies had gotten out of the baseball card business, and the gum companies, as we know them today, did not exist. What were left were some caramel candy companies and some anonymous manufacturers of low-quality strip cards. These are small baseball cards with poor art and color.

> **Learn the Lingo**
>
> **Double folder** baseball cards come folded over. When opened, they amputate the legs of the first player and reveal a second player standing on his friend's legs. **Triple folders** show an action scene flanked by head shots of two players.

Second Base: The Golden Era #2

The 1930s marked the second golden era. It saw the establishment of the baseball bubble gum card, cards most like the ones we know today. In 1933 the Goudy Gum Company of Boston issued the first major set of baseball cards. It consisted of 240 players, 40 of whom are now members of the Hall of Fame. Six years later, Gum Inc., which later became Bowman Gum, issued their first set entitled "Play Ball—America." This was the era in which some of the most attractive and sought-after cards in the history of collecting were produced.

WAGNER, PITTSBURG

MICKEY MANTLE

Would you trade these cards for a utility outfielder, a player to be named later, and an undisclosed amount of cash?

Tricks of the Trade

Before you buy any baseball cards, check the prices in a reputable guide, such as *Beckett Baseball Card Price Guide, 2000 Baseball Card Price Guide,* or *Baseball's Top 500: Card Checklist & Price Guide.*

Seventh Inning Stretch: A Break for War

Baseball card production ended with the beginning of America's involvement in World War II. The need for scrap paper during the war resulted in a scarcity of cards from this era. From 1942 to 1947, almost no cards were produced.

Third Base: Modern Baseball Cards

The embargo on the production of baseball cards ended in 1948, when the Bowman Company produced a 48-card set. The Topps Company entered the market in 1951, bought Bowman, remained virtually the sole manufacturer of baseball cards on a national scale until the Fleer and Donruss companies entered the business in the 1980s.

By the mid-1970s, baseball cards had become extremely popular. The first price guide came out in 1979. The baseball card phenomenon entered a new phase in the late 1980s. The skyrocketing values of older cards prompted an escalation in competition for a share of the marketplace among card companies. By the mid-1990s, there were at least six major companies, each producing at least two or three different major cards.

Home Run: Collecting Baseball Cards

Kids collect baseball cards because they're affordable and fun. In the good old days, you even got a slab of pink bubble gum slapped up against the cards. What happened if you didn't like the players you got in your pack? You could always put the cards in the spokes of your bicycle. They made a great noise.

Adults love baseball cards because they provide a psychic link to the past. They are easy to store, catalog, and trade—and they can be a good investment.

Big Deals

Derek Jeter has appeared on more than 630 cards since his cardboard debut in 1993—that's 90 cards per season.

House of Cards

When I wrote the first edition of this book in 1996, the boom in baseball cards had reached the point where they were the main focus of baseball memorabilia shows held throughout the country. The glossy, four-color cards featuring players from major league teams had developed into a sizzlin' collectible.

The market has certainly cooled today. For example, Darryl Strawberry's rookie card, a 1983 Topps Traded, was once in the $100 range. Now, it can be had for as little as $5.

Several factors are responsible for this decline. First, manufacturers flooded the market with too many issues or unattainable specials, which made it nearly impossible to assemble complete sets or find that special hero. Also, the hobby passed from the hands of Little Leaguers to those in the major leagues, casting a pall over the game.

Caveat Emptor

Beware of cards that have been cut down to make them look new. These cards are considered damaged and have little value to collectors. The easiest way to spot a cut-down card is to carry a test card. Place the suspect card on top of the test card. If the suspect card is smaller than the test card, run.

Nonetheless, baseball card collectors still feel passionately about this colorful collectible. It's impossible to give specific prices for cards because there are so many cards available in so many categories. Here are a few fun facts about the cards of recent players:

➤ A super-premium, limited issue 1996 Select Mirror Gold (Pinnacle) of Derek Jeter may sell for as much as $1,000.

➤ A standard issue Derek Jeter card fetches around $5; a limited issue, about $100.

➤ Greg Maddux's 1998 Donruss Elite Back to the Future card lists for a whopping $1,200 (although that doesn't mean anyone would be willing to ante up that much).

➤ Maddux's 1996 Mirror Gold card books for around $800.

➤ Roger Clemens's Mirror Gold card lists at $800; his rookie card (1984 Fleer Update), $250.

If you do decide to collect baseball cards, here are some suggestions for putting together a solid collection. First of all, start with the best. With baseball cards—as with all other collectible cards—condition should be your first consideration. A card in good condition is worth several times the same card in shoddy condition. How can you tell whether a card is *ex-mint* (the fancy-schmancy name for best possible shape)? Here's how:

➤ The card is clean.

➤ The card has its original gloss.

➤ The card has four sharp corners.

➤ The surface has no tears, creases, or smudges.

Building a Collection

Baseball card collectors are especially at risk for the collector's lament: "So much to buy … so little time." You need a plan, or you risk ending up with a pile rather than a collection. I recommend four ways to organize your collection: *year set, player, team,* and *Hall of Fame standing.* Let's look at each one in detail:

➤ **Collect by year.** Try to complete an entire set of a particular series for one year.

➤ **Collect by player(s).** Try to obtain every card ever made of a certain player or players. If this plan appeals to you, I recommend that you focus on a player who has entered the major leagues recently. Otherwise, amassing the collection could easily become your life's work.

➤ **Collect by team.** Get all the cards of the players on a specific team. Most of these types of collectors focus on their home team.

➤ **Collect by Hall of Fame standing.** Collect the cards of only those players who have been inducted into the Hall of Fame. The logic? Cards of superstars will soar in value faster than the cards of average or forgettable players. This has proven to be the case. If you want to jump on this bandwagon, guess which players will make the Hall of Fame, buy and hoard those cards, and kiss that rabbit's foot a few extra times.

Big Deals

The Honus Wagner card is the rarest of all baseball cards. Produced by the Sweet Caporal Tobacco Company from 1909 to 1911, the card was recalled when Wagner, who did not smoke, objected to the use of his picture in connection with the tobacco product. This is the prestige card among collectors. In case you intend to rummage through bins at flea markets looking for ol' Honus, start with size. The card is much smaller than today's baseball cards. The background is orange, and Wagner is wearing a Pittsburgh uniform. When you find it, remember that I sent you. You can take me out to the ball game.

Buy Smart

You can cozy up to the corner deli owner and get first dibs on his or her shipment of coleslaw and luncheon meat, but if it's baseball cards you're after, there are better ways to find what you desire. Here are the best ways to shop for baseball cards:

➤ **Internet.** On the Web, you can find shops and auctions that sell baseball cards (and other collectible cards). This is an especially good way to shop when you're trying to find that one special card. It's fast and convenient, too. For detailed information about shopping for collectibles on the Internet, see Chapter 8, "CyberShopping: Buying and Selling Online."

➤ **Conventions.** Baseball card collecting is very popular throughout the country. As a result, scores of baseball card shows and conventions take place every weekend. Conventions allow you to buy just the cards you want so you don't get stuck with stacks of useless cards. Look through the newspaper or local "What's Happening" publications to find the conventions in your area.

➤ **Mail order.** Many serious collectors get new cards wholesale through the mail. This is an especially valuable source if you live in a remote area or aren't yet wired to the Web.

➤ **Friends.** You can trade as well as buy cards from fellow aficionados. How can you meet people who are willing to help you build your collection? Set up a network of like-minded fans. Use e-mail, snail-mail, or face-time in conventions.

Tricks of the Trade

To widen your collection or to find cards not available in your hometown, consider timing your vacation to coincide with big national card conventions. You can make it up to your spouse later.

Caveat Emptor

Phony fat, phony baloney, phony phones—what's next? You guessed it—counterfeit baseball cards. Once a card is valued at about $100, the chances are someone will make a knockoff. If you're thinking of buying a big bucks card, get the current buzz from the baseball mags and rags first. Also check carefully with reputable dealers before putting any cash down.

➤ **Dealers.** Get to know the reputable dealers. Tell them which cards you need so they can help you locate them.

➤ **Family.** Every now and again, Cousin Ralph cleans his attic and comes up with a box of Great Uncle Louie's baseball cards. Let the family know you're interested in baseball cards. That way, if any turn up, you might get first crack at them.

Tricks of the Trade

There are price guides for virtually every type of collectible sports card, such as *Beckett Football Price Guide.*

Hey, Sport: Sports Cards

Some collectors have turned their attention to other types of sports cards: boxing, football, hockey, basketball, and wrestling, to name just a few. Overall, these cards are much more affordable than baseball cards. Even vintage sports cards in good condition are still available for under $10.

Like baseball cards, sports cards were first produced in the 1880s to reinforce fragile cigarette boxes and attract buyers to the thrill of emphysema and black lung. During World War I, boxing cards held center ring; by the 1930s, attention had shifted to football heroes. In 1958 the Topps Bubble Gum Company issued a series of basketball cards—a resounding flop.

In the 1950s and 1960s, hockey's tremendous popularity in Canada sparked a series of these cards, but they, too, failed to set the fans afire in the same way that baseball cards had done. But sports cards might just wind your watch, so read on to find out how to become a savvy collector.

Be a Sport: Collecting Sports Cards

I sent you to the Web, to conventions, and to dealers for baseball cards. If you're just starting to build a collection of sports cards, however, you may wish to first scope out the field to see what's available. That way, you can decide what you'd like to collect. Visit your local candy or stationery store, and study the display of sports cards. Buy a few packs to find out what's what. Here are some questions to ask yourself as you browse:

➤ How many cards make up a series?

➤ What is the format?

➤ What is the design?

➤ Which cards appeal to me? Why?

There are five basic ways to collect sports cards: by *era, type, team, player,* and *sport.* Select a category that's large enough to be fun but not large enough to be an impossible task. Remember, this is a hobby, not an obsession. For example, trying to collect all the football cards ever produced would seriously cut into your leisure time—forever.

Up the Ante

If you want to collect for investment, however, the rules change.

1. Consider going for the superstars in a specific sport. These cards appreciate much more quickly and steadily than the cards of average or forgettable players.

2. Avoid cards that have been glued into albums. Cards that are missing part of their backing are worth very little to investors.

3. Only buy cards in the best possible condition—mint or near-mint.

It's Your Deal: Playing Cards

Playing cards are almost as old as yesterday's news. In the fourteenth century, the king of France commissioned three packs of cards in "gold and diverse colors ornamented with various devices." In the days before malls and multiplexes, card games caught on fast. But such idle fun was anathema to the religious right. In the seventeenth century, when Oliver Cromwell and his Puritan killjoys seized power in England, they trashed the cards. The games survived nonetheless, and eventually the English settled on a style of suits based on a French patterned pack created in the 1300s.

Today, it's almost impossible to find any playing cards that predate the 1800s. And in case you're looking, before that time, cards had full-length pictures of kings and queens, not the two-headed variety we're used to dealing.

There are several methods for collecting playing cards. Modern cards are collected by subject matter displayed on the card backs. Advertising and pin-up art are just two of the options available. When dealing with other cards, some collectors buy full sets; others prefer single cards. It's your call, but superstition dictates that you shun the ace of spades. Here's why. Before the 1800s, playing cards were taxed. A special stamp was put on the ace of spades to show that the tax had been paid. Anyone found guilty of forging this stamp—"Old Frizzle," as the design was called—could have his nostrils slit, his ears cut off, or his body branded with a red-hot poker. This kind of fun-and-games could make a card somewhat unpopular ...

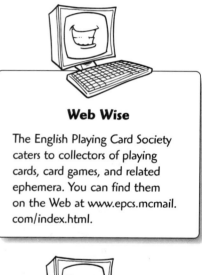

Web Wise

The English Playing Card Society caters to collectors of playing cards, card games, and related ephemera. You can find them on the Web at www.epcs.mcmail.com/index.html.

Web Wise

The official Magic homepage is located at www.wizards.com/magic/. There are many unofficial sites set up by players and collectors. Wizards of the Coast can be e-mailed with questions or comments at custserv@wizards.com.

Bewitched by *Magic* Cards

Magic: The Gathering is a collectible card game, first designed by Richard Garfield and published by Wizards of the Coast, Inc. *Magic: The Gathering,* currently available in nine languages and sold in

52 countries, is played by an estimated six million people worldwide. Its fans are a passionate lot. While the *Magic* cards in the game don't float my boat, even I have to admit that the artwork is really stunning.

Magic: The Gathering was first released on August 5, 1993. This first printing, commonly known as the "Alpha" set, contained 2.6 million cards. Shortly after, some corrections were made, and another 7.3 million cards were printed; this set is commonly known as the "Beta" set.

Magic: The Gathering *cards. The latest new craze?*

It's a Setup

The various sets of *Magic: The Gathering* include:

1. **Basic sets**
   - ➤ Classic (Sixth edition)
   - ➤ Fifth edition
   - ➤ Fourth edition
   - ➤ Revised edition
   - ➤ Alpha, Beta, and Unlimited editions

2. **Limited-edition expansion sets**
   - ➤ Mercadian Masques
   - ➤ Urza's Destiny
   - ➤ Urza's Legacy
   - ➤ Urza's Saga
   - ➤ Exodus
   - ➤ Stronghold
   - ➤ Tempest
   - ➤ Weatherlight
   - ➤ Visions

➤ Mirage

➤ Alliances

➤ Ice Age

➤ Homelands

➤ Fallen Empires

➤ The Dark

➤ Legends

➤ Antiquities

➤ Arabian Nights

3. **Special sets**

➤ Portal

➤ Portal Second Age

➤ Portal Three Kingdoms

➤ Vanguard

➤ Anthologies

➤ Promotional Cards

➤ Chronicles/Renaissance

➤ Unglued

Big Deals

Duelist magazine, published by Wizards of the Coast, is a good source for the current prices of specific cards. So far, the most expensive card is a mint condition Alpha edition Black Lotus, which sells for $500 or more.

Build a Deck

Magic cards are typically sold in 60-card *starter decks* and 15-card *booster packs*. A starter deck contains 2 rare cards, 13 uncommon cards, and 45 common cards. Of the 45 commons, approximately 20 of them are Land cards, which have virtually no value but are necessary to play the game. A booster pack contains 1 rare card, 3 uncommon cards, and 11 common cards.

Tricks of the Trade

A rare card from the newest expansion set will almost always be more valuable than an old common card.

A set of *Magic* cards will usually remain in print for several months, except for the limited-edition expansion sets, which have a single printing. A limited-edition or out-of-print set is usually available in most stores for several months afterward. After that, the only sources for old packs or individual cards are comic book/sci-fi conventions or dealers who specialize in collectible cards. Dealers can be found on the Web and in stores.

Common cards usually sell for 10 to 25 cents apiece, depending on the card and its usefulness in game play. The price of most uncommon cards may range from 50¢ to several dollars. Rare cards, depending on the card, can cost anywhere from several dollars to several hundred dollars. In general, the selling price of a card depends on the same three factors that govern all collectible cards: *rarity, age,* and *condition.*

(Much thanks to Charles Rozakis for writing this section. May your Magic *card collection grow and prosper.)*

Gotta Catch 'Em All: Pokémon Cards

Take this quick quiz to see if you're tuned in to the hottest card collectible for the younger set:

1. *Pokémon* is Japanese for …
   a. "A poke in the eye with a sharp stick."
   b. "A pig in a poke, mon."
   c. "Pocket monsters."

2. Pokémon characters include …
   a. Moe, Larry, and Curly.
   b. Clinton, Trump, and Quayle.
   c. Pikachu, Bulbasaur, and Charmander.

3. Pokémon merchandise sales are …
   a. $500,000 a year.
   b. $5 million a year.
   c. $5 billion a year.

Answers

Every answer is c. But you knew that.

Pokémon is an army of feisty and funny cartoon creatures that have become an obsession with the preteen set. The creatures battle each other with special powers. The American frenzy came with the introduction of the cartoon show, then the trading cards were added to the mix, then it gathered steam with the Nintendo video game in 1998 and marketing of toy figures, and spun into the stratosphere with the movie release in October 1999.

Pokémon Fever

Small packs of Pokémon cards cost between $6 and $10 a set, and large packs run as much as $30. Cards with holograms are the most pricey, at $50 each. Nonetheless, Pokémon cards are flying off the shelves: Over 200,000 sets are sold every month. It's clear that Pokémon cards have become the currency of choice on many school playgrounds. Serious collectors have their work cut out for them: a mission to obtain all 151 creatures. Kids flock to malls to participate in official trading bazaars.

Tykes are so preoccupied with trading Pokémon cards that some schools have banned them. Parents are up-in-arms, too, as shown by the class-action lawsuit filed by a group in California claiming Pokémon got their children addicted to gambling.

The Card Facts

Each card features a Pokémon, complete with its picture and statistics. The rarest cards—Mew and Togepi—are pictured in holographic cards layered with gold and glitter. Rare cards such as these fetch several hundred dollars apiece. As with *Magic* cards, Pokémon cards are distributed by Wizards of the Coast.

Learn the Lingo

Pokémon is pronounced *poke-ay-mon.*

Caveat Emptor

There's a rash of counterfeit Pokémon cards across the country. If you collect Pokémon cards, make sure the packages have the Nintendo seal. Further, the printing on the cards should be crisp, not blurry.

The Least You Need to Know

➤ No matter what type of cards you collect, the benchmarks are rarity, age, and condition.

➤ The market for collectible baseball cards has cooled recently, so build your collection carefully.

➤ Playing cards are a popular and traditional collectible.

➤ The hottest new collectible cards are *Magic: The Gathering* and Pokémon.

Chapter 11

Not-So-Funny Papers: Comic Books

In This Chapter

➤ Survey the history of comic books

➤ Build a collection

➤ Grade comics

➤ Learn the lingo

Historically, people saved books out of reverence for the printed word, but that reverence didn't extend to comics. That's a good thing for comics collectors. If people *had* saved their comics from the 1930s and 1940s, everyone would have copies of the super-valuable 1938 *Action Comics #1*—and it would be worth about as much as a last month's issue of *Action Comics*.

Early comic books, like most high-priced collectibles, are desirable because they are beautiful and rare (not unlike me). Comics from 1933 to 1940, for example, are very scarce in any condition, especially those from the mid- to late-1930s. Near-mint to mint copies are virtually nonexistent—known examples of any particular issue are limited to a handful of copies or less. For example, fewer than 20 copies of *Action Comics #1* are known to have survived. Old comics are almost as rare as politicians who admit to inhaling during the 1970s.

This chapter starts with a stroll down memory lane, where you will discover how comic books got their start. Then you'll find out how to start a comics collection of your own and why the condition of a comic book is so important to its value. Next, you will learn the terms unique to comic book collecting so that you'll know what the pros are talking about and so you can become a pro yourself. Then I'll teach you which books are the most valuable and why. Finally, I'll talk about comic art, the newest offshoot of comic book collecting.

Bam! Pow! Zap! A Short History of Comic Books

The comic book industry began in the mid-1930s when M. C. ("Max") Gaines decided to compile a collection of newspaper comic strips in a magazine form as a premium giveaway. Max's first comic book was a series of reprints given away to people who bought Ivory Soap. Other companies quickly saw the popularity of such magazines, and very soon all the usable strips were being reprinted.

Web Wise

World Famous Comics, at www.wfcomics.com, is a news and features Web site for comics collectors. It includes a daily column by Tony Isabella and a daily trivia quiz by Bob Rozakis.

In stepped Major Malcolm Wheeler-Nicholson, a man with a paper supply and a printing contract. This pulp-fiction writer/cavalry officer/sportsman/adventurer started his company (National Allied Publications) by printing *New Comics* and *New Fun Comics,* using all new material. With 32 tabloid newspaper-sized pages and a full-color cover, the 1935 comic established many of the features of the modern comic book: humor, adventure, sports, and the extended continuity story.

In 1936, Wheeler-Nicholson folded his package in half, creating the format that became today's standard. The following year, Wheeler-Nicholson started another new title, *Detective Comics,* the first comic book devoted to a single theme. It was an instant hit and gave the company its name: DC Comics. Later that year, Wheeler-Nicholson sold his business to his partner, Harry Donenfeld.

It's a Bird, It's a Plane ...

In 1938, looking for a lead feature to launch another new title, Gaines and his editors settled on a strip that had been created by two teenagers from Cleveland five years earlier and had been unsuccessfully offered as a newspaper strip. The character was faster than a locomotive and could leap tall buildings in a single bound. He even had a sexy secret identity. It's ... Superman! The comic book? *Action Comics.* Nineteen-year-olds Jerry Seigel and Joe Shuster had created an American icon. Superman was the first of the costumed superheroes who would define the medium in the coming years.

As quickly as they could, other publishers (and DC itself) sought to make economic lightning strike again and again. Costumed heroes arrived by the busload, including Batman, The Flash, Green Lantern, and Wonder Woman from DC; Captain America, the Human Torch, and Sub-Mariner from Timely; Captain Marvel and the Marvel

Family from Fawcett; and Plastic Man and The Spirit from Quality. It was an age of heroes that lasted through the Second World War and into the late 1940s.

By the end of the war, superheroes were yesterday's news. Publishers started looking for new hooks to reel 'em in. Crime comics, western comics, war comics, and romance comics all started appearing. MLJ Publications started a backup feature about "America's Typical Teenager"—Archie. The freckle-faced lad and his sidekicks, Betty and Veronica, are still popular today. And at EC Publications (which Max Gaines had started after leaving DC and which was now being run by his son Bill), horror comics were crawling out from the writers' fevered imaginations.

This lucky collector has a rich trove of highly collectible comics.

The Horror, the Horror!

With such titles as *Tales from the Crypt* and *Weird Science,* Bill Gaines and his crew set the industry scrambling in a new direction, one that eventually spawned a parental uproar and a congressional investigation. With each new rival publisher going for more and more gory material, it was an easy task for psychologist Fredric Wertham to gain notoriety by blaming all the ills of society on comic books. (*We* know it was rock music.)

In an attempt to forestall congressional action and public backlash, the larger publishers banded together and formed the Comics Magazine Association, with a Comics Code to label appropriate comic book material. Virtually overnight, Gaines and his schlockmeister competitors were forced to abandon comics. Only Gaines continued on the fringe of the business, publishing a highly successful comic book turned magazine: MAD.

They're Back ...

Comics languished throughout the early and mid-1950s until 1956, when DC editor Julius Schwartz proposed bringing the superheroes back for another try. He revised and revamped The Flash, and his efforts met with enthusiastic response. He followed his success with Green Lantern, Hawkman, The Atom, and the Justice League of America.

Learn the Lingo

Like Gaul, comics can be neatly divided into three stages of development. The first stage is called the "Golden Age," from June 1935 to 1955. Next is the "Silver Age," September 1956 to the early 1970s. Last is the "Modern Age," 1980s to the present. Collectors use these terms to distinguish among production eras.

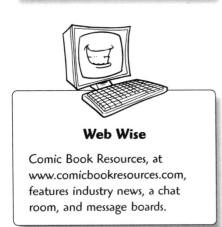

Web Wise

Comic Book Resources, at www.comicbookresources.com, features industry news, a chat room, and message boards.

Meanwhile, over at Atlas (formerly Timely) Comics, publisher Martin Goodman salivated over the success of his rivals at DC and suggested to his editor that they should start publishing superhero comics as well. The editor, a long-time wri-ter of comics for Timely/Atlas named Stan Lee, took a shot and created the Fantastic Four, Spiderman, the Incredible Hulk, and the X-Men.

It was not long before a new age of superheroes was upon us. The early 1960s saw almost as many new characters as the 1940s had; the frenzy was further fueled by the Batman TV series in 1966.

In the early 1970s, the comic book industry became aware that its audience was changing. Instead of losing all its readers around age 14 (when boys discovered girls and girls discovered telephones), these readers were staying on, looking for more diverse and challenging material. Coupled with the growth of a direct market (in which the publishers could supply books directly to comic book shops), and the utilization of new printing technologies, the industry went through its largest expansion. Record numbers of titles were produced every month.

A new generation of horror comics, many produced by fans-turned-professionals from England, began to appear, aimed at an adult audience. Far more graphic than those of the 1950s, but also with far more complex story lines, these books in particular have led former readers back into the comic book fold.

In leaps and bounds, the comic book industry dove into computerized color and art, bringing it up to techno-speed—and in some cases ahead of the curve. New printing techniques were utilized. Types of paper were reformulated to best show off the subtleties of the artwork.

Comics Today

Which brings us to the present, when comics have lost much of their luster. Sales of current books, which peaked in 1993, have steadily declined in each succeeding year. It's so bad that ...

➤ Marvel went into bankruptcy in 1997 for 18 months, emerging with its line of comic books drastically reduced.

➤ Comic book specialty shops, which numbered more than 10,000 in the early 1990s, are now estimated to be fewer than 3,000.

Caveat Emptor

Beware of reprints of classic comic books sold as originals. Look for a copyright date to distinguish the new from the old.

Taking the Plunge

So you want to be a comics collector? With the stratospheric value of investment-grade comic books from the 1930s and 1940s, it's not hard to explain their appeal. But collectors are also passionate about the art, artists, and story lines in their favorite comic books.

Quick, check the attic. See if any of the top 10 comics listed in the following table are playing hide-and-seek there. If so, nab 'em fast. They're worth a bundle.

The Most Valuable American Comic Books

Title	Date	Significance
Action Comics #1	June, 1938	First appearance of Superman
Detective Comics #27	May, 1939	First appearance of Batman
Superman #1	Summer, 1939	First comic devoted entirely to Superman
Marvel Comics #1	October, 1939	First appearance of the Human Torch
New Fun Comics #1	February, 1935	First DC comic book
Detective Comics #1	March, 1937	First in a series
All-American Comics #16	July, 1940	First appearance of Green Lantern
Batman #1	Spring, 1940	First comic book devoted to Batman
Whiz Comics #1	February, 1940	First appearance of Captain Marvel
Captain America Comics #1	March, 1941	First appearance of Captain America

Many dealers sell comic books on the Web. Collectible books are also offered for sale at online auctions.

Big Deals

Silver Age comics are the hottest collectible comics at the moment.

Most collectors start by buying new issues. That way, they can decide which titles appeal to them the most. But there is more to buying comics than plunking down some bills. You can arrange your collection in almost limitless ways. Five of the most common methods are collecting by artist, company, numbers, title, and character.

➤ **Collecting by artist.** Many collectors follow the career of a favorite comic artist as he or she migrates from company to company. Today, some artists have even approached the ranks of superstars, complete with flashy automobiles and impressive egos. Original artwork from such fan favorites as Todd McFarlane, Alex Ross, Frank Miller, and Jim Lee have held their value.

➤ **Collecting by company.** Some collectors latch on to a particular company and collect only the titles that it produces. This method can help you specialize.

➤ **Collecting by numbers.** All numbers may be equal, but some numbers are more valuable than others. With comics, it's number one that counts. For years, comic collectors have sought out first issues. It's hard to go astray with number ones: They may introduce new characters, start a new story line, or underprint to create an instant rarity.

Caveat Emptor

Sounds easy to collect by title? Remember that some titles run for decades ... and decades ... and decades.

➤ **Collecting by title.** This is an especially popular way to build a collection. Pick a title and try to nab the entire run.

➤ **Collecting by character.** Collecting by character means saving all the particular issues that feature the superhero (or villain) that you have selected. Spiderman, for example, appears in his own comic as well as in several other issues where he teams up with other characters. Collecting by character presents intriguing bookkeeping chores as well as fun reading.

Even the most minor blemish lowers the value of a comic book. Before you buy a comic to add to your collection, look it over carefully. The cover should be on correctly; the colors should be bright and crisp. The corners and staples should be straight, too.

Making the Grade

You thought your junior high math teacher was picky? You remember, the one with the ruler. She was a mastodon, but she can't hold a candle to comic book collectors. Serious collectors grade comics by a very rigid set of standards. Study the following chart to see if your comics make the grade.

Tricks of the Trade

Serious collectors often buy two or more copies of a new surefire hit comic: one to read and one to store. Speculation is always a gamble, of course, so check carefully before you start snapping up boxes of current issues. It may not be a wise investment, for example, to stockpile comics that are part of a print run of four million.

Comic Condition Grades

Condition	Abbreviation	Description
Mint	M	As close to perfect as perfect can be. The cover is flat; the ink bright. Staples are centered; the spine tight.
Near Mint	NM	Only minor imperfections, such as a few very tiny flecks of color. The bindery tears (small rips that occur during binding) are less than $\frac{1}{16}$ of an inch; the corners are square with ever-so-slight blunting allowed.
Very Fine	VF	Excellent copy, but the spine may have a few barely perceptible transverse stress lines (small wrinkles). A $\frac{1}{4}$-inch crease is allowed, if the color is not broken. Pages and covers can be off-white, but not brown.
Fine	F	The copy shows minor wear but is still flat and uncreased. A fine comic has been read a few times and handled with consideration.
Very Good	VG	This is the average used comic book: It usually has a center crease, a rolled spine, and some discoloration. A staple may be loose, but the cover is still attached—at least partially.

continues

Comic Condition Grades   (continued)

Condition	Abbreviation	Description
Good	G	The comic has all its pages and its cover, but some pages may have chunks missing. To make the grade, no missing piece can be larger than ½ inch. This is the lowest acceptable collectible grade because comics in lesser condition are usually missing pages and covers or disintegrating.
Fair	F	The book is soiled, ragged, and may be missing large pieces. This is what happens to a comic when you cut the coupon for sea monkeys from its back cover.
Poor	P	These books are badly stained, mildewed, ripped, and defaced. Often, the books are so brittle that they fall apart when you handle them.

Web Wise

Comicon, at www.Comicon.com, features news and information about comic book conventions around the country.

It's enough to make you wear white gloves when you read the comic book you just bought. Not a bad idea.

A Nip and a Tuck

Judging by what I see at the gym, few of us hesitate to have a little taken off here or added on there. A bit of liposuction down below, a touch of the scalpel under the eyes. No one's *ever* going to convince me that people of a certain age look that good without the aid of a pricey plastic surgeon. No matter how many sit-ups they do.

But the aging comic book collector who easily submits to a little personal refurbishing is likely to recoil in horror at the idea of making his or her prize books endure the same process. And with good cause. Professionally restored comic books do have a place in the collectibles market, but only under three conditions:

1. The work has been done by a professional.

2. The seller discloses complete information about the restoration.

3. The resulting book is priced fairly, based on demand and condition.

Nonetheless, all things being equal, a professionally restored book will rarely be worth the same amount as an unrestored book in the same condition. For example, an unrestored copy of *Incredible Hulk #6* in very good condition will be worth more than a fair copy of the book restored to very good condition. The latest trends at comic book auctions suggest that unrestored rare books in fine or better condition will be better investments than restored books in the future. This is because there will be fewer unrestored pieces. Conclusion? Save restoration efforts for comic books graded less than fine. And don't worry so much about your love handles.

Buzz, Buzz

Every collectible has its buzz words, and comics are no different. How can you learn all the jargon so you sound like a real fanboy? Study this handy-dandy crib sheet so you know what all the buzz is about.

Tricks of the Trade

The Overstreet Comic Book Price Guide is the industry standard. It's published once a year by Gemstone Publishing. Also consult *Wizard* magazine, a monthly, and *The Comic Buyer's Guide*, a weekly. Both carry pricing updates and other industry news.

Term	Meaning
Adult material	Sex, violence, naughty bits.
Adzine	A magazine that advertises comics and collectibles.
Annual	Published once a year.
Arrival date	A dealer or distributor hand-pencils the date when he places the comic for sale. This date is usually a month or two before the cover date.
Ashcan	Dummy title prepared to show advertisers or to copyright a trademark and title. The inside pages are often blank.
B&W	Black-and-white art.
Bad girl art	Depicts women in sexually explicit ways.
Bi-monthly	Published every two months.
Bi-weekly	Published every two weeks.
Complete run	All issues of a given title.
Con	A comic book convention.
Crossover	When a character appears in another character's story.
Debut	The first time a character appears in a comic.
Double cover	An error in binding that results in two covers being bound into the same book; not a defect, and makes the book very slightly more valuable.
Fanzine	A nonprofessional fan publication.
Foxing	Orange-brown spots caused by mold.
Gatefold cover	A cover that folds out, usually an additional page width.

continues

continued

Term	Meaning
Indicia	Copyright information; usually on the inside front cover or page 1.
Logo	The stylized title of the comic or character as it appears on the cover or title page.
One-shot	The only issue of a title published.
Pedigree	A comic book from a famous collection.
Printing defect	A defect that occurs during the printing process, such as wrinkled paper or a misfolded spine.
Provenance	The source of a comic book, such as a person's collection.
Quarterly	Published four times a year, every three months.
Rolled spine	Damage to a comic book caused by folding back the pages while reading.
Semi-monthly	Published twice a month.
Spine	The edge of the book that is folded and stapled.
Spine roll	A defect that occurs during binding. It results in uneven pages.
Splash panel	The large panel on the first page of a comic.
Stress lines	Small wrinkles along the comic book's spine.
Sun shadow	A serious defect caused by the sun.
Swipe	Art in a comic copied and modified, after changing the characters shown, from previously published material.

Tricks of the Trade

Remember when your mother used to tell you that character counts? She knew her comic books. Which character is on a page of original art matters. A page of a story that shows Super-man is worth more than a page that shows Clark Kent—even if it's the same story.

Art for Art's Sake

In addition to the actual comic books, some collectors lust after original art. These black-and-white inked drawings are usually 50 percent larger than the printed pages. The older art is highly valued and often difficult to find, but there are substantial amounts of contemporary art available.

In the past, few comic book companies returned the art panels to the artists, so few panels were available for sale. Since the 1970s, however, most companies now give the art back to the creators. The artists, in turn, are free to sell their pages to dealers and at conventions.

As with comic books, the value of original art depends on four factors:

1. Popularity of character
2. Popularity of artist
3. Rarity
4. Skill

The Least You Need to Know

➤ The comic book industry began in the mid-1930s. The most valuable comic books date from these early "golden" years. Many Marvel books from the 1960s and DC books from the mid-1950s are hot, too.

➤ Rarity and condition determine the value of a comic book.

➤ Original comic art is a popular collectible.

➤ Comic books did not corrupt America's youth. Blame it on the bossa nova.

Chapter 12

Tried and True: Collecting Stamps and Coins

In This Chapter

➤ Learn the parts of a stamp

➤ Explore collectible stamps

➤ Learn the parts of a coin

➤ Start a coin collection

➤ Invest in collectible coins

The colorful bits of gummed paper squares that move the mail may not look like much, but stamps have excited the passion of collectors for generations. In this chapter, I'll explain the different parts of a stamp, describe the best places to get the stamps you need to build your collection, and teach you how to build a collection of value.

This chapter also covers another traditional collectible, coin collecting. You'll learn the different parts of a coin and what you need to start your own coin collection. Along the way, I'll give you tips for grading, sorting, and turning coin collecting into coin investing.

Stamp Collecting 101

The world's first stick-on, prepaid stamps were introduced in Britain on May 6, 1840. Only two denominations were issued: the penny black and the twopenny blue. America issued her first stamps seven years later. Five cents bought you Ben Franklin's likeness; for a nickel more, you got George Washington's sweet puss. The stamps had to be cut apart because no one had thought of perforations. They hadn't been invented yet.

The Whole Is the Sum of Its Parts

You look at a stamp and it looks like a stamp. Like all stamps, it has a few thingies and a couple of whoosies. There is even a whatchamacallit or two. Each of those thingies has a name. Use this diagram to break the code:

Every stamp has eight main parts.

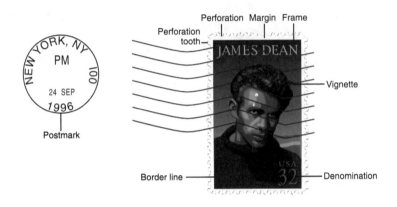

Form and Function

Stamp and stamplike substitutes come in different formats. Different collectors fancy different formats. It's your call. Here's the lowdown:

➤ **Booklets.** A complete booklet is referred to as an *unexploded booklet.* A page of stamps from a booklet is called a *pane.*

➤ **Coil format.** The stamps are issued on a roll. Coil stamps are perforated on two sides only, usually the left and right sides. They are generally collected in pairs.

➤ **Covers.** A *cover* is any kind of envelope that has traveled through the mail. It's called a "cover" because it covers the message—the letter—inside.

➤ **E-stamps.** A method of purchasing, downloading, and printing postage directly from your computer. These have no collectible value—yet.

➤ **First day covers.** First day covers contain a postmark for the first day the stamp was put on sale. Usually, only one lucky city gets first crack at selling the stamp. The next day, any post office can offer the stamp for sale. Many collectors of first day covers prefer their covers unaddressed. They send away for them and write their name on a removable label. When the cover arrives, they peel off the label.

➤ **Permit imprints.** Used when you are mailing more than 200 pieces or 50 pounds at one time.

Learn the Lingo

Stamp collecting is called **philately**; a stamp collector is called a **philatelist.**

➤ **Plate blocks.** This is a block of stamps that includes on the selvage the number of the printing plate used to print the stamps. Some plate blocks contain four stamps. Stamps printed by the flat-plate method are collected in blocks of six; multicolored stamps can have as many as 10 or 20 stamps per block. Stamps with "floating plate numbers" may contain almost half a sheet of stamps per plate block.

➤ **Plate-number coils.** The U.S. Postal Service started putting plate numbers on coils in 1981. Collectors usually save plate-number coils in strips of three or five. The plate number is printed in the middle.

➤ **Postal stationery.** There are three types: *prestamped envelopes, aerogrammes* (letter sheets for foreign postage), and *postal cards* (not the same as picture postcards but rather blank cards with the stamp already printed).

Tricks of the Trade

If you get an envelope with a canceled stamp you like, don't be too quick to soak it off the envelope. Sometimes the entire envelope may be worth more than the used stamp alone because of the postmark. Check the value with a dealer or in a stamp price guide.

➤ **Postage meters.** Legal substitutes for stamps, used primarily by businesses.

➤ **Self-adhesive stamps.** The stamps are peeled from their backing; they don't have to be licked. They were first issued in 1974.

➤ **Sheet format.** Perforated sheets of stamps.

➤ **Souvenir sheets.** A small sheet of one or more stamps, having a commemorative inscription or special artwork surrounding the stamp or stamps.

A Sticky Acquisition: Acquiring Stamps

Notice that I said "acquiring" stamps rather than "buying" them. There are many ways to get stamps, and buying is just one of the methods. How you acquire stamps depends on which stamps you want, where you live, and how much time and money you have to devote to your collection. Here are the methods; take your pick.

Used, Not Abused

Used stamps have fulfilled their life's work: They have helped a letter get somewhere. As their reward, they have been canceled to prevent reuse. Don't sneer at used stamps. Some collectors seek out used stamps only; virgin stamps, they argue, are nothing more than fancy labels. There are two big advantages to collecting used stamps:

1. You don't have to worry about the gum being pristine. It ain't. As a matter of fact, it's all gone. You soaked it off to get the stamp off the envelope.

2. Used stamps are generally cheaper than new stamps.

Big Deals

So, you want your cute face on a stamp? Different countries have different rules. In America, it's a little hard to lobby on your own behalf for stamphood, because you have to be dead for at least 10 years before you can appear on a stamp. (If you were the president, you have to be dead for only one year.) Significant events are commemorated only on anniversaries in multiples of 50 years. Only events and anniversaries of widespread national importance are eligible for consideration. Stamps are not issued to honor fraternal, political, sectarian, or service organizations whose main *raison d'être* is to solicit or distribute funds. If you have an idea for a stamp, send your suggestion to this address:

Citizens' Stamp Advisory Committee
Stamp Information Branch
United States Postal Service
Washington, DC 20260-6352

Some used stamps are valuable because of the cancellation they bear. But except for the cost of neat-o cancellations, used stamps are inexpensive. They can even be free if you soak them off your own mail and hit up your near and dear kinfolk for their used stamps.

Mixtures and Packets

Stamp mixtures are just what they sound like: piles and piles of assorted stamps. They can be used or new. Stamp mixtures are sold in large quantities—even by the thousands—as well as by weight. You can buy them *on paper* (with part of the envelope) or *off paper* (soaked off). I recommend that you buy packets labeled *all different* as opposed to *assorted*. The former term means that every stamp will be different; the latter, that you may get duplicates.

Buying mixtures is not like playing the lottery. You won't find the prize in the Cracker Jack box, either.

Tricks of the Trade

To get a stamp off an envelope, place the stamp in cool water so that the paper becomes moist—not the stamp. Peel the paper from the stamp, not the stamp from the paper. Lay the stamp facedown on blotting paper. When the stamp is dry, store it between pages of clean blotting paper.

128

Say the mixture label reads, "1,000 stamps! Total catalog value $50—for only $5!" This means that you have bought 1,000 stamps for $5. Doing your division shows that each stamp is worth 5¢, the minimum value assigned to a stamp in *Scott's Catalog,* the stamp catalog. Trust me; there's no needle hidden in this haystack—you won't find a $5 million stamp or even a $5 one.

But the picture is even more grim. Even though the catalog value is indeed $50 for the lot, you won't be able to get that. The 5¢ per stamp ($50 total) represents the dealer's time more than the stamp's actual value.

Why would anyone buy mixtures? They help you acquire a lot of stamps quickly, cheaply, and easily, so you can learn about stamp collecting and decide how to limit and refine your collection.

Web Wise

The Philatelic Society, the national American stamp society, is on the Web at www.west.net/~stamps1/aps.html. The American Philatelic Research Library has a super online catalog at www.stamps.org.

Dealing with Dealers

Cozy up to a neighborhood stamp dealer. They are the most knowledgeable stamp mavens you will find. Most stamp dealers are fair and ethical people, savvy to the reality that only by establishing a steady, repeat clientele are they going to retire happily.

But this is a quid-pro-quo relationship. They teach; you buy. You cannot hang around the store and pick the stamp dealer's brain without buying enough stamps to make it worth his time. You most especially cannot pick Dealer #1's brain and then buy from Dealer #2 because his or her prices are better. Tacky, tacky.

Try to find a dealer who will be your mentor and help you learn what you need to know to be a successful stamp collector. A good stamp dealer can help you with more than stamp education. Say you want to collect stamps related to zeppelins, but your dealer doesn't have any particular interest in the *Hindenberg.* Nonetheless, your dealer probably knows another dealer or several collectors who do groove on blimps and so can help you network. This same advice applies to coin dealers, as you'll learn later in this chapter.

Mail Order and Internet

Mail-order and Internet sales are not for those who require instant gratification. But ordering stamps this way does allow you a much wider range of possibilities. It's also the best way to buy if you don't have a stamp store within reach.

Here are two ways to use mail order:

1. **Approvals.** *Approvals* means that you can see the stamps before you buy them. On your request, a dealer will send you a selection of stamps for your approval. You keep the stamps you do want and return payment for them along with the stamps you reject. However, if any stamps are lost or damaged while they are in your possession, you're responsible. So lock up your pet stamp-eating iguana when the approval package comes.

2. **Wanted: Stamps.** Here's the scoop. You send the dealer a list of stamps you want. This is called your *want list*. The dealer goes over your list, reviews his or her stock, and lets you know what you can get at your price. You're not under any obligation to buy anything, but you must respond to the dealer's offer with an acceptance or refusal.

Auctions

You can attend an auction in person or bid by mail or Internet. Some auctions are by mail only or on the Web only. Since this method of buying stamps and coins normally involves some serious money, it's important to know and understand the terms of sale. You learned this in previous chapters.

Another Opening, Another Show: Stamp Shows

Stamp shows (also known as *Philatelic Exhibitions*) are a good way to dive right into the world of stamps. They offer you a way to see a lot of stamps at one time. You'll also get a chance to scope out stamps you might not otherwise get to see—especially those that cost as much as a week in the south of France.

Some stamp shows have a *bourse,* or exchange, where dealers have come to sell rather than play show-and-tell. Like a good consumer, you can comparison shop and schmooze new dealers. Stamp shows are also great places to meet representatives from stamp clubs and see if they offer what you need. You might be able to find a club that's right for you.

Some large shows also feature a temporary U.S. Postal Service station where you can mail letters and buy stamps. Convenient postage is nice, but the zowie! part of the kiosk is the special postmarks, usually pictorials. The letters you mail from the show will bear these special pictorials. Don't want to mail your envelope? The show's sponsors usually sell a special envelope, which you can decorate with a stamp of your choice and have canceled with the show's postmark. You can take the envelope with you. It makes a nice souvenir.

Caveat Emptor

It costs very little to print a stamp; thus, many small countries issue reams of stamps every year. These stamps are colorful, attractive— and usually worthless. There is even a term for these no-account stamps: *wallpaper.* Most collectors look upon these money-making gimmick stamps with contempt, but it's your money.

Big Deals

The world's most valuable stamp is a 1¢ black-on-magenta British Guiana (now Guyana) printed in the capital, Georgetown, in 1856, when supplies from Britain failed to arrive. Yet the young colonial collector who found the only known copy among some old stamps in 1873 sold it for the equivalent of a few pennies because he thought it was dull and uninteresting. In 1934 it sold for $32,000; by 1980 the price had skyrocketed to $850,000.

The stamp is now believed to be a true one-of-a-kind. An intriguing story about the stamp relates an incident that happened around the turn of the century, while it was owned by the American millionaire Arthur Hind. A British merchant seaman called on Hind with another genuine one-cent black-on-magenta. Hind is said to have paid the seaman a huge sum for the second stamp—and then burned it. He told his friends, "Now there is still only one."

Even-Steven: Trading

As you have learned in previous chapters, many collectors trade rather than purchase collectibles. The same is true of stampmeisters. Often, trading allows you to get the stamps you want without forking over cash. It's a great way to fill out a collection, too.

You can meet potential trading partners through stamp clubs at shows and through the Web. Dealers are often willing to trade as well. Over a period of time, you can trade up to quality stamps you could otherwise not afford to buy. This same advice applies to trading coins.

What to Collect?

You can collect any stamps you like: individual issues, plate blocks, first day covers, and so on. The simplest collection is the general one; it is also dauntingly large. Monstrous even. As a result, some collectors specialize in the stamps of a particular country. That's still a big mother of a collection. Topical themes narrow down a collection nicely, and many collectors favor them.

Big Deals

The most worthless stamp ever issued—taking only face value into account—was a 3,000-pengo stamp issued in Hungary on February 5, 1946. At the time of issue, one U.S. penny would have bought 25 billion of the stamps.

As with any paper collectible, the condition of a stamp is very important. Stamps are graded *mint* (never used), *extremely fine, very fine, fine, very good,* and *good.* How can you assess a stamp yourself? Here are 10 factors to consider:

Web Wise

The American Air Mail Society provides many services for the aerophilatelic at www.ourworld. compuserve.com/homepages/aams.

1. How even is the gum on the back?
2. Are there any creases and tears?
3. In what condition are the perforations?
4. Are the colors vivid?
5. How much fading has occurred?
6. How brittle is the paper?
7. Has the stamp been regummed?
8. Is one area thinner than another?
9. Has the stamp been repaired?
10. Has the stamp been singed when someone tried to iron out a crease?

Don't Bet the Ranch: Stamps as Investments

The scene: Anywhere, U.S.A.

The plot: A stamp collector is trying to sell his collection to a reputable dealer.

Dealer: (examining the piles and piles of stamps) "You've got postage here. It can be used to mail letters. It's worth 80 percent of face value."

Collector: (incredulous) "What?! Less than face value?"

Dealer: "Yes, that's its value."

Collector: "How can that be? Stamps are supposed to be good investments." (Pause.) "I don't want to sell at a loss. Someday they will be worth more. What do you think?"

Unfortunately, time alone will not cause *mint postage* (unused stamps) to rise in value. Rising prices are created when increased demand exerts force on a limited supply. Demand is the key factor; rarity comes next. Age, by itself, has little to do with value. In order for a sheet of post-1945 mint stamps to increase in value, the collectors (demand) must absorb the vast hoards (supply).

Look Before You Leap

Stamps are generally considered good investments. As is the case with any collectible, however, some stamps are—and some stamps are not. The majority of all stamps— the new issues, the packets, the mixtures, the approvals, the new commemoratives you get at the post office, the designer first day covers, and so on—are not good investments. But they were never intended to be.

Stockpiles of commonplace stamps will not pay off your mortgage, send your kids to college, or finance your retirement. The math is easy enough for even me to do: If one person puts aside one extra sheet of each new commemorative, there is a supply of 50 stamps (assuming 50 stamps per sheet). That will make 50 new collectors of that stamp happy campers. But if you put aside 5 or 10 sheets of every new stamp, you have enough to satisfy hundreds of new collectors. If *every* collector squirrels away sheets and sheets of new stamps, the vast supply will far outstrip the demand and will saturate the market. And that is what is going on now.

A Little Face Time

"You can't go wrong at face," the time-honored stamp-collecting mantra goes. People who subscribe to this maxim argue that the logic of buying new mint sheets at face value is the same as buying Disney stock at its original issue price. Would that it were so; it's not the same thing at all.

Buying new mint issues at face value is the same as buying shares of *every* new penny stock issued. For every one that becomes a blue chip, thousands and thousands will be losers. Buying new-issue stamps willy-nilly at the post office is not picking winners. It's buying piles and piles of stamps.

Mindless buying does not a collector make. It makes a person with a lot of postage to store.

Try this instead. If you collect single stamps, buy *one* stamp of each new issue. If you collect plate

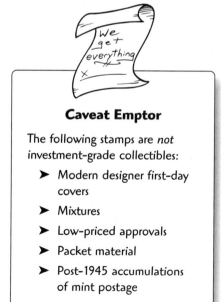

Caveat Emptor

The following stamps are *not* investment-grade collectibles:

➤ Modern designer first-day covers

➤ Mixtures

➤ Low-priced approvals

➤ Packet material

➤ Post-1945 accumulations of mint postage

blocks, buy *one* plate block ... and so on. Advantages: You will spend only a few dollars. The money you would have tied up in duplicates can be better spent in acquiring more-valuable earlier stamps.

Don't Take Any Wooden Nickels: Collecting Coins

Coin collecting is an equally time-honored hobby. Ancient Romans collected coins from even more ancient Romans. Popes in the 1200s and 1300s were avid coin collectors. The famous Flemish painter Rubens collected coins; so did John Quincy Adams and King Farouk of Egypt. According to some estimates, about five million Americans collect coins today. Let's explore coins as collectibles.

Making Heads or Tails of It: Learning the Parts of a Coin

Before you can start a collection, you have to know what you're collecting. The key to a successful collection is to learn as much about coins as you can. Let's start with a typical U.S. coin. Here is a list of the different parts of a coin.

Learn the Lingo

Coin collectors and scholars are called **numismatists.**

➤ **Date.** The year, which does not have to be the date when the coin was struck

➤ **Designer's initials.** Optional, identifying the coin's designer

➤ **Device.** The major part of the coin's design

➤ **Edge.** The thin curved surface of the coin

➤ **Exergue.** The area that contains the value and date

➤ **Field.** The flat surface of the coin, between the ridge and the devices

➤ **Legend.** The lettering (also called "inscription")

➤ **Mint mark.** Letters or another symbol that shows where the coin was made

➤ **Motto.** A religious/patriotic phrase, such as "In God We Trust"

➤ **Obverse.** The front of the coin, the "heads" side

➤ **Reverse.** The back of the coin, the "tails" side

➤ **Rim.** The slightly raised border, just inside the edge

Pocket Change or Priceless? Grading Coins

You know the collector's mantra by now: *age, rarity,* and *condition.* It applies to anything you collect, but especially to stamps and coins.

There is no universally accepted standard for grading coins, because grading is an art rather than a science. However, the following categories of currency grades are generally accepted in the industry. Knowing this system can help you assemble and refine your collection.

Grading	Meaning
Proof coins	The coins have a mirror-like finish and are struck from polished dies especially for collectors.
Uncirculated	Mint condition, apart from marks caused by the coins rubbing together.
Extra Fine	Almost perfect.
Very Fine	Shows slight wear.
Fine	Shows signs of wear.
Very Good	The design shows clearly, but the detail is worn away.
Good	The coin is very worn, but the outline of the design is still visible.
Fair	A coin can just about not be identified.

A Penny Saved Is a Dollar Earned: Sources for Coins

You can get pennies from heaven, but there are more reliable sources. I recommend circulation, other collectors, and coin dealers. Let's take a look at the advantages and disadvantages of each method of getting coins.

Look Further Than the Couch Cushions: Circulation

Circulation is the most convenient way to get coins. The drawback? Many coins are no longer circulated. For example, pre-1965 U.S. dimes, quarters, and half-dollars no longer circulate because their silver content (bullion value) is worth more than their face value (fiat value).

Even commonplace coins that have only face value can be difficult to get. For example, "wheat cents," Lincoln pennies made before 1959, are rarely seen. Since billions of these pennies exist, their value is low, so the hoarding is irrational.

Want an easy entry to the world of coin collecting? Assemble an album of *Lincoln Cents* by date and mint mark. Start with 1959 coins. They are the least expensive set you can make, and they will teach you a great deal about putting together a coin collection.

Web Wise

You can find out coin values at www.coin-universe.com/sites/index.html.

The Exchange of Change: Coin Dealers

Coin dealers are the #1 source of coins for serious collectors. Dealers have the knowledge and the coins. There is no shortage of coin dealers, so keep looking until you find someone you feel comfortable dealing with.

You can find reputable coin dealers by asking your fellow collectors whom they like. I recommend that you first check out your local coin shop. It's convenient, and you're more likely to develop a professional relationship, which will help you in many ways. You'll get better discounts, hints, and perhaps even supplies, because your dealer will know what you need. In addition, a local coin dealer who knows you is more likely to buy back coins as you trade up. He or she may even be willing occasionally to buy less-desirable coins from you to keep your business.

If I Had a Nickel for Every Coin Collector ...

Network via the Web or work to find other people who share your interest in coin collecting. Tap into coin collector clubs; check the local community bulletin boards for news about coin collector clubs. Coin dealers can often put you in touch with other collectors; in fact, you may meet collectors at coin shops. Try attending some local conventions and coin shows, too. Many of the collectors you meet will be willing to trade coins with you and share their knowledge.

When Four Quarters Equal More Than a Dollar: Collection vs. Investment

If we could see into the future, we'd all have bought Dell stock and given up red meat. (Well, maybe not the meat.) Who can tell which coins will be hot and which ones will flop? Remember the mantra: age, rarity, and demand. And follow these guidelines:

➤ Use common sense and evaluate your dealer's reputation and reliability *before* you send money or authorize a credit card transaction.

➤ Comparison shop. Visit at least three dealers before making any major purchase.

➤ Check prices in leading coin publications to make sure that you're not being overcharged. Check prices at online auctions, too.

➤ Beware of any "coin investment" promotion that promises "guaranteed profits," "limited quantity," "lowest price in the world," "limited sale time," and "guaranteed grading."

You can check the value of a coin in the annual *A Guide Book of United States Coins* by R. S. Yeoman. Called the "Red Book" by those in the know, it is the standard U.S. coin catalog for determining retail coin prices, mintages, and popular collectible coins. Since the *Guide Book* is published only once a year, there will sometimes be a time lag if the coin market is changing rapidly, as it did during the 1970s.

Plunking Down Your Spare Change

Okay, so your mother calls you up. She's at a garage sale pawing through a pile of coins. She wants to know whether she should buy the nickel marked 1912D. It's only a dollar. The answer is an enthusiastic "Yes!"

Here are some other coins to consider learning more about as possible investments. There are many more; these are just a few suggestions. Mom will likely never find these in a garage sale, but you never know.

➤ Scarce twentieth-century coins, such as *Mercury Dimes,* in uncirculated condition

➤ *U.S. Bust* coins in high grades

➤ *Indian Head* cents with low mintages in uncirculated condition

➤ Ancient coins in silver and gold (I know, this is a no-brainer; you already figured this one out for yourself.)

➤ Nineteenth-century European silver *crowns* or gold coins with small mintages in uncirculated condition

➤ "Key dates" in popular coin series, such as 1877 *Indian Cent,* 1895 *Morgan Dollars*

➤ *U.S. Pioneer* gold coins

➤ Nineteenth-century U.S. proof sets in uncirculated condition

➤ *U.S. Half Cents* and *Large Cents* in uncirculated condition

➤ Popular U.S. classics, such as *Barber coinage, Liberty Seated,* preferably in uncirculated condition

Caveat Emptor

Be especially leery of coins sold by telemarketing. Reputable coin dealers with high-quality goods don't have to smooth-talk you over the phone while you're trying to eat dinner.

Web Wise

The American Numismatic Society is at www.amnumsoc.org/. The American Numismatic Association is at www.money.org/.

The Least You Need to Know

➤ When it comes to stamps and coins, repeat after me: age, rarity, condition.

➤ Don't be penny-wise and pound foolish: Buy quality stamps and coins.

➤ Knowledge is power: Learn as much as you can about stamps and coins before you invest in them.

➤ Beware of fraud and counterfeit stamps and coins.

Chapter 13

~~Love~~ Money Makes the World Go Round

In This Chapter

➤ Learn the history of paper money

➤ Start and maintain a paper money collection

➤ Get to know each part of a bill

➤ Discover which U.S. and foreign issues are hot

It's been called *moolah, cash, bread, dough, lettuce, clams, bills, folding money, fins, ten-spots, C-notes, travelin' money, bucks,* and *greenbacks*. But no matter what we call it, we know what we mean—paper money. The word *money* comes from the Latin *moneta* (from *moneo,* "to warn"). Juno was the Roman goddess of warning and finances, known as *Juno Moneta*. Since ancient times, money has fascinated people in a way that few other tangibles have.

Compared with stamp and coin collecting, paper money collecting is a relatively recent hobby. In the past, people looked upon paper money as something to spend, not admire—and besides, who had extra money to *collect?* The purchasing power of bank notes from the 1800s and earlier was so much greater than today's money that few people could afford to hoard any paper money at all, much less be crazy enough to collect it. Hoarding meant you weren't earning bank interest. In addition, banks went under so fast—and thus invalidated their paper money issue—that smart people spent their bank notes rather than collected them.

In this chapter, you will learn the history of paper money. Then you'll get a little cozy with some folding money so you can familiarize yourself with each part of a bill. Next, I'll teach you how to start and maintain a paper money collection. Finally, you'll discover which U.S. and foreign issues are hot. Along the way, I'll show you how to take care of your collection, including storing, displaying, and insuring it.

If These Bills Could Talk: A Brief History of Paper Money

Paper money is any type of currency printed on paper. Besides the traditional wood pulp and cloth rag, "paper" money has also been made from tree bark, leather, and silk. Paper money itself has no intrinsic value—after all, you can't eat it or wear it— but it can be converted (or *redeemed*) for metals that people perceive as valuable, such as gold and silver.

The First Money

The world's first true paper money originated in China, but scholars argue over the specifics. Some claim that the first paper money was created as early as A.D. 650, during the Tang (or T'ang, take your pick) Dynasty, but none of these notes survived. Others contend that paper money was not freely circulated until the ninth century, during the Tang Dynasty, and they can buttress their claims with actual paper money from the era.

We're in the Money: The Development of Money in America

Visiting our shores in the early nineteenth century, the Frenchman Alexis de Tocqueville commented on the relationship of Americans to their greenbacks: "I know of no country, indeed, where the love of money has taken stronger hold on the affections of men," he said. He was onto something.

Web Wise

The Society of Paper Money Collectors, Inc., is open to anyone interested in paper money or related areas such as checks, stocks, engravings, and other fiscal ephemera. Their Web site is www.spmc.org/.

American paper money dates from 1690, when the Massachusetts Bay Colony printed *Bills of Credit* to pay military expenses for the soldiers sent to fight against the French colonists. Other states quickly followed suit. From the term *Bills of Credit*, we get our slang term "bill"—a piece of American paper money.

Colonial currency arose from a constant shortage of coins and insufficient British paper money. In 1775 the Continental Congress issued their own paper money, in $1 to $30 denominations. Over $240 million in *Continentals* (as the money was called) was in circulation by 1779. Rising inflation and rampant counterfeiting made the bills virtually worthless; at the end of the war, they were redeemed at the rate of one cent on the dollar.

Alexander Hamilton organized the First Bank of the United States in 1791, and it soon issued its own notes. The bank was liquidated in 1811, leaving the country flooded with paper money from private, state-chartered banks. The Second Bank of the United States was founded in 1817. It was soundly managed and brought a uniform paper currency to the country by the 1820s.

The South Will Rise Again— but Its Money Won't

When South Carolina seceded from the Union in 1860, about 5.6 million white people and 3.5 million black slaves were living in the 11 states that would become the Confederate States of America. About 22.3 million people lived in the North. The Confederate government found it impossible to pass up the reckless printing of unbacked paper money to finance its war, and so it issued over $2 billion in Confeder-ate notes. Not a good move. By the end of the war, the money was so worthless that some Confederate soldiers refused to accept their pay in Confederate money, insisting on being paid in Union currency!

Tricks of the Trade

Want to collect *Confederate currency?* All types are available, making it easy to plan a long-term collecting strategy. Get to know which notes are rare and which ones are commonplace. Buy notes that are in good condition, and go for notes that give you a matched color set, all bright or all faded, for example.

Dollars and Sense: Why Collect Paper Money?

There are so many things to collect—so why collect paper money? Here are my Top Five Reasons.

1. **It's beautiful.** A finely made bank note is a work of art.
2. **It's historic.** You can chronicle the rise and fall of empires on their paper money.
3. **It's valuable.** Nearly all paper money is worth something aside from its collectible value. Drop a few twenties on the sidewalk, and you'll see what I mean.
4. **It's interesting.** You meet fascinating people through this collectible.
5. **It's fun.** Everyone likes money.

Learn the Lingo

Collectors of paper money and bank notes are called **notaphilists.** The slang term "rag picker" is used by those Philistines who can't spell "notaphilist."

The Almighty Dollar

Quick—without looking—can you name the different parts of a dollar bill? In case you've been spending your time collecting (shudder) credit cards, here are the parts of a modern U.S. bank note.

➤ **Back plate number.** The small green number on the back that identifies the printing plate. It is in the same shade of green as the entire reverse design.

➤ **Check letter, letter plate letter, quadrant number.** The letter or number that identifies the printing plates and plate positions of the note.

➤ **Denomination.** The face value of the note. It appears on our money both in lettering and in numerals.

➤ **Federal Reserve seal.** The seal of the Federal Reserve District Bank. New bills display the seal of the United States Federal Reserve System.

➤ **"Fort Worth Letters."** The letters "FW" that appear before the check letter and face plate number on notes made at the Fort Worth, Texas, Bureau of Engraving.

➤ **Inscribed security thread.** The clear polyester thread embedded in the paper. "USA" and the bill's denomination is printed on the thread, visible when you hold it up to the light. The security thread cannot be reproduced on modern color copiers.

➤ **Legal tender clause.** Wording that states that the money is legal. U.S. notes have this legal tender clause: "THIS NOTE IS LEGAL TENDER FOR ALL DEBTS, PUBLIC AND PRIVATE."

➤ **Microprinting.** The lettering "THE UNITED STATES OF AMERICA" printed over and over outside the portrait oval. You can see it only with a magnifying glass. The new bills have this inscription printed twice on both sides of the base of the portrait oval.

➤ **Motto.** "IN GOD WE TRUST."

➤ **National identification.** The issuing country's name. Our bills say "The United States of America" at the top of the note, on both sides.

➤ **Portrait.** The picture of the famous American on the bill.

➤ **Scrollwork.** The elaborate designs on the note's borders. Scrollwork is done to make counterfeiting the note more difficult.

➤ **Serial numbers.** The official set of letters and numbers that designate the individual number of each note. The serial number is printed twice in green on modern Federal Reserve notes.

➤ **Series.** The year when the bill's design was adopted. It does not have to be the same year that the note was printed. When a small design change is made, a letter is added after the date.

➤ **Signatures.** The written names of the authorizing officials. Modern bills are signed by the Secretary of the Treasury and the Treasurer of the United States.

➤ **Treasury seal.** The seal of the U.S. Department of the Treasury.

➤ **Type of note.** The words "Federal Reserve Note" in white letters at the top of the face.

➤ **Vignette.** The scene portrayed on the note. It includes the portrait on the front and the central design (such as the building) on the back.

Big Deals

The Federal Reserve removes worn and mutilated notes from circulation. Every year, about 6 billion bills, weighing 7,000 tons and having a face value of $60 billion, are trashed. Between 1960 and 1990, about $474 billion in paper money was burned, shredded, or compacted because it was unfit for circulation.

Before we go any further, here's a crib sheet for the most common circulating notes.

Denominations and Portraits

Denomination	Portrait	Back Design
$1	Washington	Great Seal of the United States
$2	Jefferson	Signing of Declaration of Independence
$5	Lincoln	Lincoln Memorial
$10	Hamilton	U.S. Treasury Building
$20	Jackson	White House
$50	Grant	U.S. Capitol
$100	Franklin	Independence Hall
$500	McKinley	FIVE HUNDRED DOLLARS
$1,000	Cleveland	ONE THOUSAND DOLLARS
$5,000	Madison	FIVE THOUSAND DOLLARS
$10,000	Chase	TEN THOUSAND DOLLARS

Web Wise

The International Bank Note Society is on the Web at www. public.coe.edu/~sfellar/IBNSJ/ map.htm. There's a nice Paper Money WWW Directory, too, at web.idirect.com/~mjp/mjpwww. html.

Building Your Collection

Whether you collect rare bills or commonplace ones, domestic or foreign, old or new, some guidelines stay the same. Here they are:

➤ **Go for quality, not quantity.** You can learn a lot from a box of cheap bank notes, but you'll never lose sleep from buying the best.

➤ **Know the market.** This can help you avoid overpaying or getting stuck with a stinker.

➤ **Go for variety.** Avoid duplication, whenever possible. Variety helps you reduce risk.

➤ **Specialize.** Build your collection around a logical theme.

➤ **Avoid damaged money.** Don't shell out for notes that are severely damaged. There's a reason why they're cheap; they're not worth anything.

Top U.S. Notes for Collectors

You can start a collection of U.S. notes by reaching into your wallet, but if you wish to collect notes that are obsolete (no longer in circulation), you will have to get them from dealers or other collectors. The collector's rule holds here, too: Your cost will depend on the bill's rarity, condition, and demand. What follows is my list of the most popular types of U.S. bills for collectors:

1. **Colonial and Continental currency.** The most valuable specimens are bright, flawless notes with broad margins.

Tricks of the Trade

Criswell's *Confederate and Southern States Currency* is the reference text for collectors of Confederate currency.

2. **Broken bank notes.** Also known as *obsolete currency, wildcat bank notes, state and local currency,* and *private bank notes,* the bank notes from the 1800s are collected by time period, design, denomination, locale, etc.

3. **Confederate currency.** Collected by state, denomination, vignette, locale, and so on. Confederate and Civil War currency affords a wide variety of collecting opportunities.

4. **U.S. fractional currency.** "Fractional currency" refers to notes issued from 1862 to 1876, when people hoarded coins because of Civil War hysteria. Denominations include 3, 5, 10, 15, 25, and 50 cents.

5. **Large-size notes.** "Large-size notes" refers to those notes issued from 1861 to 1929. Nick-named "horse blankets" because of their larger size, these notes come in many different varieties, including Compound Interest Treasury Notes, Interest Bearing Notes, and Treasury Notes.

6. **Small-size U.S. currency.** These are the bills we see everyday, first issued in 1929. There are over 1,000 different varieties, so specialization is the way to go unless your pockets are very deep.

7. **Rare American Colonial notes.** All Colonial notes issued before 1755 are rare; so are Delaware notes from 1729 to 1739. Check with guidebooks and dealers for many other examples.

8. **Rare obsolete currency.** Much commonplace obsolete U.S. currency is available, but some collectors seek out only the rare notes. See a guidebook for specific examples.

9. **Rare U.S. military payment certificates.** The real rarities are *Replacement Notes*. They don't have a suffix letter at the end of the numbers.

10. **Nineteenth-century Hawaiian bank notes.** Another rare collectible, these were first "discovered" by Captain Cook in 1778.

Hot Foreign Money

Does your taste run to French wines, Italian leather, and Swiss chocolate? Then foreign notes might be for you. You can collect foreign currency in many ways, including by country, region, political party, ruler, and chronological order. Some of the most popular notes are Australian pounds/shillings pre-1966, anything Fiji pre–World War II, and Russian notes from the Czarist empire. Following are some other foreign issues that are popular with collectors. There are many, many more hot issues, but space doesn't permit me to list them all.

1. **Canada.** Anything with premium over face value.

2. **China.** Over 10,000 basic notes are available. Be selective.

3. **France.** Notes from 1900 to 1950.

4. **India.** British colonial issues from the 1800s to 1947 (the date of Indian independence) are desirable.

5. **Mexico.** Hot areas include provincial bank issues, revolutionary bank issues, and modern government issues.

6. **Norway.** Notes from the 1800s and earlier are very pricey; as a result, most collectors focus on modern issues.

Learn the Lingo

Hell's Notes are fake Chinese currency burned at a funeral to provide the deceased with money in the afterlife. The notes are *not* prized by collectors.

Web Wise

Bank Note Reporter is a monthly newspaper for collectors of U.S., Confederate, and foreign paper money. They're on the Web at www.krause.com/coins/br. The Professional Numismatists Guild is an organization of rare coin and paper money experts. They're at www.pngdealers.com.

7. **Portugal.** Many collectors favor notes from 1900 to 1910 that show historical scenes.

8. **Switzerland.** All the money is valuable; what else would you expect from Europe's most stable country? Trilingual notes are expensive and much sought-after by collectors.

9. **Tibet.** Notes from 1912 to 1950, when the Chinese Communists seized control.

10. **Yugoslavia.** Notes from the 1920s to 1930s for their beauty.

You Can't Go Wrong with Money

A 1985 Federal Reserve study concluded that about 75 percent of the circulating U.S. money (coins and paper money) cannot be located—amounting to $154 billion. Possibilities include foreign hoarding of American money, tax-evading cash transactions, and illegal drug deals. Numismatic collectors have very little of it.

Nonetheless, the 1970s saw a collecting boom in paper money. As speculation fever reached a pitch in the 1980s, paper money that had sold for $100 just a decade earlier was up to $1000. How can you get into the action? First, let me teach you how to grade paper money.

Making the Grade

There is no universally accepted standard for grading money, since grading paper money is an art, not a science. Nevertheless, the following categories of currency grades are generally accepted. Knowing this can help you get your collection together.

Paper Money Grades

Grade	Meaning
Gem Crisp	As fine as a newborn baby's bottom.
Uncirculated	May have a few smudges or bent corners.
Extremely fine	Has three light folds or one major crease, but no major stains or tears.
Very fine	Has several creases, some dirt and limpness.
Fine	Has many folds and creases; some wear and tear.

Grade	Meaning
Very good	Shows much wear, but no missing pieces.
Good	Is as limp as a wet noodle; missing small pieces.
Fair	Is missing large pieces, big holes, filthy.
Poor	Shows severe damage—missing large pieces, stained, may be torn in half.

Cash on the Barrelhead

Now that you know how paper money is graded, how can you discover which bills are available to collect? Use this chart to see how dealers and collectors classify the availability of paper money.

Classifications for Availability of Paper Money

Classification	Definition
Unique	One of a kind
Very rare	Offered for sale very infrequently, perhaps every 5 or 10 years
Rare	Offered for sale a few times every year
Scarce	Missing from most routine collections, but usually available from major paper money conventions
Common	Easy to find (but may be very pricey!)

Pass the Bucks: Handling and Preserving Money

Store your collection in protective plastic holders. You can buy inexpensive soft-plastic holders for literally pennies apiece. Sealed on three sides, they are open at the fourth side so you can insert the bill. They come in many different sizes.

Prized notes belong in hard-plastic holders. These holders consist of two clear panels fastened to each other with plastic screws, so that you can see both sides of the note. They are more expensive, but, hey, your finest pieces deserve the best.

Wash and Wear Money

Should you clean your money? When in doubt, don't. Unless you're a professional paper cleaner and restorer, less is more. You can always do more, but it may be impossible to undo what you have already done.

Furthermore, make sure that everything you do can be reversed—that the bank note is not permanently changed by your actions. I recommend that you practice your cleaning and repairing techniques on pocket currency (you know, the stuff we use every day) before you try it on a collectible. You may even wish to practice on a less valuable note of the same period before you try your technique on an especially valuable piece.

Start small. For example, you might try to erase a small pencil mark. Later you might attempt to tape a small- or medium-size hole. Don't try to repair anything large, though. Leave major repairs to the experts. They have to make a living, too.

Strut Your Stuff ... Not

Many old paper notes are delicate because of chemically destructive inks, thin paper, and wear and tear. Even notes in good condition can be damaged in many ways. Follow these guidelines to keep your collection in optimal condition.

1. As you'll learn in later chapters, humidity spells danger for all paper collectibles. Don't stash your paper money collection in the freezer in an old head of lettuce. Instead, store your collection away from high humidity sources.

Tricks of the Trade

Collectors sometimes iron their money to smooth out wrinkles. Ironing can scorch the paper or make it shiny or brittle. If you can't resist the urge to press, place the bill between two smooth pieces of cloth or blotting paper. Iron both sides, but never touch the iron directly to the money. Or you could come and do my shirts. They're really piling up.

2. Keep your collection away from direct sunlight, because light causes inks to fade.

3. Critters love the taste of money. Termites, silverfish, mice, and bookworms will eat up your money faster than inflation. If you are prone to creature features, invest in a quality exterminator.

4. Store paper money above the floor, away from sources of dust: heaters, windows, bookcases. Dust off your albums before you handle them.

5. I know your money never seems to stretch far enough, but avoid tug-of-war with your bills. Be gentle when you pass a note to someone else. Also, don't force notes into holders and store currency albums upright.

6. Air out your collection on a regular basis to prevent mold and mildew from forming.

7. A great deal of money has been destroyed by fire. To prevent this from happening to your collection, store your paper money away from fireplaces and heaters. You may also wish to store valuable specimens in fire-resistant containers.

8. Wash your hands before you handle your money. The natural oils on your hands, combined with lotions, dirt, and cosmetics, spell trouble for paper money. Paper money was meant to be handled, you protest. Yes, I answer, but when you collect valuable examples of paper money, you want to protect them.

Caveat Emptor

Resist the temptation to frame prized bank notes and hang them on your wall. Fading will soon make your dollars as worthless as donuts.

Penny Wise, Pound Foolish

You've invested considerable amounts of time and money in your collection, so it would be foolish to store it improperly. Of course, it's neat to have your paper money at home to show off to friends, relatives, and the occasional burglar. But resist the temptation to flash your wad. Paper money is easy to hide, but if you keep valuable notes at home, consider insuring them or storing them in a safe.

All safes are not safe. A burglar-resistant safe is not the same thing as a fire-resistant safe. A burglar-resistant safe has thick walls and a tough combination lock, and is often bolted to the floor. However, it may not be fire-resistant. Some fire-resistant safes

Tricks of the Trade

You still need insurance if you store your collection in a bank safe deposit box. The contents of a safe deposit box are rarely insured by the bank.

have heat-resistant walls, but others spray chemicals or water that sounds the death knell to valuable paper money. Consider fully insuring your collection and storing it in a burglar-resistant safe.

Bank storage is another option. As an added incentive, many bank vaults are climate-controlled, making them the ideal environment for paper money. If you go this route, rent a safe deposit box large enough to comfortably accommodate your collection and perhaps even leave a little room for growth.

The Least You Need to Know

➤ When selecting bills to add to your collection, follow the collector's mantra: rarity, condition, demand.

➤ Like any paper collectible, money requires special handling and storage.

➤ A fool and his money are soon parted.

Part 4
Feathering the Nest

Thimble Collectors International (TCI) recently held its 10th Biennial Convention in Bloomington, Minnesota. The convention featured seminars on a wide variety of topics, as well as a sales mall where conference attendees could shop for that special addition to their collections.

Thimbles don't do it for you? How about toothpick holders? The annual convention of the National Toothpick Holder Collectors Society was held this summer in Eugene, Oregon.

Is glass your thing? Then consider dropping by the Westmoreland Glass Society's annual meeting. They promise glass and a good time.

Thimbles, toothpick holders, glass, books, china, toys, beer bottles, household items, clocks, quilts, radios, records, tools—collecting offers a myriad of fabulous everyday objects. Take your pick. So let's go shopping already.

Chapter 14

Cute, Cuddly, and Costly: Collectible Stuffed Toys

In This Chapter

➤ Beanie Babies

➤ Other collectible plush toys

➤ Teddy bears

In 1997 the Chicago Cubs negotiated a deal with Ty, Inc., the makers of Beanie Babies, to hand out 10,000 Cubbie the Bear Beanie Babies along with a commemorative card to fans aged 13 and under. The moment the promotion was announced, Beanie Baby collectors went berserk. The game sold out at once—all 37,000 seats. A few months later, the Cubs tried it again, with Back to School Cubbie. This time the frenzy was even greater as fans mobbed the streets days before the tickets went on sale.

Not to be outdone, the Chicago White Sox ran a Beanie Baby promotion in July of 1997. You guessed it: That game garnered the biggest attendance of the season (nearly 33,000), thanks to Blizzard the tiger. What can we conclude? People go wild for Beanie Babies. But Beanies are the new kids on the block; for generations, collectors have had a love affair with plush toys.

For example, *arctophily,* or teddy bear collecting, is an increasingly serious hobby. The most expensive teddy bear ever sold at an auction was a 1926 Steiff teddy bear named "Happy." It recently sold at Sotheby's (London) for $55,000.

Are Beanies still hot? If so, which ones make the best collectibles? How can you build an enjoyable and valuable collection of stuffed toys? What about fakes and frauds? That's what you'll learn in this chapter.

Spilling the Beans

What's a half-pound handful of polyester plush filled with plastic pellets worth? Plenty—if it's packaged as a Beanie Baby. Since their debut in 1993, about one billion of these toys have been sold. According to reliable estimates, over 20 million people collect Beanie Babies. Clearly, Beanies are a collectible phenomenon. Who gets the credit (and the cash)?

The lucky winner is H. Ty Warner, a 1962 Kalamazoo College alum who got his start selling Dakin stuffed animals to gift shops in the Midwest. Sensing a good thing, Warner left Dakin in 1980 and created his own line of stuffed creatures, full-sized Himalayan cats. Thirteen years later, he scaled the toys down and the numbers up to create Beanie Babies. Nine Beanies made their debut at a toy fair in 1993:

➤ Chocolate the Moose

➤ Cubbie the Brown Bear

➤ Flash the Dolphin

➤ Legs the Frog

➤ Patti the Platypus

➤ Pinchers the Red Lobster

➤ Splash the Black Whale

➤ Spot the Black-and-White Dog

➤ Squealer the Pig

Web Wise

Beanie Babies have scores of sites on the Internet. Most are devoted to selling Beanies; some are fan pages. The "official" Beanie Baby site is Ty's at www.ty.com.

Beanies sold well, but they were nothing to write home about until Christmas 1996, when the toys suddenly caught on and sales zoomed into the stratosphere.

Bean Town

H. Ty Warner is no media hog; in fact, he's so reclusive that he makes J. D. Salinger look like a party animal. Warner won't grant interviews, release the company's unlisted telephone number, or deal with the shopping network. He holds his company close and tight. He holds his Beanies even tighter.

As new Beanies are issued, older ones are "retired" by being put out of production. Through this policy, Ty has succeeded in tapping our fear of being left out: Buy now or miss the Beanie boat. This brilliant "retirement" policy has created a whole new level of demand for endangered plush species. Hoarders try to figure out which Beanies will be yanked next so they can stock up and (hopefully) make a financial killing.

As you learned in the beginning of this chapter, Ty sponsors promotional events that send even the most staunch anti-Beanies into a tizzy. Among the most popular of these promotions are free Beanies at sporting events and fast food franchises. Desire flames into frenzy as adults elbow kids out of the way to snatch the Teenie Beanies from Happy Meals.

Has Beans?

On August 31, 1999, Ty struck terror into the hearts of collectors and speculators alike when it announced that all Beanie Babies would be retired on New Year's Day. Was it the end of Beanie Babies? Were Beanies being sandbagged?

The announcement provoked a great deal of conjecture and second guessing in the collecting industry. Some speculated that it was unlikely the company would completely stop producing Beanies because of the backlash from people who have bought heavily into the line. These pundits of plush argued that Ty has just created a gimmick to pump up profits on its pint-sized collectibles. "A lot of retailers have not been able to sell what they have," says John Porter of *White's Guide to Collectible Figures.* "The secondary market has collapsed in the last six months," said George Papania of George's Video Games and Collectibles in Las Vegas. Now, however, George plans to stock up on every Beanie he can locate.

Tricks of the Trade

If you pick up a Beanie Baby at a promotional event, save all the assorted ephemera, too. These souvenirs include ticket stubs, programs, Happy Meal boxes, and so on. To some serious collectors, such related paraphernalia can add greatly to the Beanie's collectible value.

Big Deals

Princess the bear, a Beanie created in 1997 to honor Princess Diana's memory, was an instant collectible. The purple bear presold over the Internet for $400 to $600. It's currently listed in price guides at far less than $100.

Others felt that the retirement was a marketing gimmick for launching a whole new line of more expensive Beanies. Mary Beth Dvorak Sobolewski, editor of *Bean Bag World* (which tracks the industry), predicted that Ty will introduce a new set of Beanies with hologram hangtags to help thwart counterfeiters.

Still others believed that Ty was indeed bowing out, yielding the territory to the new kid on the block, Pokémon.

Is it lights out for Lucky the Lady Bug? Requiem for Ringo the Raccoon? Around the New Year, Ty asked its Web site readers whether they wanted Beanie Babies to be retired. By an overwhelming margin, voters concluded that Beanies should be continued. Not only did they want more Beanie Babies, but they also felt that Ty should increase the retail price! So what's the scoop on new Beanies? Ty has an unlisted phone number (yes, you read that correctly), but their Web site lists Beanies 2000, so we can assume that new Beanies are being issued.

A Hill of Beans

Each new Beanie costs about $5.00 to $7.00 and comes with its own birth date. The most eagerly sought-after Beanies are the retired ones. A few are sold for astonishing prices on the secondary market. Here are some recent prices:

Beanie Baby	Price
Ants the Anteater	$5 to $7
Bernie the St. Bernard	$9 to $12
Chops the Lamb	$135
Happy the Hippo (gray)	$600
Happy the Hippo (lavender)	$11
Humphrey the Camel	$1,500
Peanut the Elephant (dark blue)	$4,500
Peanut the Elephant (light blue)	$11
Quackers the Duck (without wings)	$1750
Quackers the Duck (with wings)	$11
Wrinkles the Bulldog	$8
Zip the Black Cat (with white paws)	$30
Zip the Black Cat (all black)	$1,650

However, the secondary market for Beanies is extremely volatile. When it comes to investments, collectibles in general and Beanie Babies in particular are in the high risk category. "People overpaid and drove the prices up too far," claims Les Fox, co-author of *The Beanie Baby Handbook*. Fox believes Beanie Babies will decline in value from 15 to 20 percent.

Teenie Beanie Baby Twigs and Teenie Beanie Baby Peanut the Elephant, both valued at around $15.

Chocolate the Moose is currently valued at around $5 to $7; Seaweed the Otter is valued at $15 to $20.

And remember: None of us has a crystal ball. It's hard to predict what will be collectible 20 years from now and what it will be worth.

Fake Out

I'm very bearish on Beanies because they are so easy to knock off. Most of the counterfeit Beanies come from China, and some of them look very good indeed. For a beginning collector, it can be impossible to tell the difference between a genuine Beanie and an impostor. Even some experienced collectors have been duped.

The best way to protect yourself from being duped into buying a counterfeit Beanie Baby is by using common sense. If a deal seems too good to be true, you betcha it is. If you do decide to invest in Beanies, always buy from reputable dealers and get items

Caveat Emptor

Remember that a collectible is worth only as much as someone is willing to pay for it. A price listed for any collectible in a price guide is not guaranteed in any way. All quotes are estimates.

Caveat Emptor

Beware: Even some legitimate Beanie Baby hangtags have mistakes. Sometimes, the mistake on a hangtag can increase the value of the Beanie, depending on a collector's desire for that oddity.

in the best possible condition. Learn as much as you can about Beanie Babies, as you would with any collectible. Here are some aspects to check:

1. **Beans.** The PVC pellets in real Beanies are small and round. Many imitations use larger pellets or ones with an irregular shape. Squeeze the Beanie and feel the pellets.

2. **Color.** You can make sure the colors are accurate by comparing a suspect Beanie to a real one. It's not hard: Ty, Inc., uses the same plush on many of its Beanies. For example, the body plush on one Beanie will turn up on the wings of another and the beak of a third. That way, if you can't get the identical Beanie to use as a comparison, you can get one that has a bit of the same-color plush.

3. **Fabric.** Beanie Babies have soft plush; fakes are made with cheaper fabric (that's why they're cheaper).

4. **Shape.** Try to handle real Beanies to get used to their shape. If that's not possible, study pictures. Make sure the one you want to buy matches the picture.

5. **Size.** Most Beanies are the same size. If you find one that's too big or too small, alarms should sound.

6. **Stitching.** Ty Beanies are well stitched, whereas counterfeits tend to be sloppy. Make sure that the stitches are small and even.

7. **Tags.** The Beanie style number and name are printed on the back of every tag. There are five different versions of the *hangtag*, depending on the year the toy was issued. *Tush tags* are cloth tags sewn into the seam of the Beanie toward the rear (hence, "tush"). Make sure the style of the tag matches the time the toy was released. To find the hangtag style for each year, consult a Beanie Baby price guide.

8. **Thread accent.** Some Beanie Babies have a small piece of thread sewn onto their faces to define their features. If the Beanie you want to buy is supposed to have this feature, check to see that the thread is there. Is it placed correctly? Is it the right color?

Using Your Bean

If you're thinking of collecting Beanies or you already own some trademarked plush, here are some guidelines:

1. **Educate yourself.** As with any collectible, learn as much as you can before you start laying down some bucks. Even though each new Beanie costs only a few dollars, those few dollars add up fast. If you buy 25 Beanies at $7 each ... well, you can do the math. Searching for Beanies? Try these sources:

   ➤ Online auctions

   ➤ Garage sales

   ➤ Beanie Baby conventions

   ➤ Flea markets

   ➤ Swap meets

   ➤ House sales

   ➤ Newspaper ads

   ➤ Collectibles stores

Tricks of the Trade

To a Beanie Baby collector, the hangtag helps determine value. Figure 25 percent less for a bent tag and 50 percent less for no tag, right off the bat. A Beanie Baby with a perfect hangtag can be worth twice as much as one with no tag at all. Protect your hangtags with tag protectors, plastic covers sold by several different companies.

But remember: Always buy from the most reputable source to protect yourself against counterfeits and fraud. This is especially important if you're collecting Beanies for investment rather than for pleasure.

2. **Catalog your Beanies.** As you learned in Part 1, "Why Is There a Boom in Collectibles?" it's important to track what you own. If you know what you have, you can buy what you need. Catalog your Beanies by making a spreadsheet or chart with the following information:

   ➤ Name

   ➤ Type

   ➤ Day purchased

   ➤ Place purchased

   ➤ Cost

   ➤ Condition

   ➤ Current estimated value

Here's a sample chart:

Name	Type	Purchased	Place	Cost	Condition	Value
Lizzy	Tie-dyed	7/11/95	Mel's Toys	$5.00	mint	$1,000
Lizzy	Blue	8/11/95	Toy Whiz	$5.99	mint	$35
Lucky	Felt spots	10/1/95	Toy Whiz	$6.99	mint	$225
Lucky	Printed	9/1/95	Bonnie's	$5.00	mint	$25

3. **Store your Beanies properly.** If you're a serious collector, you'll want to keep your Beanies in mint condition. The best way is to wrap your Beanie Babies in acid-free archival tissue paper and place them in special boxes made of archival board. Of course, store them away from light and heat. The next best method is to store your plush treasures in clear plastic or acrylic boxes. Again, away from light and heat, please.

Caveat Emptor

Storing Beanies in zip-lock plastic bags is not recommended. The bags could trap moisture and mildew the Beanie. Few things worse than a musty Beanie.

Learn the Lingo

Meanies are bad-tempered takeoffs on Beanies.

Stuffed to the Gills

Beanie Babies aren't the only collectible plush toys—far from it. Plush treasures come in all shapes and sizes, including promotional toys. Below is a representative sampling. Remember that this is only a sampling; there are plenty more where these came from.

➤ Attic Treasures
➤ Bammers
➤ Bear Den
➤ Care Bears
➤ Coca-Cola Bean Bags
➤ Country Cousins
➤ Disney Classic
➤ Dog House
➤ Kitty Klub
➤ Mattel Disney Toy Story 2
➤ *Meanies*
➤ Nickelodeon Rug Rats
➤ Pillow Pals
➤ Planet Plush
➤ Pooh Plush
➤ Scooby Doo
➤ Warner Brothers
➤ Wildlife

Devoted collectors of Beanie Babies regard anything but an authentic Beanie Baby as an abomination, a "WannaBeanie," if you will. They claim that these plushies are riding on the coattails of Beanie Babies. They get annoyed that some of these plush toys are used to promote products, such as television shows and movies. How could Coke create a plush toy polar bear from their spokesbear? What nerve of Disney to link plush toys to animated movie characters! Harrumph. Never mind that Ty has several other lines of collectible plush toys, such as Pillow Pals and Attic Treasures.

Whatever wets your collector's whistle works for me, as it should for you. In general, non-Beanie plush collectibles are priced in the same range as Beanie Babies. Some look very different; some are almost identical to Beanies. (This is probably not an accident ....)

Whatever plushies you decide to collect, the same rules hold for collecting all of them:

1. Age
2. Rarity
3. Condition

So you want a cute plush toy to put on your dashboard, stuff into a Christmas stocking, or display on your mantel. Buy whatever you want, and enjoy it. But if you want a cute plush toy that will one day be worth a million, whoa there, partner. Since so many of these plush toys are available and the prices are so volatile, I strongly suggest that you explore the market in depth before you plunge in for profit. That said, let's turn to the granddaddy of plush toys, teddy bears.

Grin and Bear It: Teddy Bears

We have the twenty-sixth president of the United States to thank for the invention of teddy bears. On a hunting trip in Mississippi in 1902, Theodore Roosevelt refused to shoot a bear cub. It must have been a slow news day because the *Washington Post* publicized the incident in a cartoon. An enterprising Boston shopkeeper, Morris Mitchom, cashed in on the publicity by making toy bears and christening them "Teddy Bears." By the way, Theodore hated the nickname "Teddy."

The Bear Facts

Other soft toys come and go, but the teddy bear soldiers on. It has proven to be a fertile creature, bearing many progeny. Among its most notable descendants is Winnie-the-Pooh, named after the teddy bear that belonged to Christopher Robin Milne. The arrival of the first giant panda at the London Zoo in the 1930s led to a stampede of stuffed panda bears. A few years later we were attacked by stuffed koalas, many created with real kangaroo fur. As Koala Bear slipped in the popularity ratings, the hideous stuffed troll arose from Scandinavian mythology to take its place on the toy shop shelves.

This is the political cartoon that launched the bear known 'round the world.

Big Deals

As an American, I am duty-bound to uphold my country's claim to the creation of the teddy bear. Nevertheless, it is undeniably true that in Germany at the same time Margaret Steiff was also manufacturing a soft toy bear. Our bear was better than your bear, so there.

Tricks of the Trade

Steiff bears are the most prized among collectors. Their trademark ear button makes identification a snap.

Popular around the globe, Mr. Ted Bear resembles the country of its origin. European teddies, especially those made in Germany, tend to be slenderer and long-limbed, while British bears are chubbier and stubby. Some even squeak, growl, or jingle.

The Bear Body

The basic form of the teddy bear has undergone significant changes since 1903. As with nearly all collectibles, the value of a teddy bear depends on its age, rarity, and condition. You can use a teddy bear's shape to roughly determine its age and when and where it was made.

Here's my cheat sheet. Now it's yours, too.

Year	Body Shape
1900s	Long limbs, curved at wrists, pronounced snout, prominent back hump, small ears
1920s	Shorter arms, smaller feet, torso the same as bears from the early 1900s
1930s	Rounded heads, softer snout, larger ears
post-1945	Chubbier and less realistic, stumpier limbs, larger head, no back hump

The Least You Need to Know

➤ Beanie Babies debuted in 1993 and have become a popular collectible. At present the market is depressed, although some "retired" Beanies still sell for thousands of dollars.

➤ If you decide to collect Beanie Babies, watch for counterfeits. Examine the feel of the beans as well as the toy's color, fabric, shape, size, stitching, tags, and thread accents.

➤ There are many other collectible plush toys, including the ever-popular teddy bears.

➤ Whichever plushies you decide to collect, the same rules hold for collecting all of them: age, rarity, and condition.

Fun and Games

Collecting toys, games, and dolls is a relatively recent activity. At first, some antiques mavens refused to take toys seriously. "Kid's stuff," they sneered. "Give us real antiques and collectibles like china, art, and jewelry."

Now, however, toys are widely regarded as a bona fide area of serious collecting. International auctions are devoted to selling rare and beautiful toys. Special appraisers deal with pricing dolls and mechanical metal banks. Some antique toys are even selling for more than traditional antiques and collectibles such as paintings and furniture! Who's laughing now?

In this chapter, you'll first learn about dolls, dollhouses, and miniatures. Next comes detailed information on Disneyana, including a bibliography. Then I'll teach you all about mechanical and die-cast toys. Marbles, puzzles, and lunch boxes? They're all covered here, too. Let the fun begin!

All Dolled Up

Dolls have been made of every material—terra-cotta, glazed stoneware, wood, alabaster, rags, leather, papier-mâché, wax, cornhusks, and even gold. Dolls are known to have existed in ancient Egypt and ancient Greece, where they served as religious artifacts rather than as children's toys. Antiquarians eagerly hunt for these ancient dolls, but today's hard-wired collectors want only children's dolls, dating from the 1600s onward. In the past two decades, collecting dolls has reached new heights. Judging from the prices that dolls get in auction houses, they are sound investments. Here's the lowdown on dolls.

Learn the Lingo

Doll collectors are called **plangonologists.**

Tricks of the Trade

Also look for **bebe dolls,** luxury dolls with large eyes and open or closed mouths. Those with closed mouths are more desirable—a fact that shows that some people have always preferred that women be seen and not heard ....

Blockheads: Wooden Head Dolls

Perhaps seventeenth-century woodpeckers were a particularly assertive lot, much taken with wooden dolls. More likely, no one thought to save their daughters' wooden dolls. Whatever the reason, few wooden dolls made it through the 1600s to the present. The best of the lot that survived are known as "Queen Anne" dolls and date from the eighteenth century. The earliest ones are more finely carved and painted than later specimens. Wigs made of flax or real hair are perched on their wooden heads. If you're lucky enough to find one of these dolls, you can approximately date it by examining the eyes: The early dolls had dark eyes spaced far apart; later dolls had blue eyes, more closely set.

Bisque Heads

During the last quarter of the nineteenth century, Parisienne or *poupee* dolls made their appearance. These French dolls had *bisque* (fired but unglazed) ceramic heads. Among the most beautiful and highly prized of all dolls, they were made for daughters of the uptown set. On French bisque dolls, you can usually (but not always) find the mold number and/or the maker's initials carved into the back of the doll's head or stamped on the body. Reproductions are common, so identification is very tricky.

By the 1800s, the Germans had become the preeminent makers of bisque head dolls. The early German dolls look like the French ones but have thicker bodies. The top manufacturers include Armand Marseille, Kammer and Reinhardt, Gerbruder Heubach, Cuno and Otto Dressel, and Max Handwerk. By the by, having the doll's original clothes and shoes increases the value.

Papier-Mâché Heads

Ludwig Greiner, America's first doll maker, worked in the mid-nineteenth century. The doll heads were identical, but the bodies were made to suit the consumer's own specifications. Look for a gold or black label on the body to clinch identification and distinguish Greiner's American papier-mâché dolls with painted eyes from the glass-eyed babies produced in Germany during the same time.

Another type of papier-mâché doll was called a "milliner's doll" because of its wild hairstyles, often arranged in bunches of ringlets like grapes. These dolls are much sought after by today's doll collectors.

Caveat Emptor

Beware of overly restored dolls. This severely decreases the doll's value to a collector.

You Can't Be Too Rich or Too Thin: Paper Dolls

Nearly all old paper dolls are highly desirable collectibles. Marilyn Monroe paper dolls, in particular, are as hot as the star was herself. The trick is to find uncut paper dolls in good shape.

Only the doll's hairdresser knows for sure, but the following chart can help you figure out when specific paper dolls were made.

Dating Paper Dolls

Date	Hairstyle
1840s	Hair curled on the neck
1850s	Short curls
1860s	Chignons

Although most old paper dolls are behind glass in museums, many paper dolls from the 1960s are still available for affordable prices. For example:

➤ A 14-inch uncut Amy Carter paper doll sells for around $25.

➤ A *Welcome Back, Kotter* paper doll from 1976, in excellent condition, lists for $15.

Barbie: The Plastic Bombshell

When Barbie was introduced in 1959, the buyers didn't like her, and the parents didn't either. It wasn't until Mattel started running commercials for her during *The Mickey Mouse Club* that she started selling. And *selling*. According to Mattel, two Barbies are sold every second, worldwide.

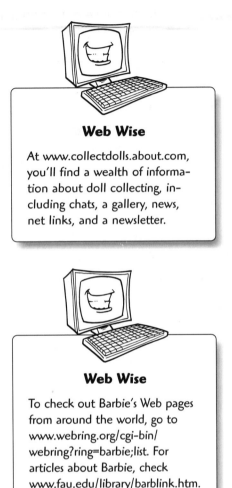

Web Wise

At www.collectdolls.about.com, you'll find a wealth of information about doll collecting, including chats, a gallery, news, net links, and a newsletter.

Web Wise

To check out Barbie's Web pages from around the world, go to www.webring.org/cgi-bin/webring?ring=barbie;list. For articles about Barbie, check www.fau.edu/library/barblink.htm.

Even Barbie's critics—those who claim that her body is unrealistically perfect or that she's a poor role model for girls—cannot deny that she's made great strides. For example, Barbie no longer has holes in her feet (originally used to secure her to a doll stand) and no longer comes clad only in a swimsuit. She's much more successful than Ken—he's really no more than an accessory. From her humble start to her icon status, Barbie has become one of the most eagerly collected, sold, and traded modern dolls.

Barbie collectors can verify the icon's staying power. The original version of the curvy doll fetches $3,000 to $5,000, notes Gigi Williams, co-owner of Gigi's Dolls and Sherry's Teddy Bears in Chicago.

It's important to save everything associated with a modern toy, including all boxes and instructions. For example, if Barbie is your doll, be sure to save all those minuscule combs, brushes, and other accessories. The more pristine the toy's condition, the more it will be worth when we're all sporting with Saint Peter.

Character Counts

In addition to Barbie, other hot modern dolls include character movie dolls (*Snow White, Ariel the Mermaid,* etc.), Chatty Cathy dolls, and many more. To find the exact price for each of these dolls, as well as others not mentioned here, consult one of the scores of doll price guides available. In addition to guidebooks, many magazines and newsletters specialize in specific kinds of dolls.

Less Is More: Dollhouses and Miniatures

Dollhouses and miniatures are no Johnny-come-lately collectibles: Collectors have been fascinated by scale-size objects since the seventeenth century, and very likely before. Artisans in Germany and Holland began producing the forerunners of today's dollhouses: elaborate cabinets that opened to reveal miniature furnished rooms.

Because every item was made by hand, only the wealthy could afford to trade up into dioramas of two or more rooms. By the end of the eighteenth century, dollhouses moved from the parlor to the nursery and became the toys we know today. The exteriors became more realistic, and the interiors now had staircases to make the rooms accessible to each other.

These adorable playthings are serious collectibles for serious collectors. If you like antique miniatures from the 1920s and 1930s, be prepared to ante up some real money. Most of the early 1930s furniture, for example, was made in Europe. It's beautifully detailed down to the last dovetailed drawer. Tiny sewing machines sewed; mini-Grandfather clocks had swinging pendulums. Japan sent Satsuma vases the size of a thumbnail; China contributed tiny Ming sculptures. Dedicated collectors cherish hand-painted tea sets a quarter-inch high and Venetian glass tumblers. A tiny library can be furnished with a thumbnail-size, leather-covered printed version of Sherlock Holmes—stamped in 14K gold.

Tricks of the Trade

Condition is paramount to a toy collector. A crack on the face of a bisque doll, chipped paint on a dollhouse, or metal fatigue in a Dinky toy lower the value of the toy considerably.

Look for craftsmanship, scarcity, and the quality of the materials used. Figure on laying out $150 for a 19-inch 1875 set of miniature kitchen furniture. A 1900 three-story Victorian dollhouse (56 by 40 by 27 inches, good condition, circa 1900) fetches well over $1,000.

This modern reproduction, built from a kit by Mark and Heather Rosenberg, retails for over $500.

The Magic Kingdom of Collectibles: Disneyana

What is Disneyana? A semiradioactive mineral? A distortion in the time-space continuum? A time-honored Italian dessert? No mouse ears for you. Disneyana is actually any item associated with the Walt Disney Company or its affiliates, past or present. People who buy Disneyana fall into four groups:

1. **Consumers** who buy Disney toys, games, and dolls to be used. The items are then discarded, thrown out, or given away.

2. **Tourists** who buy a Disney article as a souvenir or display piece.

3. **Collectors** who buy Disneyana to add to their collection. Motives include personal enjoyment, investment, and an inability to distinguish between art and kitsch.

4. **Dealers and investors** who buy Disneyana to make a profit.

I'm not a fan of Disneyana, no doubt because the perennially cheerful theme park depresses me. But I'm clearly the party pooper when it comes to this collectible. Fans of Disneyana claim it is art. Some even claim it's good art. But then again, some people claim that frozen bagels are really bagels and that mocha latte decaf is really coffee.

Fans of Disney collectibles further point out that Disneyana has been produced in large quantities since the 1920s and it can be found worldwide. The tremendous quantity produced argues against its worth, but some examples of Disneyana do bring high prices at major auctions. Go figure.

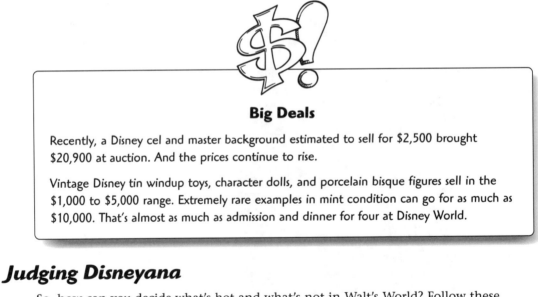

Big Deals

Recently, a Disney cel and master background estimated to sell for $2,500 brought $20,900 at auction. And the prices continue to rise.

Vintage Disney tin windup toys, character dolls, and porcelain bisque figures sell in the $1,000 to $5,000 range. Extremely rare examples in mint condition can go for as much as $10,000. That's almost as much as admission and dinner for four at Disney World.

Judging Disneyana

So, how can you decide what's hot and what's not in Walt's World? Follow these three guidelines:

➤ With Disneyana, rarity doesn't always equate with value. In Disneyana collecting, the strongest demand is often generated by people who want to obtain items of special value.

Character popularity, crossovers to other collecting fields (such as plates, books, and dolls), and the type of item (anything showing Mickey Mouse, for example) can be strong factors.

➤ Price has regional influences. Prices run high on the coasts; lower in the Corn Belt.

➤ The completeness of the box or package is a big factor with this collectible, as it is with Barbie. In some cases, the box is more desirable than the item itself. Some boxes include instructions and extra parts, too. A complete box in mint condition can add 20 to 50 percent to the price.

It's a Small World After All

Tomart's Illustrated Catalog and Price Guide by Tom Tumbush (Tomart Publications) is one of the standard guides to Disneyana. Here are some other guides to Disneyana that you may wish to consult for more detailed information on pricing:

➤ Dunn, Ann, ed. *Brookman Price Guide for Disney Stamps* (Krause Publications, 1999).

➤ Edwards, Scott, and Bob Stobener. *Cel Magic, Collecting Animation Art* (Laughs Unlimited, 1991).

➤ Finch, Christopher, and Linda Rosenkrantz. *Sotheby's Collectors Guide: Animation Art* (Henry Holt, 1998).

➤ *The Greenbook Guide to Walt Disney Classics Collection* (Greenbook, 1999).

➤ Heide, Robert, and John Gilman. *The Mickey Mouse Watch: From the Beginning of Time* (Hyperion, 1997).

➤ Longest, David, and Michael Stern. *The Collector's Encyclopedia of Disneyana* (Collector Books, 1992).

➤ Lotman, Jeff. *Animation Art, The Early Years 1911–1953* (Shiffer, 1995).

➤ Lotman, Jeff. *Animation Collectibles: A Price Guide to Animation Art Limited Editions* (Shiffer, 1999).

➤ Tumbush, Tom, and Bob Welbaum. *Tomart's Value Guide to Disney Animation Art* (Tomart Publications, 1998).

Mechanical Toys

The early makers of mechanical toys were a clever lot. In the 1870s and 1880s, they used flywheels—simple and reliable gizmos. The mechanism could be set in motion either by twirling a knob with your fingers or by using a piece of string. Here are some of the most famous early mechanical toys:

➤ Schuco produced a model Beemer.

➤ Lehmann is famous for clockwork models, such as the "Stubborn Donkey," "Lehmann Beetle," and "Bucking Bronco."

Caveat Emptor

The early die-cast toys have a dangerously high lead content. As a result, they were—and still are—quite unsafe for handling. But at these prices, who's going to play with them?

➤ The American firm of Ives created mechanical rowing men, trains, and dancing figures.

Prices were kept reasonable by using recycled parts and slot and tab fittings. More-expensive cars used all-new materials and were soldered. The invention of paper lithography in 1895 gave toy makers an inexpensive way to decorate their toys; before that time, toys had to be either hand-painted or stenciled.

The Die Is Cast

Die-cast cars have only recently incited lust in collectors' hearts. Here are some of the most collectible ones:

➤ **Tootsie toys.** Die-cast toys were first produced in the early twentieth century by the Dowst Manufacturing Company, an American firm. In 1914 Dowst introduced the Tootsie Toy range of cars, including models of Fords, Chevys, and Buicks.

➤ **Dinky toys.** The famous Dinky toys were first produced in 1933 by Liverpool entrepreneur Frank Hornby. His "O" gauge Hornby train sets of the 1920s and 1930s were tremendously popular; their accessories gave rise to the Dinky toy. The Dinkys include motor trucks, delivery vans, tractors, tanks, and two sports cars.

Production of die-cast mechanical toys largely ceased after 1945, with the notable exception of a model of a gasoline tanker with POOL (the German term for rationed gasoline) stenciled on its side. Today, Tootsie Toy, Dinky, and Solido die-cast models are much sought after by collectors as irreplaceable period pieces.

A Penny Saved Is a Penny Earned: Penny Banks

The first mechanical banks were made in the 1870s. During that period, iron ore and skilled foundry workers were in plentiful supply, and people were eager for new products. Here are some of the most important companies and their mechanical toy banks:

➤ **The J. & E. Stevens Company.** This was the first and most prolific company to manufacture mechanical banks; it remained a leader in the field for 50 years. J. & E. Stevens produced some of the finest mechanical banks: the *Darktown Battery, Girl Skipping Rope, Calamity, Two Frogs, I Always Did 'spise a Mule,* and *Eagle and Eaglets*—as well as various mechanical churches, houses, and toy safes.

➤ **The Shepard Hardware Manufacturing Company.** This early and important mechanical bank maker entered the field in the early 1880s. Notable banks include *Uncle Sam, Humpty-Dumpty,* and *Punch and Judy.*

➤ **Kyser & Rex.** *Roller Skating, Lion and Two Monkeys,* and the rare *Bowling Alley* are their most famous mechanical banks.

➤ **The Weeden Manufacturing Company.** This firm produced such mechanical banks as *Weeden's Plantation, Ding Dong Bell,* and the very rare *Japanese Ball Tosser.* All the Weeden banks are windups.

Two criteria determine the value of a mechanical bank: its action and its rarity.

➤ **Action.** Some collectors value banks that work on clockwork mechanisms; others seek spring-, lever-, or sustained-action banks.

➤ **Rarity.** Banks produced in limited quantities and delicate banks are especially rare and thus desirable. Exceptionally rare banks (and thus exceptionally valuable) include the *Freedman's Bank, Clown, Harlequin, Queen Victoria, Bowling Alley, Girl in the Victorian Chair,* and *Red Riding Hood.* Banks of this rarity and value fetch prices in the five figures.

Losing Your Marbles

Are marbles your bag? At the top of the line are sulfide marbles—only those marbles made before the twentieth century. Especially desirable are those marbles made by hand in East Germany from 1840 to 1926. Purists might argue that these marbles were first produced in 1878, but both sulfide and swirl marbles ("thread" and "figure" marbles) were made as closely guarded family secrets passed down through the generations. Sulfide marbles contain metal figures of birds, fish, and so on; the rarest contain numbers and figures. There are also marbles made of clay, china, stone, jade, onyx, and jasper.

Like anything else worth collecting, marbles are being reproduced. Nicks alone don't make an antique. To distinguish authentic marbles from reproductions, hold the marble up to the light. Old marbles will have a greenish blue tint. In addition, they will be heavier than the new ones.

Caveat Emptor

Restoration of a toy should be undertaken only by an expert and only as a last resort. It's better to have some original rust than a spanking new finish that completely obliterates the original paint.

Tricks of the Trade

Old mechanical banks work smoothly. The parts of recast banks, in contrast, rarely fit together well. Old banks feel silky; recast banks lack the same rich patina.

Puzzle Me This

Puzzle collectors are a passionate bunch, too. Here are some of the most sought-after puzzles:

1. Pre-1970
   - ➤ Pastime puzzles (Parker Brothers)
   - ➤ PAR puzzles
   - ➤ Madmar
   - ➤ Joseph K. Straus puzzles (especially the purple boxed "Regals")
   - ➤ Tuck's puzzles
   - ➤ U-nit puzzles

2. **1970 to present day**
   - ➤ Stave puzzles (Vermont)
   - ➤ Pagemark (Massachusetts)
   - ➤ Elms puzzles (Maine)
   - ➤ PAR puzzles (New York)
   - ➤ Rainy Lake puzzles (Wisconsin)
   - ➤ J. C. Ayer Puzzles (Massachusetts)

Web Wise

Collectible Board Games at www.members.iex.net/~rfinn is a Web site devoted to collectible board games and related topics.

Puzzle collectors will often consider buying puzzles that are missing a piece or two, but the overall condition must be good. Puzzles missing many pieces or those suffering extensive damage have no value to collectors.

Here are some sample puzzle prices:

- ➤ **Air Fleet Picture Puzzle.** Set of three, Madmar, 1930s, $60
- ➤ **Tarzan Big Little Book Picture Puzzles.** Whitman, 1938, $150
- ➤ **Howdy Doody Magic Show.** Frame tray, poll-parrot advertisement, paper envelope with picture guide, ca. 1950s, $8\frac{1}{4}$ by $7\frac{1}{4}$ inches, $50

- ➤ **A Pioneer Christmas.** Parker Brothers, Pastime Picture Puzzle, 1932, 104 pieces, 7 by 5 inches, $25
- ➤ **Six Million Dollar Man.** Puzzle in a can, 1975, complete, $15
- ➤ **Starsky and Hutch.** 150-piece, 14 by 10 inches [photo], very good condition, $8
- ➤ **Welcome Back Kotter.** 1977, puzzle tray, $8\frac{1}{2}$ by 11 inches, Whitman [photo], excellent condition, $10

Not Brown Baggin' It: Lunch Boxes

Modern toys continue to rise in collector popularity. Lunch boxes were a new category 10 years ago. The market has declined somewhat since their discovery. The newest lunch box collectible category is vinyl lunch boxes. Lucky for collectors, lunch boxes are still affordable, for example:

➤ A 1984 Gremlins lunch box in very good condition sells for about $15.

➤ An Evil Kenieval lunch box with thermos in very good condition will set you back $70.

➤ A 1985 Rambo lunch box in very good shape lists for $16.

Here are some plastic/vinyl examples:

➤ *Monkees,* vinyl, with Thermos, 1967, $150

➤ *Scooby Doo,* plastic, dome, with Thermos, $30

➤ *Welcome Back, Kotter,* Barbarino, vinyl, with Thermos, $65

This metal lunch box, based on the 1970's Japanese cartoon show Speed Racer, *is in unusually good condition.*

The Least You Need to Know

➤ Toys are very hot collectibles, whether they are antiques or modern.

➤ Among the most eagerly collected toys are dolls, dollhouses, and miniatures, Disneyana, mechanical toys, die-cast toys, marbles, puzzles, and lunch boxes.

➤ Age, rarity, and condition determine the value of a toy.

➤ If you collect modern toys, save the whole kit and caboodle: the toy, the box, the directions.

➤ Toys aren't kids' stuff anymore.

Chapter 16

Home Sweet Collectible

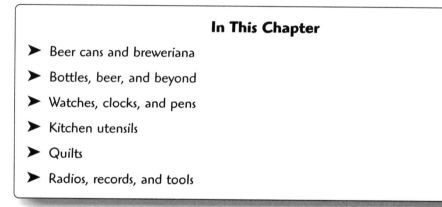

In This Chapter

➤ Beer cans and breweriana

➤ Bottles, beer, and beyond

➤ Watches, clocks, and pens

➤ Kitchen utensils

➤ Quilts

➤ Radios, records, and tools

> 'The time has come,' the Walrus said,
> 'To talk of many things:
> Of shoes—and ships—and sealing-wax—
> Of cabbages—and kings—
> And why the sea is boiling hot—
> And whether pigs have wings.'

History does not record what Lewis Carroll's Walrus and Carpenter collected, but if this passage is any indication, this famous literary duo certainly shared the collector's spirit. This chapter is devoted to the little collectibles that mean a lot, things like beer cans, bottles, clocks, and kitchen tools.

We've all dropped some serious money on the small things that make our home special. This bric-a-brac often expresses our personal taste more than our furniture and big collections do. In this chapter, you'll discover which collectibles have moved from the living room, den, and pantry to the marketplace. I'll teach you the basics of collecting today's hottest household items: beer cans, bottles, clocks, pens, quilts, radios, and tools. You'll learn what factors make these commonplace items a collector's dream come true.

Having Your Hobby and Drinking It, Too: Beer Cans

Do you get weepy when you hear der Bingster croon "White Christmas"? Do Al Capone's escapades send a little tingle down your spine? Do you have a thing about World War II, coneheads, pinups, or the Bicentennial? If so, beer cans may be your collectible of choice. Their colorful history reflects many possible interests, for example:

➤ As many beer cans as evergreens are festooned for Christmas—and beer cans are easier to get into the car.

➤ Scarface Capone once owned the Manhattan Brewing Company.

➤ World War II beer cans were colored a dark brown-black and lettered in dull orange. This kept the cans from attracting the enemy's attention. Since so few of the cans came back to the United States, they are great rarities.

➤ The first commercial use of the beer can was an American Can flat top. It contained Krueger Cream Ale and was first sold in 1935.

➤ The Miss Rheingold series made from the 1940s to the early 1960s carried a line of luscious "pre-p.c." pinups. A variety of Miss Rheingolds—including actress Diane Baker—had their faces and figures plastered on the cans.

Tricks of the Trade

A series of revolving shelves is an attractive way to display beer cans.

Web Wise

For collectors of breweriana and those interested in brewery history, check out www.a-b-a.com.

Get Your Cold Beer Here!

Considering the popularity of malt liquor, it's no wonder that beer can collecting is such a widespread hobby. Fortunately for those so inclined, a collection of beer cans is easy to start. Most collectors begin by buying as many local varieties of canned beer as they can; others comb dump sites and recycling centers. (Hey, I said it was an easy hobby, not a *clean* one.) You can drink the beer and save the empty can; but if you do drink the beer, open the can from the bottom so the "flip tab" is kept intact. Beer can collectors highly value "perfect" specimens.

You can attend some of the many "canventions" held across the country to get rare varieties of cans. These gatherings of like-minded beermeisters are advertised well in advance in newspapers and in beer can collectors' publications. It's not unusual for rare cans to sell for hundreds of dollars at these events. They must be in top condition, however: clean, dent-free, and unscratched.

On Tap

The most popular categories of beer can collecting are *brand name, era, region, design,* and *size.* Some collectors specialize in the expensive cone-tops; others have a broader focus, seeking out beer cans in their travels throughout the United States.

Breweriana is the term given to the wide variety of items that have to do with the production of beer. This includes the following items:

➤ Beer tap holders and foam scrapers

➤ Calendars advertising beer

➤ Brewery hardware such as meters and plaques

➤ Beer coasters

➤ Beer barrel plugs

➤ Signs advertising beer

➤ Napkins with beer brand logos

➤ Beer trays

Learn the Lingo

Any product connected with the production of beer is considered **breweriana.** This includes everything from advertising posters to the plugs on beer barrels.

Tricks of the Trade

Got a little rust on one of your beer cans? Rub some oil on it to prevent the rust from spreading.

Although all of these items are legitimate fodder for the collector of breweriana, some items are more desirable than others. An original beer barrel meter is not likely to fetch as much as a colorful poster advertising a popular brand of beer. The latter has greater visual appeal and so would likely be a hotter collectible.

The Many Ways to Spin the Bottle

Bottle collectors, like kindergartners, rarely divide neatly into groups. One group includes collectors of bottles made before 1900, when the bottle-making machine was invented. Within this group are those who specialize in hand-blown bottles, mold-blown bottles, historic flasks, snuff bottles, medicine bottles, and inkwells.

Another group looks for bottles in the shape of famous people, animals, and objects. A third group collects twentieth-century bottles created especially for the collector. Then you have people who seek out Mason jars and those who want barber bottles. There are so many different kinds of bottle collections that you can rest assured you'll find a place in Bottle Collector Land, bunkie.

Prices range as widely as collector tastes. You can get a New Orleans 7-Up seltzer bottle in a pretty pinkish rose for $30. Or, you can buy a green Crump & Fox "Superior Mineral Water" bottle for a mere $750. To figure out what *your* bottles are worth, see Appendix B, "Further Reading," or access one of the Web sites listed in the sidebars for a list of price guides. Here are some of the most popular kinds of bottles that collectors covet.

- ➤ Avon
- ➤ Barber
- ➤ Beam
- ➤ Beer
- ➤ Bitters
- ➤ Cologne
- ➤ Figural
- ➤ Food
- ➤ Fruit
- ➤ Liquor (miniature and full-size)

- ➤ Medicinal bottles
- ➤ Milk bottles
- ➤ Mineral water
- ➤ Modern
- ➤ Poison
- ➤ Sarsaparilla
- ➤ Scent
- ➤ Soda
- ➤ Whiskey

Web Wise

The Federation of Historical Bottle Collectors (www.fohbc. com), the National Association of Milk Bottle Collectors (www. collectoronline.com/club–NAMBC–wp.html), and the Antique Bottle Collectors Haven (www.antiquebottles.com) all provide sources for bottle collectors.

Let's look at the most collectible bottles in more detail. Here are the top five types of collectible bottles:

1. **Avon bottles.** Dingdong, Avon calling. Avon was founded in 1886 by a whiz kid named David McConnell and his wife. Working out of their Manhattan pied-a-terre, they illogically named themselves the California Perfume Company and sent women door-to-door hawking their powders and perfumes, ointments and unguents. In 1928 they introduced a new line of products called "Avon."

Avon collectors save anything produced by the California Perfume Company and/or Avon. The most popular collectibles are novelty perfume and cologne bottles in various shapes, such as cars, flowers, and animals. People also collect the boxes and advertisements that came with the products. On the average, bottles range in price from $5 to around $50.

2. **Whiskey bottles.** Here's looking at you, kid. Many different types of whiskey bottles are collected. In general, the most desirable ones were produced in the nineteenth century. You can roughly assess age by the bottle's size: Before 1860 bottles were made in both large and small sizes; afterward they came in the standard "fifth" size. Bottles come in many intriguing colors, including purple, amber, green, and blue. Figural Jim Beam bottles form a subgenre of collectible bottles. Other collectible whiskey bottle makers include Ezra Brooks, Garnier, Luxardo, and Ski Country. Collectible whiskey bottles range from a low of $5 per bottle to a high of around $250.

3. **Medicine bottles.** There are two main categories of collectible medicine bottles:

   ➤ *Bitters bottles.* Bitters were quack remedies that were sold before the passage of the Pure Food and Drug Act in 1907. Their heyday was from 1875 to 1905. True bitters bottle collectors want only those specimens that have the word "bitters" on the glass or label. Most of these bottles are reasonably priced ($25–$50), but some of the rare ones have sold for hundreds of dollars. Some of the rarest ones have sold for over $1,000.

   ➤ *Other medicine bottles.* The most popular bottles are those that were produced between 1845 and 1907 and that have an unusual shape and a rare color. All other factors being the same, a light red bottle is more desirable than a clear one, for example. Unusual labels, like those for "Barker's Poison Panacea" and "Baker's Vegetable Blood" are also hot.

Big Deals

In 1999 a bid of $22,000 snagged a 1-quart Millville Atmospheric fruit jar at the Norman Heckler & Company auction held in Woodstock Valley, Connecticut. The jar has a cobalt blue body and a glass lid with an iron clamp. Made in the United States from 1860 to 1870, it's extremely rare and was estimated to sell for $12,000 to $15,000.

A William Pogue jar for preserving fruit captured a high $11,000 bid. The jar was made in the 1845 to 1860 era and is a greenish aquamarine color.

4. **Soda bottles.** Whether you call it "soda" or "pop," these bottles have collector's cool. Strictly speaking, bottle collectors seek carbonated-beverage containers that date from 1840 on. Because many city water systems were contaminated, the

wealthy drank bottled carbonated water. From 1840 to 1850, the bottles were made of stoneware; later they were made of glass. Hundreds of different varieties exist, and nearly all are reasonably priced at $10 to $150.

5. **Inkwells.** In 1810 the first inkwells were imported to America. These early varieties were made of ceramic. Soon American artisans began to produce glass and silver inkwells.

   Inkwells vary widely in price, depending on age, composition, rarity, and condition. You can find affordable inkwells at flea markets and swap meets ($35 and up), but the finest examples are sold only in upscale venues such as antique bottle shows and auctions. If you want to go the high-end route with this collectible, I recommend that you gather as much information as possible by attending bottle shows and auctions. Study the wares and catalogs. Be especially aware of reproductions fobbed off as authentic articles.

Beauty in a Bottle

Whichever types of bottles set your blood a' tingling, you can find beautiful old bottles in many ways.

➤ **Dig we must.** For the athletically inclined, you can dig for bottles at village, town, or city dumps. Dump sites that date back a hundred years or more are often the most fertile hunting grounds. Mining camps are another rewarding site. I don't recommend this method for those of you who, like me, are convinced that staying at any hotel without that crucial fifth star is tantamount to (shudder) camping.

➤ **Swimming with the fishes.** Forget snorkeling in the warm turquoise waters of the Caribbean. Who wants to look at all those boring fish when you can dive in the icy green North Atlantic for bottles? Seriously, a surprising number of bottle collectors snag their greatest finds in lakes, rivers, and streams near old hotels and resorts. Talk to town historians and consult old maps and town documents to find promising locations to plumb.

➤ **Shoppers of the world, unite!** Couch potato collectors like me go to conventions, flea markets, and antique shops to find neat bottles. Always look for bottles in the best possible condition. Very, very carefully feel the rims for chips and nicks.

Caveat Emptor

Before you go on a bottle dig, always get permission from the property owner. I also recommend that you bring along a sturdy pair of gloves, a shovel, newspapers, and plastic bags.

Cleaning Bottles

If your hunt in the dump has been a roaring success, you're apt to stagger home with a pile of greasy, mucky bottles. In this case, your best bet is to leave them soaking overnight in a solution of water and gentle liquid dishwashing detergent.

The next day, clean the inside of each bottle with a test-tube brush. Dry the bottle carefully and lay it on its side on a towel. Allow several days for the bottle to dry out completely.

Never, never, never soak a bottle that still bears its label, however. The label often adds a great deal to the value of the bottle. To clean these bottles, fill them with warm, soapy water and let them soak a while. Then empty out half the water and gently shake the bottle. Rinse and repeat until the bottle is clean. If necessary, scrub the inside with the test-tube brush. Wipe the outside with a damp cloth. Be careful not to damage the label.

Tricks of the Trade

Medicine bottles are most valuable when the label is intact.

Whatever Winds Your Watch

Galileo, that old heretic, gets credit for inventing pendulum clocks. Clocks with movements carved from cherry wood and oak were made in the United States until the mid-eighteenth century because brass was then both expensive and difficult to obtain in North America.

By the mid-1800s, imposing grandfather clocks and more-modest mantel and shelf clocks were commonplace accessories in wealthier American homes. These are called "case clocks." By the end of the century, clocks were being mass-produced, and so were found in even modest homes. Take a hike through a flea market some Saturday; you'll find numerous wooden case clocks. Some will be authentic; others, reproductions and fakes.

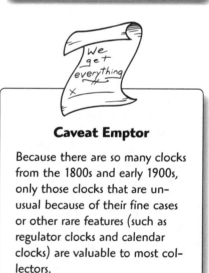

Caveat Emptor

Because there are so many clocks from the 1800s and early 1900s, only those clocks that are unusual because of their fine cases or other rare features (such as regulator clocks and calendar clocks) are valuable to most collectors.

Buying Time: Purchasing a Clock

Prices for so-called antique clocks can be staggering—and an astonishingly large number of people pay the going rate. Prices range from $50 (New Haven, art nouveau, small) to $10,000+ (Pierre-Phillippe Thomire, Empire, ormolu-mounted, 15 to 20 inches). Before you invest in an antique or collectible clock, be sure that you're

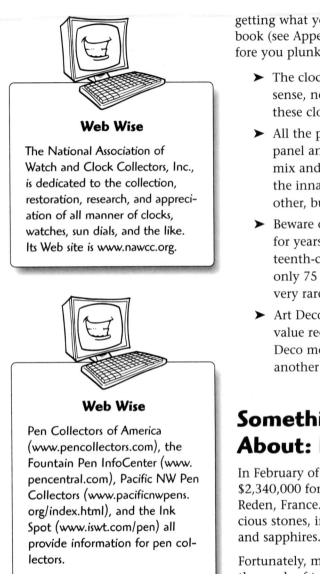

Web Wise

The National Association of Watch and Clock Collectors, Inc., is dedicated to the collection, restoration, research, and appreciation of all manner of clocks, watches, sun dials, and the like. Its Web site is www.nawcc.org.

Web Wise

Pen Collectors of America (www.pencollectors.com), the Fountain Pen InfoCenter (www. pencentral.com), Pacific NW Pen Collectors (www.pacificnwpens. org/index.html), and the Ink Spot (www.iswt.com/pen) all provide information for pen collectors.

getting what you've been promised. Check a guidebook (see Appendix B), and follow these guidelines before you plunk down your money:

➤ The clock should work. Sounds like common sense, no? You'd be surprised how many of these clocks are clinkers.

➤ All the parts should be original—even the glass panel and all parts of the case. You may wish to mix and match by creating your own clock with the innards from one and the case from another, but that's a whole 'nother kettle of fish.

➤ Beware of banjo clocks. They have been copied for years and are often sold as early seventeenth-century clocks, when they are actually only 75 years old. Real period banjo clocks are very rare and very expensive.

➤ Art Deco shelf clocks have been appreciating in value recently, especially those with obvious Art Deco motifs. Clock/lamps from the 1930s are another up-and-comer.

Something to Write Home About: Pens

In February of 1988, a Japanese collector paid $2,340,000 for the "Anemone" fountain pen made by Reden, France. The pen is embellished with 600 precious stones, including emeralds, amethysts, rubies, and sapphires. It took more than a year to create.

Fortunately, most writing implements are well within the reach of today's collector, but signs indicate that the market is rising. Glass fountain pens, those decorated in Art Nouveau and Art Deco styles, and early masterpieces of design such as Mont Blanc and Waterman are among the most desirable collectibles in this category.

All types of pens are collected, including ballpoint pens as well as fountain pens. A 1967 Monkees pen costs about $3; a ballpoint Martin Luther King picture pen, around $35. Pens often become part of another collection, such as Beatles memorabilia or presidential keepsakes. Some collectors also seek out pencils. The most desirable pencils now are automatic pencils of unusual designs. (And let us not forget pencil boxes and sharpeners!)

Big Deals

As of April 29, 1992, Vilma Valma Turpeinen of Tampere, Finland, had collected 14,492 different pens. Vilma's collection earned her a place in the *1996 Guinness Book of World Records.*

Domestic Goddess Strikes It Rich!

Slap the bread into the old toaster and drift off into a reverie: A collector of Art Deco pieces from the 1920s to 1940s taps on your screen door and offers you some serious money for your 60-year-old toaster. You think, "Okay, it has a sleek, rounded style, but it's still an old toaster. Who would want an old toaster?"

Think again. Streamlined toasters, irons, and Mixmasters from the 1920s, 1930s, and 1940s are some of the newest collectibles. So are Bakelite radios and other kitchen-ware from the past. Collectors of kitchen kitsch look for plastic, chrome, and hand-hammered aluminum items. Bright colors add to the item's value, as does design. Geometric shapes and snazzy silhouettes are most desirable.

Most old kitchen utensils and furnishings have value to collectors. The most popular categories of collecting are *personal appeal, era,* and *purpose.* Here are some of the most eagerly sought household collectibles:

➤ Appliances, such as hand-operated washing machines, iceboxes (wooden or metal), irons, Mixmasters, and toasters
➤ Baskets
➤ Butter, candy, and chocolate molds
➤ Caddies and containers
➤ Cookie cutters, cookie jars, cookbooks
➤ Dishes
➤ Egg beaters
➤ Funnels
➤ Jell-O molds
➤ Kitchen glassware, such as measuring cups, reamers, shakers, and pitchers
➤ Measuring devices

➤ Milk pails and jugs

➤ Mortar and pestle

➤ Nutmeg graters

➤ Pots and pans

➤ Pressure cookers

➤ Racks of serving spoons and other utensils

➤ Rolling pins

➤ Sausage grinders, stuffers, etc.

➤ Thermometers

➤ Trivets

➤ Utensils and racks

➤ Waffle irons

➤ Washboards

Now you know which kitchen utensils to look for when you blitz through flea markets, garage sales, and antique shows.

With the exception of kitchen items such as books and catalogs, collectors do not require kitchen collectibles to be in mint condition. The item must be in working order, however. This is especially important for things such as cake tins and toasters. Avoid buying items that have rust, holes, or missing pieces.

Living in an Amish Paradise: Quilts

Quilts are three-layer fabric sandwiches: the top (the design), the filler, and the backing. The layers are held together by the stitching, called "quilting." In the old days, quilts were filled with wool or cotton; today, many synthetic fibers are used. The four most common types of quilts are

➤ **Appliqué quilts.** These quilts are made by sewing, or appliquéing, different pieces of fabric onto the top cover to form a design, which can be very elaborate.

➤ **Crazy quilts.** Popular during the Victorian era, these quilts consist of different-size pieces of fabric, flags, ribbons stitched together in a random pattern.

➤ **Patchwork (or pieced) quilts.** These quilts are made by stitching together small pieces of fabric in geometric patterns.

➤ **Trapunto quilts.** These quilts have a decorative high-relief pattern made by stitching the design through two layers of fabric and then slitting the bottom fabric in order to stuff the design from behind.

The quality of each quilt must be individually determined by its design, the quality of the work, the color, age, and condition. If the quilt is documented with the year and possibly the name of the maker or owner, it will assume much more value. Among the most valuable quilts are "Baltimore quilts," named for the city where they were stitched by young women preparing for marriage. These quilts date from the middle of the last century.

Today, collectors can find outstanding examples of contemporary quilting at the annual Mennonite auctions held in Harrisburg, Pennsylvania. This is the largest quilt auction in the world, attracting about 10,000 people every year. No matter where you buy your collectible-quality quilt, figure on putting down at least $300. Fine examples of this handiwork go from around $1,200 to $2,500.

This quilt, made by master quilter Debbie Greenberger, is quite valuable because it is entirely hand-stitched.

This quilt has little value to a collector because it is made entirely by machine.

Catch the (Air) Wave: Radios

Entertainment devices are interesting—and expensive—collectibles. Radios, for example, were manufactured in great quantities after World War I. Examples made during the late 1930s and 1940s are especially popular with collectors. Made of *Bakelite* or *Catalin,* early types of plastic, they are usually about 14 inches long and 10 inches high. Prices for Catalin radios with an Art Deco flair range between $600 to $1,000.

Web Wise

The Antique Radio Collector is located online at www.wrldradio. home.att.net.

If you're looking for exotic radios, concentrate on early Atwater Kent, Majestic, RCA, and Polle Royal. To some collectors, the most desired of all are the Scott all-wave receivers of the 1930s. They were built on two chrome chassis: the upper tuning section and the lower amplifying section. These sets contained as many as 30 tubes, guaranteeing superb reception. An especially desirable model is the Philco 690 XX made in 1937. Collectible Philco radios start at $80 to $250. Other collectible radios range from $30 to $4,500.

There is also a growing interest in shortwave reception. If this is your field, look to the early Scotts. Those built today most likely cannot exceed the quality and reception of the earlier models.

Dust Off That Turntable: Records

The scene: A cocktail party. I am nursing a diet cola and minding my own business.

The conversation: A friend of a friend of a friend says to me, "I hear you know something about collectibles. I have a fortune in old opera records. Collectors will give me a bundle for them."

Web Wise

The Record Collectors Guild at www.members.tripod.com/ ~theRCGuild and the Vinyl Tourist at www.catalog.com/arts/ tourist.htm might be worth a look if you're thinking of collecting records.

I think, "Not bloody likely. Records aren't valuable merely because they're old. There are records from the early 1900s that you can't give away, but then there are records from the 1960s that are very hot." But for once in my life, I say nothing and head for the peanuts. A smart move.

Most of the records that collectors covet today are desirable because they were originally produced in small supply for a limited audience and have since developed a cult following. Records can also become popular collectibles if they were made by certain companies. A record bearing a scarce label will be valuable to some collector even if the music isn't terribly popular.

Record collectors are especially demanding about the condition of the record. A chipped, cracked, or warped record is as good as worthless unless it is extremely rare. A record that is scuffed is worth less than half the same record in mint condition. The condition of the album cover is also crucial. In the case of records from the 1950s, 1960s, and 1970s, the sleeve can be as valuable as the record itself.

Learn the Lingo

Record collectors are known as **discophiles.**

Here are some types of records that are highly popular at this time:

➤ Early recordings of people who later became stars

➤ Rare record labels

➤ Original-issue records of the 1950s and 1960s featuring rock and roll stars and bands such as Elvis Presley and The Beatles

Records offer something for every collector.

On average, collectible albums range from $5 on up. Unless exceedingly rare, wax cylinders are not especially pricey: They cost from $6 to around $50. Here are some recent prices from an online auction of LPs. Notice how much condition affects price:

➤ *Beatles LP Introducing the Beatles,* Vee Jay Records, 1964. Record is in good condition and cover is great, $40.

➤ *The Beatles—Yesterday and Today.* A sealed, first state, stereo copy of this 1966 Capitol LP first sold for $28,500. That buyer later turned down a solid offer of $40,000!

➤ *Stay Away Joe,* by Elvis Presley. A near-mint copy of this 1967 promotional LP first sold for $1,300 at auction. Within just weeks, the buyer had already turned down offers in excess of $20,000.

➤ *Good Luck Charm,* by Elvis Presley. A "very good" copy of this 1962 Compact 33 RCA Victor single first sold for $14,000. Shortly afterward, that buyer resold this record and picture sleeve for $24,000.

➤ Blues singer Robert Johnson issued about a dozen Vocalion label 78 rpm singles in 1937. Any that have been offered in recent years have fetched from $2,000 to $5,000.

➤ *The Freewheelin' Bob Dylan.* Several first pressings of this 1963 Columbia LP have traded hands—with prices ranging between $15,000 and $30,000.

➤ *River Deep—Mountain High,* a 1966 Philles LP by Ike and Tina Turner. Several sales have been reported, all in the $15,000 to $20,000 range. This is especially amazing considering no cover exists for this disc.

➤ *The Caine Mutiny,* a 1954 RCA Victor original soundtrack album. It last sold for $10,000. The LP contains music and dialogue from the film.

➤ Just the picture sleeve for *Street Fighting Man,* a 1968 hit by the Rolling Stones, sold for $12,000. Since it's the sleeve that's so rare, whether or not the sale included the disc is irrelevant.

And before you ask: Unless exceedingly rare, those old Edison-type cylinders are neither pricey nor in demand. They usually sell for $5 to $15.

Tool Time

Wrenches Do Well at Bailey Auction

The auction of antique wrenches conducted in December 1999 by Bailey & Associates Realty & Auction, in York, Nebraska, proves that tools is a collecting area of growing importance and seriousness.

A large Planet Jr. #312 cutout implement wrench, one of only three known to exist, brought $1,800. A 21-inch Acme monkey wrench sold for $300; an Alexander implement wrench, $190; an American Wrench Co. adjustable wagon wrench, $120; a patent-applied-for adjustable buggy wrench, $210; a John Deere King Corn Silo wrench, $500; Deer & Co. wood-handle nut wrench, $70; and an Indian Motorcycle 7-inch pocket wrench, $100.

Tools are a hot collectible at the moment. Collectible tools are desirable because they're rare, so chances are most tools you'll find aren't going to pay off your

Caveat Emptor

There are numerous guides to the prices of antique tools, but take them with a pound or two of caution. Prices for this collectible often vary widely.

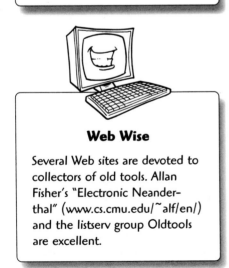

Web Wise

Several Web sites are devoted to collectors of old tools. Allan Fisher's "Electronic Neanderthal" (www.cs.cmu.edu/~alf/en/) and the listserv group Oldtools are excellent.

mortgage. However, there *are* plenty of rare things out there. Especially desirable are tools from the turn of the century up to the 1930s. Here are the guidelines:

➤ **Rarity.** As a rule of thumb, the more unusual the tool, the greater its potential for value. For example, tool collectors scramble for wooden planes and brass-mounted rulers.

➤ **Name recognition.** Well-known names in tools (such as Stanley) add value.

➤ **Condition.** All things being equal, tools in excellent condition fetch higher prices than rusted wrecks, but never assume that a rusted or worn tool is worthless. Just the opposite is often the case.

➤ **Original packaging.** Like many other collectibles, tools are worth more if they are in their original boxes.

The value of a tool varies greatly, depending on the tool's condition and the geographic location. The patina itself gives a lot of the value to the tool, especially with wooden tools. The ultimate rule is to avoid irreversible changes.

The Least You Need to Know

➤ Beer cans and related memorabilia are popular collectibles. Bottles are also a fan favorite, especially Avon, whiskey, medicine, and soda bottles.

➤ Inkwells, watches, clocks, and pens send collectors' pulses racing.

➤ Household appliances from the 1920s, 1930s, and 1940s are among the newest collectibles.

➤ Quilts are cozy as well as costly collectibles.

➤ Radios, records, and tools are eagerly sought after by aficionados.

➤ Condition, age, rarity, and design distinguish the valuable from the merely old.

Chapter 17

Book Learnin'

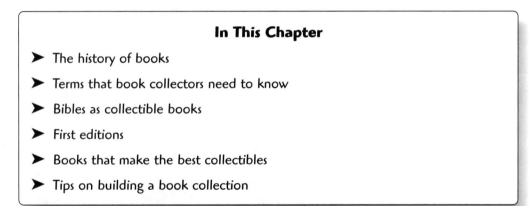

In This Chapter

➤ The history of books

➤ Terms that book collectors need to know

➤ Bibles as collectible books

➤ First editions

➤ Books that make the best collectibles

➤ Tips on building a book collection

I remember the time I snagged what I gleefully assumed was a treasure trove of early nineteenth-century books. My source was a garage sale, no less. Certain that the books were extremely valuable, I made a list of the books and planned for my retirement in Barbados. The expert book dealer I called was gentle when he broke the news that my "treasure" was trash. He was right—no one wanted my old books. I couldn't even re-coup my initial (admittedly modest) investment. I finally ended up donating the books to the library. And I'm sure they took them only because I'm on the Board of Trustees.

This experience taught me that when it comes to collectibles, age is not enough. Desirability and the law of supply and demand set the price for old books. With the exception of *incunabula* (books printed before 1501), a book must have much more than age going for it to be a valuable collectible.

Book and manuscript collecting is an area that requires a lot of studying if you want to keep up with the latest and greatest. This chapter is designed to get you started. First, you'll get a capsule summary of the development of printing and learn the language of book collecting. Then I'll tell you whether Bibles are collectible books.

Next, you'll learn about first editions, one of the most potentially rewarding areas of book collecting. Along the way, I'll cover children's books, atlases, and other intriguing collectible books. Finally, I'll explain how you can build your own book collection. You'll find out which books to collect and which books to avoid, like those with dry rot, fading, and mold.

I picked up this first edition for pennies at a huge book sale.

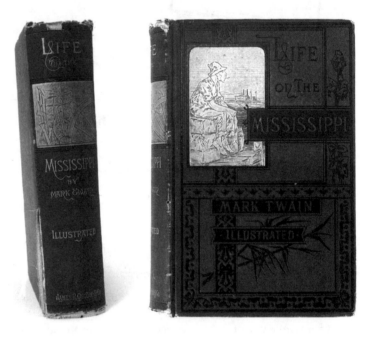

Book 'Em, Danno

The success of printing, mass-production at its most noble, has led to the survival of a vast body of collectible materials. The printing revolution of the mid-1400s was the result of the invention of movable type, a method of mass-producing individual metal letters that could be rearranged into any combination and used over and over again. Its big buzz was its speed. Johann Gutenberg, a German who lived from around 1399 to 1468, gets credit where credit is due.

As I mentioned earlier, books produced during the first 50 years of printing are called *incunabula,* which literally means "in swaddling clothes." Because of the typeface used, most of these books look very much like the manuscripts from which they were copied.

Printing presses soon were established in all the important commercial centers. Vellum was too costly to be used to feed all these presses, so the papermakers put the pedal to the metal to keep the presses rolling. The durability of early paper has ensured that many examples of early printing still exist.

Mass Wants Class

In the early years, most books were religious. By the middle of the 1600s, however, historical, scientific, and fictional works became far more popular. Along the way, printing became publishing and an industry was born. Book reviews, book advertisements, book catalogs, and many related products were offshoots. By the early nineteenth century, the entire printing process had become mechanized and production had soared.

Paperback Writer

Increased literacy and disposable income resulted in the beginning of the throwaway age: Cheap, discardable books became the rage with the masses. In 1935 Allen Lane founded the Penguin paperback series in England, making quality books available at little cost. The paperback revolution followed on its heels.

Learn the Lingo

Incunabula are books produced before 1501. Incunabula fetch high prices even though most of them are astonishingly dull theological works.

Web Wise

The Philobiblon Club is Philadelphia's club for book collectors, booksellers, and anyone interested in books. They're on the Web at www.dept.english. upenn.edu/~traister/philo.html.

Book Speak

Every collectible has its specialized terms, as you've already learned in previous chapters, and books are no exception. Before you decide which books to collect, let me teach you the terms you need to know.

For example, *antiquarian* booksellers sound like a stuffy group with expensive wares, but they include not only the vendors with the most rarefied books, but also those with the most commonplace ones. Antiquarian books are not necessarily old, and even prestigious sellers of expensive modern editions may refer to themselves as antiquarian booksellers.

Tricks of the Trade

Ahearn's *Book Collecting: A Comprehensive Guide* is the most extensive guide for identifying and pricing modern first editions and some older titles, too.

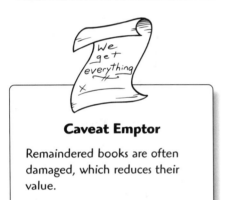

Caveat Emptor

Remaindered books are often damaged, which reduces their value.

Here's a glossary of useful terms for book collectors:

➤ **ARC.** Advanced reading copy, typically sent out by a publisher to solicit reviews and promote sales before a book is published.

➤ **Association copy.** A copy with extraordinary associations, usually because it belonged to a famous person.

➤ **BAL.** The Bibliography of American Literature, the standard source for the bibliographic identification of a book.

➤ **Book club.** An edition of a book printed especially for a book club. Book club editions are usually less valuable than other editions.

➤ **Exlib, ex-lib.** A book from a library, usually with library markings.

➤ **First edition.** The first printing of a book. First editions are often, but not always, more valuable than later editions.

➤ **Foxed.** Brown spots on paper. Foxing makes a book less valuable.

➤ **Limited edition.** An edition limited to a specified number of copies.

➤ **Mint.** Unread or as new.

➤ **Remainder.** A copy sold by a publisher after withdrawing the book from publication.

➤ **Slipcase.** A paper, cloth, or leather book cover.

➤ **Trade edition.** A special edition of a book that is issued before the full commercial publication of the book.

How *Not* to Get Rich Quick Collecting Books

For some odd reason, many people think that more is better. This is especially noticeable at salad bars and diners, but it spills over to book collecting as well. Here's the faulty reasoning I hear all the time: "If a specific book is a best seller, it must be a hot collectible." Say it ain't so, Joe. It ain't. More copies published is not better, especially when in book collecting.

If so many copies of each book have been printed, how can any one copy be worth much? It can't. And it never will be. That's why specialization was invented. Let's take a look at a very special book: the Bible.

A Good Book—but Not a Good Investment: Bibles

The Good Book has many things going for it, but collectible value isn't one of them. Two factors work against making the Bible a collector's item. First, the Bible is the most frequently printed book, which keeps the price down. The Bible has been published in more editions and in more countries than any other book. Second, millions of copies survive because no one is willing to destroy any. Large supply equals low collector value. However, there is a ray of hope: early Bibles. Some of these are very valuable. The following tips may help you if collecting Bibles is your area of interest:

➤ **Age.** The rule of thumb is that in order for a Bible to be of interest to a book collector, it must date to the eighteenth century, when the early presses and wooden type were still used.

➤ **Photo op.** Bibles with wood-block pictures are valuable, more for the pictures than the Bible itself. If the pictures were colored by hand, the value is even greater.

➤ **Illumination.** Among the most valuable Bibles are those with hand-painted illustrations. This painstaking work was most often undertaken by monks.

➤ **Bible bonanza.** A Bible that has been both handwritten and hand-painted is the Holy Grail of all collectors. Even single pages from such Bibles sell for staggering sums, which is unfortunate because it means the Bible has been torn apart.

Learn the Lingo

Illuminated books are those with hand-painted pictures.

Caveat Emptor

Religious books in general are poor collectibles and usually sell for only a few dollars each.

➤ **Errata.** Other rare Bibles include those that have printed errors. For example, the "Place Makers Bible" states, "Blessed are the place makers, for they shall be called the children of God." (If I have to explain the error, you don't deserve to find the Bible.) The "Place Makers Bible" is otherwise known as the Geneva Bible, second edition, published in England from 1561 to 1562. You might chance upon the "Vinegar Bible" ("the Parable of the Vinegar" instead of "the Parable of the Vineyard") and the "Basket Bible," which had a whole basketful of errors.

Leader of the Pack: First Editions

An *edition* is defined as all copies of a book printed at any time from one setup of type. An *impression,* in contrast, comprises the entire number of copies of that edition printed at any one time. The distinction seems picky, but it's crucial for the collector.

Say that a mistake is found while a book is being printed. The mistake is corrected on the spot, and the printing and binding continues. The first books to roll off the presses will have the mistake—*but the other copies won't.* Ironically, a collector will prefer the first edition over the second, even though the first contains an error. Since it's the first, it's more valuable. First editions of books by noted authors are a "must have" for some book collectors. "First edition" alone is not enough to make a book a collectible, how-ever—especially since the first edition might very well be the last edition. Walk this way to get the primo first editions:

➤ The author must be famous.

➤ The book must be important.

➤ The book must be in excellent condition.

Here are some notable examples of pricey first editions:

➤ A first edition of Theodore Dreiser's *Sister Carrie* (1900)

➤ A first edition of F. Scott Fitzgerald's *The Beautiful and the Damned* (1922)

➤ A first edition of William Faulkner's *The Wild Palms* (1939)

➤ A first edition of George Orwell's *1984* (1949)

Each of these first editions is special in some way. For example, the first edition of *Sister Carrie* is valuable because it was suppressed by the publisher on the grounds of obscenity. Dreiser was forced to rewrite the book and change the ending. Only re-cently has the original copy been republished.

Let's assume that you're at a garage sale or a flea market, nice places to find (poten-tially) valuable first editions. How should you go about determining whether the books you've grabbed have any collectible value? Ask yourself these four questions:

1. Is it a real first edition?

2. Is the author or illustrator hot?

3. Is the book in collectible condition (including the dust jacket)?

4. Are there other features that make the book a desirable collectible (such as being a limited edition/print run)?

Read on to learn about each of these four criteria.

Learn the Lingo

Book dealers and collectors refer to the characteristics that iden-tify a first edition as **points.**

Identifying a First Edition

How can you tell a first edition? A first edition, like a ripe melon, is not always easy to distinguish. On a very lucky day, you might get a break because the copyright page will actually say "first edition." If this happens, buy a lottery ticket right away. Sometimes the date is clearly printed on the title page—and it matches the copyright on the reverse side. In these instances, buy another lottery ticket. Hey, you never know.

There are other clear ways to identify first editions. Some publishers use a code to indicate the book's print run. For example, the publisher might use a numeral system to denote the run, printing the numbers 1 to 10. As each successive printing is completed, a numeral is dropped to indicate which printing the book comes from.

In the past, though, some editions were not marked. Others have been found marked with the first year the book was published, although they may have been reissued years later from a new print run.

With many books, however, you have to do some serious detective work to identify the edition. A detail about the color of the binding or a misspelled word (not corrected until the second edition) can help you authenticate a first edition. Bibliographies are available that list these important points.

Who's Hot ... and Who's Not?

First editions by well-known authors, including such Nobel laureates as Saul Bellow, Ernest Hemingway, William Faulkner, and Toni Morrison, are desired by some collectors. But how about the lesser-known writers whose books may be far more valuable because they are suddenly politically correct? Unfortunately, there's no substitute for hitting the books. You have to study dealers' catalogs and get to know your authors. Once is not enough, either. You have to keep up with the trends here; an author who's hot one year may very well be tepid the next.

Like authors, certain illustrators are desirable to collect. Many twentieth-century illustrators are popular with the book-collecting crowd, and here are some of the most popular ones. I make no claims for completeness; and remember, the list changes with shifts in public taste.

Caveat Emptor

Authors love selling their tomes to book clubs because they bring in big bucks, but collectors shun these editions as worthless first edition wannabees. If you see the logo from the Literary Guild or the Book-of-the-Month Club, pass the book on by—unless, of course, you want to read it!

Web Wise

The International Book Collectors Association helps sponsor a Rare Book Ring devoted to collectible books. Their Web site is www.webring.org/cgi-bin/webring?ring=rarebooks.

Edwin Abbey	Alfred Miller
Thomas Hart Benton	Gerald Nailor
Pierre Bonnard	Maxfield Parrish
Marc Chagall	Edgar Samuel Paxson
Howard Chandler	Pablo Picasso
Warren Chappell	Beatrix Potter
Walter Crane	Howard Pyle
Salvador Dali	Arthur Rackham
Edwin Deakin	Frederic Remington
W. W. Denslow	Norman Rockwell
Maynard Dixon	Charles M. Russell
Edmund Dulac	Frank Schoonover
Thomas Fogarty	Maurice Sendak
A. B. Frost	Kate Sewell
Christy Edward Gorey	Ernest Shepard
Kate Greenaway	Jessie Wilcox Smith
Thomas Hanford	Ben Stahl
Maude Humphrey	Arthur Szyk
Peter Hurd	Garth Williams
Rockwell Kent	Andrew Wyeth
Robert Lawson	N. C. Wyeth
Henri Matisse	

Jacket Required: Collectible Condition

The presence of the original dust jacket often makes the difference between a book being a collectible and just another (dusty) old book. Without a dust jacket, a twentieth-century first edition is worth only a fraction of its dust-jacketed value.

Check the book for signs of wear. Is it ripped, stained, damaged? Does it look like it's been through the Crimean War? Check the hinges and spine, too. Are they overly worn? About to give up the ghost? Collectors expect first editions published after 1950 to be in very good condition because they are not that old.

Gilding the Lily

A first edition signed by the author is one of the book collector's ultimate trophies. Signed books are especially valuable if they are signed by an author reluctant to autograph books—even if the book isn't a first edition. Autographs by J. D. Salinger and Vladimir Nabokov, for example, are highly prized by collectors because they are so rare.

First editions that contain manuscript emendations in the author's own handwriting are highly prized. So are books with presentation inscriptions ("Mary—Never forget Paris—Ernie").

Tricks of the Trade

When you buy a new book today, try to have the author sign it whenever possible. This enhances the value of the book immediately and may even elevate it to collector's status down the road.

Hot Tip: Old Atlases

One area of book collecting that commands steady interest is atlases produced in the 1800s. Invaluable as a means of researching American history, old atlases are of special interest to the residents of the areas covered in the books. Lawyers also seek out old atlases for the regions in which they ply their trade, since genealogies, property lines, and past ownership of items are often revealed in these books.

Old atlases also have the advantage of being easy to collect, since you can learn all you need to know fast. After all, the number of atlases produced for each region was usually very limited. Keep in touch with your local book dealer to find out which atlases are in demand. With this collectible, age increases value, because not many copies of a specific printing survive.

Caveat Emptor

Most collectors of old atlases don't care as much about age or historical value because they're looking for content. Be sure to find out which old atlases are being reprinted, since reprinting seriously lowers the value of this collectible.

A Novel Idea: Books with Collectible Potential

You're a grownup. That means you can stay up past 10 P.M. (if you can keep your eyes open), eat ice cream before dinner, and collect whichever books tickle your fancy. Some collectors buy books that they want to read; others look for investment-grade books.

Valuable books do share some common traits: They tend to be rare, limited, old, and in great condition. But what can you do if your tastes are rich but your purse is poor?

Caveat Emptor

In general, avoid old school books. They have very little value to most collectors. There's a lesson here somewhere.

Tricks of the Trade

Some nineteenth-century books are collected for the wood-block prints they contain. In some cases, the prints are cut out and individually framed because they are worth far more money than the book. Some of these wood-block prints or steel engravings are the only record of certain scenes executed by famous illustrators. Look for prints by Winslow Homer and Frederick Remington.

Following is a list of some collectible categories of books that are still affordable but likely to rise in value with time:

➤ Old books on art
➤ Old books on antiques
➤ Old auction catalogs
➤ Books about native heroes
➤ Diaries
➤ Sailor's logs
➤ Captain's logs
➤ Nonfiction books on hunting
➤ Nonfiction books on fishing
➤ Nonfiction books on the military
➤ Nonfiction books on sports

Whichever books you buy, remember your collector's mantra: *condition, condition, condition.*

Each to His (or Her) Own Taste

Book collectors generally limit their collection by concentrating on categories, such as *genre, author, illustrator,* or *period.* The most popular genres are as follows: *horror, biography, science fiction, crime, fiction, fantasy, history,* and *erotica.*

Serious Shopping

Where you shop for books depends on your collection. Lower-priced collectible books are readily available at garage sales, flea markets, estate and tag sales, and library book sales. Most of the real finds have probably already been located by savvy collectors who zipped through the sale before you were even in the shower, but you may still find something to your liking. In general, avoid first editions that were library books, because the library stamps and card jackets make the book far less valuable.

If your collection is more upscale, consider shopping through mail order, from an online auction, or from a reputable book dealer. Most book dealers feel that if they can't charge at least $25 to $50 for a first edition, it's not worth listing in their catalog. Secondhand bookstores are usually stocked to the rafters, but the condition of the books is often a problem. The books have usually shed their jackets and may have been annotated by previous owners.

The Least You Need to Know

➤ Age alone does not make a book valuable to a collector.

➤ Bibles and other religious books are rarely hot collectibles.

➤ First editions are valuable only if they were written by a first-rate author or illustrator, still have their book jackets, and are in good condition.

➤ When you're collecting books, use the collector's mantra: rarity, condition, and age.

➤ Read.

Chapter 18

China and Crystal Collectibles

In This Chapter

➤ The china syndrome: earthenware, stoneware, bone china, porcelain, and ironstone

➤ Highly prized china

➤ Nifty glass collectibles

➤ Different grades and types of collectible glass

Among the most popular collectibles are china and crystal, largely because they're functional as well as beautiful. This chapter starts with a brief history of china. Then I'll teach you everything you always wanted to know about earthenware, stoneware, bone china, porcelain, and ironstone. Next, I list and describe the hottest china collectibles. You'll learn which manufacturers and pieces are the most eagerly sought after.

In the second half of this chapter, you'll learn about the hottest collectible glassware today, including fine crystal, Depression glass, carnival glass, Waterford, Tiffany—even those Bugs Bunny juice glasses you thought were worthless. There's also a section on glass paperweights. Finally, I'll show you how to buy collectible glass with assurance.

Shards of History

The first ceramic pieces were pots as fragile as a teenager's ego. As a result, only shards survive. It was not until the early eighteenth century that Europeans cracked the china code. Even after American china gained a place on our shelves, French, English, and German china remained so popular that Americans never really became big names in the china biz. Even today, most fine china collected in America is imported.

All ceramics are made from clay. The type of ceramic is determined by the composition of the clay, the way it is prepared, the temperature at which it is fired, and the glazes used. The most common types of ceramics are earthenware, stoneware, china, ironstone, and porcelain. Let's look at each one in detail.

Salt of the Earth: Earthenware

Earthenware is porous pottery, usually fired at the lowest kiln temperature. To be waterproof, it must be glazed. Nearly all of our everyday dishes are earthenware.

American art pottery runs the gamut from one-of-a-kind treasures to mass-produced items with the look of individually crafted pieces. Like many desirables, some art pottery that is highly valued today sold for very little when it was first produced. As it emerged from attics and basements, it promptly flew into the eager arms of collectors.

Below is a short list of American art potters whose work is actively collected. There are far more potters whose work is remarkable, but space limitations prevent their inclusion here. Since collectors of art pottery often favor examples from their region, I have listed the potters by their state:

➤ Arkansas: Niloak

➤ Colorado: Van Briggle

➤ Louisiana: Newcomb

➤ Massachusetts: Dedham Pottery, Grueby

➤ Minnesota: Red Wing

➤ New Jersey: Fulper Pottery

➤ New York: Buffalo Pottery

➤ Ohio: Cowan; Hull; Knowles, Taylor, and Knowles; McCoy; Rookwood; Roseville; Shawnee; Weller

Tricks of the Trade

Regional potters who are starting out today may soon be highly regarded, so don't disregard the potter next door.

Tin-glazed earthenware (earthenware with a white glaze) dates from the 1700s. Here are the most common types of tinware:

➤ **Delft.** Italian immigrants settled in the Netherlands in 1508 and soon began producing a tin-glazed earthenware. Many towns, including Delft, had factories making this earthenware. In the early 1600s, two ships arrived in Amsterdam, groaning with piles of Chinese blue-and-white porcelain. Henceforth, the distinctive blue-and-white earthenware produced in the Netherlands became known as "Delft."

Big Deals

The difference in value between eighteenth-century Delft and later Delft is astonishing—an early Delft piece is worth more than six times the value of a modern piece of the same size and design. A signed 1750 Delft bowl, for instance, sells for over $3,000. In contrast, a modern Delft ashtray shaped like a shoe sells for under $10, and a modern butter dish with a lid is valued around $16.00.

These three Delft collectibles range in price from $20 to $50.

➤ **Faience.** Characterized by a wide variety of highly colored designs, this earthenware took off in 1661, when a group of Dutch religious refugees in Germany opened the first faience factory. A four-inch, two-handled bowl made in France is valued at $55, and a 10-inch figurine sells for around $200.

➤ **Majolica (or "Maiolica").** This earthenware is distinguished by its bright colors and intricate patterns. These wares were widely exported via Majorca (hence the term "majolica") to Italy. A small shell-shaped bowl sells for about $175; a signed cake plate, $650.

Caveat Emptor

Be aware of the reproduction line of Quimper that imitates the peasant motif. It's worth far less than the original line.

➤ **Quimper.** You can identify Quimper ware by its bright paintings of French peasants and farm animals. Quimper is more popular today than ever; a small Quimper ashtray will set you back a mere $15; a pair of coasters, $60; a large signed platter, around $3,000.

Solid as a Rock: Stoneware

Stoneware comes in many forms, Wedgwood being one of the most collectible types. Inspired in the mid-eighteenth century by a revival of ancient classical art, Wedgwood is associated almost exclusively with blue-and-white jasperware (hard, fine-grained stoneware). Wedgewood also comes in Queen's ware (a creamware), variegated ware, pearlware, black basaltes, caneware (straw-colored), and all kinds of colored and plain stoneware. Fortunately for collectors, Wedgwood is clearly marked.

A modern Wedgwood ashtray is valued at around $35; an eighteenth-century black basalt bowl, $300. A signed, 1925 Wedgwood bowl is worth around $3,700.

Roll 'Dem Bones: Bone China

In the mid-eighteenth century, English potters invented *bone china,* a somewhat harder ware that gained whiteness, translucency, and stability through the inclusion of calcium phosphate in the form of calcined (fired, chemically altered) ox bones. *Aynsley* and *Lenox* are desirable brands of bone china.

Always a Bridesmaid, Never a Bride: Ironstone

Ironstone (a.k.a. semiporcelain) used to play Betty to china's Veronica. But now that rare porcelain (such as patterns decorated with rich cobalt blue and gold borders) is out of reach of the average collector, ironstone has become a hot collectible. Extremely fine nineteenth-century English ironstone such as Mason's is much sought after, especially the large serving pieces. The following chart can help you rank the value of ironstone pieces:

Excellent Quality	Fine Quality	Good Quality
Coalport	Franciscan	Hull Pottery
Mason's	Metlox	Johnson Brothers
Villeroy & Boch	Russel Wright	Mikasa
Wedgwood	Vernon?	Pfaltzgraff
Sango		

This Botanic Garden pattern by Portmeirion is popular with collectors because it's affordable as well as beautiful: Pieces range from $20 up.

For the purpose of collecting, buy what you like and enjoy it. For the purpose of investing, buy items of the finest quality in the best condition that you can afford. Check several price guides to get the current value of each piece. Here are some of the most popular English and American varieties of ironstone:

➤ **Lusterware.** Luster is created by applying a thin layer of a precious metal to pottery. Gold results in a luster of copper to pink. Platinum yields a silver luster. Figure on spending about $150 for a good-quality piece.

➤ **Staffordshire.** The term is used to indicate any English figurine or decorative ironstone that matches our idealized version of bucolic British life.

➤ **Toby jugs.** The true Toby jug was a fat old man seated on a chair and holding a pint pot. Now there are hundreds of varieties of Toby jugs with portraits of famous people, such as Ben Franklin and Winston Churchill. A "Frowning Man" Toby jug is valued at $25; a jug showing Mamie Eisenhower goes for $50.

Putting on the Ritz: Porcelain

Collector alert: There are two kinds of porcelain: *hard paste* (porcelain made with kaolin as its main ingredient) and *soft paste* (largely bone ash).

Web Wise

The Pfaltzgraff America Collectors' Club (PACC) can be found on the Web at www.quint@wholenet.net.

Tricks of the Trade

The market is flooded with cheap copies of lusterware; so if the real thing tickles your fancy, check the bottom to see whether the piece is marked "England" or "Made in England." That's a good sign that you may have the real McCoy.

Caveat Emptor

American china companies freely reworked European names and hallmarks. American companies, for example, often used European hallmarks such as the lion, crown, horse, and unicorn. Check your guidebooks carefully to identify pieces of china.

Learn the Lingo

The term **porcelain** is used interchangeably with **china** to mean high-quality and expensive dinnerware.

Here are some of the most-collected varieties of porcelain:

➤ **Belleek.** A popular Irish porcelain, Belleek is ivory with delicate yellow or green decorations. A creamer is valued at $80; a six-inch bowl is worth about $300. Figure on spending over $1,500 for a dinner set for eight.

➤ **Bing & Grondahl.** A Danish china best known for its porcelain figurines, Christmas plates, and other commemorative items priced at about $35 and up.

➤ **Capodimonte.** These collectibles have embossed Italian or Mediterranean designs. A square six-inch ashtray is worth $45; a 10-inch box, $225.

➤ **Dresden.** The quality of delicate Dresden figurines greatly depends on their condition and details (such as meshlike crinoline lace skirts). There are also serving pieces, such as an openwork compote ($200) and a five-inch dish ($20).

➤ **Haviland.** You can find a lot of Haviland modestly priced in antique shops—which suggests that it is not as valuable as some collectors would like to think. Budget $10 for a five-inch berry bowl, $200 for a five-piece set, and around $1,000 for an 1890s seven-piece ice-cream set.

➤ **Hummel.** Regardless of my long-standing personal revulsion for cute china, coveys of collectors eagerly gobble up this stuff. There are clubs devoted to collecting Hummels. Like music groupies waiting for a new CD, Hummel fans line up at the shop when a new figurine is about to be released. Value is based on subject, age, size, and condition. Prices generally range from $75 and up. The Hummel shown on the following page, "Little Fiddler," is worth about $200; a No. 8 bookworm, $250.

The marks on the bottom of the figurine reveal the piece's age and help you deduce its rarity. See Hummel guidebooks for more information.

➤ **Imari.** Imari is a deep orange-red color and cobalt blue, highlighted with gold. Imari bowls and plates are widely collected, but the less frequently seen items—candlesticks and vases—are more valuable. A single plate can cost more than $100.

Sometimes you feel like a Hummel; sometimes you don't.

➤ **Lladro**. These are a line of very popular china figurines, characterized by pale, anemic colors and elongated lines. A Christmas tree ornament sells for around $35; Figurine No. 1495, "A Lady of Taste," goes for around $650.

Dating Porcelain

Here are the two numbers you need to know: 1891 and 1914.

If the name of the country appears on the china, it was made after 1891, in accordance with the McKinley Tariff Act. If the additional words "Made in" appear, the china was produced after 1914. China made before 1891 is much harder to date; if the china does not have a date marked on it, do not assume that it is "antique." It may indeed be valuable, or it may simply be unmarked breakable dreck.

Tricks of the Trade

Much of the china marked "Nippon" was made by the Noritake Company. Most pieces cost only a few dollars. Truly exceptional pieces range in the low hundreds.

Even when you buy cheap china at a flea market or antique store, look at the back or bottom of the piece for identifying marks. Compare this to what you just learned—and with what the seller tells you.

The marks on the back of your china can help you identify the piece.

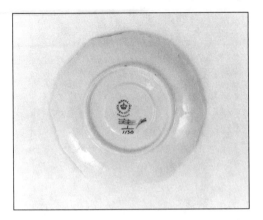

McCollectibles: Limited Editions

In recent years, collectors have become more knowledgeable and cultivated. There are also more collectors, and they have more money. As a result, the availability and affordability of prime collectible ceramics has decreased. In response, "limited edition colectibles" were born. Like takeout and drive-thru, this idea was an instant hit.

Today more than seven million people are registered collectors of "limited edition collectibles"—and that's only the people who have *registered*. Millions more are collecting these articles. Limited edition collectible clubs have sprung up around the world, laced together by national and international conventions and a tower of publications. If you like these items, buy them to grace your home. I do not recommend them for investment.

Now, let's turn to another popular collectible that can grace the table as well as the display case, crystal.

In Your Dreams: Building a Collection

By now, I've hammered it home that you should collect whatever gives you pleasure. For example, let's say the china guidebook says that New England salt glaze and slip crocks are hot this year. But you think crocks are as clunky as clogs. Solution? Don't collect 'em. Pick what you like and can live with. That way, you'll never be saddled with pieces you selected for investment because someone said they would be the latest and the greatest.

But no matter what type of china you collect, you must know how to authenticate it. That's what the following section discusses. I've also included some useful guidelines that can help you get the best value for your money. Read on!

Fill It with Leaded, Please: Cut Crystal

Fine crystal is called "lead crystal" because it contains lead oxide, the ingredient that makes the glass clear and gives it the bell-like ring when the rim is tapped or "pinched," a sound not found in other stemware.

Cut crystal made between 1890 and 1915 (the so-called brilliant period) is the most desired by collectors and commands steep prices. About 25 to 28 percent of this cut glass was lead. Today's cut glass (also called "cut crystal") has only 10 to 12 percent lead, which accounts for its lack of glitter when compared with its ancestors. Items made with cut glass and sterling silver (such as powder jars and pitchers) are also highly desired by many collectors. The value of the piece depends on the following qualities:

➤ **Condition.** Chips or cracks can render a piece valueless.

➤ **Brilliance.** The more sparkle, the more value.

➤ **Rarity.** Unusual shapes are more valuable. A heart-shaped piece will be more valuable than an oval, all things being equal.

If this is really your lucky day, you might find the manufacturer's signature on your cut glass. This is a long shot, however, since only about 10 percent of the cut glass made between 1880 and 1900 was signed. In case you're looking, check the uncut side of the glass. Like autographed books, signed pieces are usually more valuable than unsigned ones. Following is a list of the most highly collected cut glass.

Tricks of the Trade

Many modern collectibles are aimed at different markets. Lladro, for example, produces many figurines for its domestic market only, or its European market only, or its duty-free stores only. Americans find these items while traveling abroad and come back convinced they have discovered something rare and enormously valuable. They haven't.

Learn the Lingo

Bohemian glass is made by fusing together a layer of clear glass and a layer of colored glass and then cutting designs into the two.

Venetian glass has come to be a generic term for many types of glass that originated in Venice. Some are valuable; some aren't.

1. **Waterford.** None of the Anglo/Irish glass made before 1851 was known to have been marked, but Waterford glass produced after 1951 is clearly etched with the "Waterford" name. Collectors prize this heavily cut crystal.

2. **Steuben (Corning).** Steuben is considered the greatest continuous producer of American glass. Pieces are expensive, and quality is exceedingly fine.

3. **Pressed glass.** When pressed glass was first produced in the nineteenth century, it was as popular as a water fountain in the Sahara. Fashionable hostesses had complete sets of pressed glass, not difficult since the stuff was sold in five-and-dime stores and dry goods stores, and through catalogs. Eventually the craze abated.

Cut glass decanters like this one are popular collectibles. This Waterford decanter costs about $100.

By the late 1920s, however, pressed glass emerged from dusty shelves to become one of the most popular items for American glass collectors. Today, a pressed glass compote sells for about $100, but you can still pick up a six-inch Georgia pressed glass compote for under $25. Study the following chart to learn the different patterns.

air-twist stem · diamond motif · flared lip · quarter fan motif

baluster stem · etched floral motif · globe shape · scroll motif

faceted stem · notched motif

Pressed glass has unique patterns.

Other Twentieth-Century Glass

The craft of glass making has continually been refined and adapted to current tastes and needs. A tremendous amount of collectible glass has been produced in the last century. Let's take a look at some of the best.

Beauty and Bucks: Art Glass

American art glass dates from 1880 to 1900. During this time, some of the finest designed, colored, and decorated glass appeared. Some types are identified by color, such as ruby, black amethyst, and cranberry. Others are known by their names, such as Peachblow, Burmese, Amberina, and Crown Milano.

Tricks of the Trade

It can be difficult to distinguish cut glass from pressed glass. You can tell the difference most easily by letting your fingers do the work. Feel for sharp edges.

They range in price from about $300 for a tumbler to a high of $7,000 for a 1925 seven-inch bottle by the designer Maurice Marinot. Figure on spending $100 for a bowl.

The most famous art glass was produced by Louis Comfort Tiffany and Tiffany Studios. Tiffany is especially well known for vibrant stained-glass windows and beautifully colored lamp shades.

Poor Man's Tiffany: Carnival Glass

Often given out at carnivals and fairs, carnival glass was also used as a freebie by tea and cereal companies. Long regarded as a stepchild in the glass collectors' extended family, the pieces made with more care have recently become popular collectibles.

215

The top favorites are Northwood pieces, made by the Northwood Glass Company in Wheeling, West Virginia. Prices vary widely, depending on age, maker, and pattern. Also, color can affect value. Although marigold is the color most often associated with carnival glass, blue, green, and purple are also commonly found colors. Small pieces, such as a tumbler or punch cup, cost about $20 each, while nine-inch bowls fetch about $100. A fine six-piece set sells for about $1,000.

Learn the Lingo

Depression glass tumblers with decal decorations of palm trees, nudes, or geometric designs were often sold as containers for processed-cheese spreads. Collectors call those containers used by Kraft Foods **swankyswigs.**

Tricks of the Trade

Collectible drinking glasses featuring TV puppet Howdy Doody and those with early Disney characters continue to grow in popularity and value. A 1950s Howdy Doody juice glass can sell for as much as $20. A Disney glass at the same price is considered a bargain.

Crystal on Steroids: Depression Glass

Depression glass is America's first mass-produced glassware, as different from crystal as sushi is from fish sticks. It was made in the Depression years, from the 1920s to the collector cutoff date of 1940.

Depression glass was produced in many colors, including clear, black, red, blue, and pearly white. The opaque white is often called *milk glass*. The most common colors were green, pink, amber, and yellow.

Since there is still so much Depression glass around, greed can be your worst enemy. Try these guidelines for collecting Depression glass:

1. **Quality.** Look for undamaged pieces and unusual items, such as gift and decorative pieces.

2. **Category.** Consider specializing in one category instead of trying to find a matching service for twelve.

3. **Companies.** Depression glass collectors often buy glassware made by specific companies. The most popular ones are Cambridge Glass Company, Imperial Glass Company, Mac-Beth Evans, Federal, Hazel Atlas, Indiana, or Hocking Glass Company, Jeanette Glass Company, and Fostoria Glass Company.

4. **Colors.** Red is the most prized color, followed by cobalt blue. Clear is the least desired after pink.

5. **Styles.** The famous Nuart and Nucut lines from Imperial are especially popular with collectors.

6. **Authenticity.** Be careful when you buy Depres-sion Glass because many patterns have been reproduced. Color and pattern definition are clues to a piece's authenticity.

American and European Glass of the 1940s and 1950s

In addition to Levittown, Frank Sinatra, and the Man in the Grey Flannel Suit, the 1940s and 1950s saw the creation of some beautiful American glass. Following is a list of some of the glass manufacturers of this era whose products have attracted the most attention among collectors. Space limitations prevent me from listing all the different glass manufacturers, so don't hold it against me for the ones I couldn't fit in.

➤ **Crystal glass.** Produced by the Crystal Art Glass factory in Cambridge, Ohio, it is also called "Degenhart," the name of the firm's owners. Many of the items were made of rich, opaque slag glass in amethyst and off-white. You can find such novelty items as paperweights, salt and pepper shakers, and toothpick holders.

➤ **Heisey glass.** The most desirable Heisey glass is Verlys, frosted in various patterns. Prices start at $20 for a small nut dish, cheese plate, or punch cup and can range up to $250 for large pitchers.

➤ **New Martinsville glass.** Collectors lust after this firm's black glass, produced in bold modern shapes.

➤ **Westmoreland glass.** Known for its novelty items (such as high hats, pistols, and ashtrays shaped like turtles), Westmoreland glass comes in black, ruby, white, and amber. Items made after 1949 are marked with the intertwined letters *W* and *G*. Ashtrays run about $15, bowls about $100, and milk-glass cookie jars about $250.

Passionate for Paperweights

Paperweights are important glass collectibles. Look for those by the Boston and Sandwich Glass Company and the New England Glass Company. The latter specialized in flowers, animals, letters, and stars. The Pairpoint works in New Bedford and the Millville works in New Jersey produced some elegant samples.

Novelty paperweights will likely never be worth enough to put your child through college, but they can make an interesting collection for the budget-minded among us.

217

Collecting Glass

Gotta have it? Memorize these Top Five Rules to use the next time a yearning for glass overtakes you:

1. **Learn your glass.** Visit factories, museums, other people's collections. If you learn to recognize the Real Thing, you will be much more likely to get great deals that other people don't recognize.

2. **Labels.** Always check labels. Some unscrupulous sellers copy early labels and attach them to unmarked pieces. An original label will be worn and faded.

3. **Attend estate sales.** You can often find great examples at excellent prices—because other bidders didn't follow Rule #1.

4. **Rummage around.** Always check box lots of kitchen and household items for sale at flea markets, swap meets, house sales, and the like. You may find an excellent item buried in a box of junk.

5. **Condition, condition, condition.** Don't buy damaged pieces. They have little value.

The Least You Need to Know

➤ Delft, faience, majolica, and Quimper are all tin-glazed earthenware.

➤ Wedgwood is a type of stoneware. Lusterware and Staffordshire are ironstone.

➤ Porcelain is the same as china. Belleek, Bing & Grondahl, Capodimonte, Dresden, Haviland, Hummel, Imari, and Lladro are all types of porcelain.

➤ Avoid buying "limited edition" china collectibles for investment.

➤ Depression glass and carnival glass are affordable and popular collectibles.

➤ Learn as much as you can. Glass is especially easy to fake—and fakes abound with this collectible.

Part 5

Master of Arts: Photographs, Prints, and Paintings

"This is not art to me, all these squares and things. Real art has, you know, like a Madonna in it."

—Unknown (from the guest book at an exhibition of modern art)

"I'm glad all the old masters are dead, and I only wish they had died sooner."

—Mark Twain

No other aspect of the antiques, collectibles, and desirables world is as sexy as the art market. The prices of fine paintings boggle the mind: $51 million for a Picasso, $49 million for a (relatively) minor van Gogh. The cost of exquisite photographs is almost as high. It's a world of highfliers: Singer Elton John, for example, collects contemporary black-and-white photographs for his apartment in Atlanta and collects the portraits of eighteenth-century artist Arthur Devis for his English country mansion. "No way I could collect fine drawings and paintings," you think. Wrong.

There's plenty of magnificent collectible art, photographs, prints, and lithographs—enough to suit every taste and budget. Let me show you how to get your feet wet in the wonderful world of art.

Loch Ness

Chapter 19

Say Cheese, Please: Photographs

In This Chapter

➤ Purchasing collectible photographs

➤ Focusing on the most expensive photographs ever sold at auction

➤ Buying and storing daguerreotypes

➤ Creating a photography collection for every budget

➤ Storing modern photos

➤ Collecting cameras

Is photography art? Yes, and a highly collectible one at that. Most of the art photographers of the nineteenth century were ignored in their day but are highly prized in our own. Right now, American photographs from the 1920s and 1930s are smokin' collectibles. The images of contemporary photographers are also widely sought after.

For some photography collectors, the appeal of this art lies in the fact that the camera captures a moment that can never be repeated again. For others, the allure lies in photography's realistic base. But whatever their reasons for seeking out fine photographs, these collectors are passionate about their interest.

In this chapter, you will first learn about the earliest photographic images, *daguerreotypes*. Then you'll discover which nineteenth-century image makers are prized. Next I'll take you on a survey of contemporary American and British photography; you'll see what other people are collecting and why. Finally, you'll get ballpark figures for a representative sampling of collectible photographs, so you can price your own portfolio.

Look at the Birdie

Collectors of photographs cut across all class lines, but inquiring minds don't care that Mr. and Ms. John Q. Average collect snapshots. We care about the glitterati. So I'll just drop some names of famous collectors of photographs: actress Jodie Foster, musician Elton John, actress Diane Keaton, designer Ralph Lauren, and pop culture icon Madonna.

Photographs greatly increase in value if they are autographed, like this one.

What photographs do they collect? Some favor the classics:

➤ Edouard Baldus

➤ Lewis Carroll

➤ Henri Cartier-Bresson

➤ Edward S. Curtis

➤ Walker Evans

➤ Hiro

➤ Dorothea Lange

➤ Tina Moditti

➤ Irving Penn

➤ Man Ray

➤ Alexander Rodchenko

➤ Alfred Stieglitz

➤ Edward Streichen

➤ Edward Weston

Others crest the new wave:

➤ Patrick Demarchelier

➤ Adam Fuss

➤ Mario Giacomelli

➤ Karel Hajek

➤ Alfred Cheney Johnston

➤ William Klein

➤ Mary Ellen Marx

➤ Steven Meisel

➤ Francesco Scavullo

➤ Neil Winokur

➤ Max Yavno

More on this later, shutterbugs.

What do the top-of-the-line photographs go for? Here are some of the most expensive photographs ever sold at auction:

Pricey Photographs Sold at Auction

Photographer	Photo	Price	Auction/Date
Edward S. Curtis (American, 1868–1952)	*The North American Indian 1907–30*	$662,500	Sotheby's, New York, 1993
Alfred Stieglitz (American, 1864–1946)	*Georgia O'Keeffe: A Portrait—Hands with Thimble*, 1930	$398,500	Christie's, New York, 1989
Alfred Stieglitz	*Equivalents (21)*, 1920s	$396,000	Christie's, New York, 1989
Edward S. Curtis (American, 1868–1952)	*The North American Indian 1907–30*	$396,000	Christie's, New York, 1992
Man Ray (American, 1890–1976)	*Noir et Blanc*, 1926	$354,5000	Christie's, New York, 1994
Man Ray	*Hier, Demain, Aujourd'hui*, 1930–32	$222,500	Christie's, New York, 1993
Man Ray	*Glass Tears*, ca. 1930	$195,000	Sotheby's, London, 1993

continues

Pricey Photographs Sold at Auction (continued)

Photographer	Photo	Price	Auction/Date
Tina Moditti (Mexican, 1896–1942)	*Two Callas*, 1925	$189,500	Christie's, New York, 1993
Alexander Rodchenko (Russian, 1891–1956)	*Girl with Leica*, 1934	$181,450	Christie's, London, 1992
Tina Moditti (Mexican, 1896–1942)	*Roses, Mexico*, 1925	$165,000	Sotheby's, New York, 1991

And you threw away your Instamatic.

But people who collect photographs are too diverse to categorize. If you can describe yourself as a philosopher, investor, aesthete, detective, or explorer, then this may be the collectible for you. Let's start with the birth of photography, *daguerreotypes*.

America in Amber: Daguerreotypes

Jacques Louis Mande Daguerre announced his picture-taking process in 1839. Although Daguerre's announcement marked the official birth of photography, it was actually a photographic dead end because of the process he used. A daguerreotype is produced by light striking a silvered copper plate. As a result, there is no negative. The image on the plate cannot be reproduced or enlarged. Bad for customers; great for collectors.

Big Deals

One of the best daguerreotype collections in America has been amassed by Matthew Isenburg of Connecticut. It includes over 2,000 daguerreotypes and 3,000 pieces of related gear such as cases, equipment, books, documents, and of course, cameras. The collection cost Isenburg $4 million and almost 30 years to assemble. It's now worth an estimated $20 million.

Smile!

Nonetheless, daguerreotypes were enormously popular through the late 1850s. They were beautifully accurate images, and although not cheap by the standards of the time, still cost less than the alternative, painted portraits. Thousands of "daguerreian artists" and itinerant photographers combed the countryside, seeking people who wanted their mugs immortalized. Around 30 million daguerreotypes were taken in America between 1840 and 1860. That's not counting the millions and millions taken throughout the rest of the world.

Daguerreotypes are especially collectible because each one is unique—unlike photographs today that are made from negatives—and each captures people, places, and events from the first period in history ever to be recorded by photographic images.

But, as with any item that becomes a collectible, over the years the vast majority of these daguerreotypes were lost or damaged. By 1860 daguerreotypes had been supplanted by *ambrotype,* tintype, and paper images.

Picture Perfect

When determining what to buy, here are the criteria.

➤ **Size.** A "full plate" measures 6½ inches by 8½ inches. Other sizes are divisions of a full plate. Most daguerreotypes were sixth plates, so anything larger is out of the ordinary and thus potentially very valuable to collectors.

➤ **Condition.** As with most other collectibles, buy daguerreotypes in the best condition you can afford.

➤ **Subject matter.** Collectors of daguerreotypes seek out photos of animals, outdoor scenes, men at work. They also lust after portraits of people who became famous after their death and so were not widely photographed. Fan favorites include the writer Edgar Allan Poe and the philosopher Henry David Thoreau. Images of these men start at $10,000 each.

➤ **Maker.** The more famous the "daguerreian artist," the more the daguerreotype will be worth. All things being equal, a signed daguerreotype is worth more than an unsigned one.

Web Wise

The Daguerreian Society, devoted to the history, science, and art of the daguerreotype, is on the Web at www.abell.austinc.edu/dag.

Tricks of the Trade

You can distinguish daguerreotypes from other images by their mirrorlike reflection and precise detail.

➤ Aesthetic beauty. As with any artistic creation, form matters to collectors of daguerreotypes. Look for the interplay of composition, line, shape, and shadow.

Market Forecast

The market for daguerreotypes is stronger now than ever. A standard small "ancestor" daguerreotype sells for under $100, but for anything special, prices rise more quickly than a successful soufflé. For example, an early panorama of Paris and a portrait of Daguerre were sold privately for more than $100,000. In a 1992 auction, a half-plate Cincinnati scene by African-American James Presley Ball sold for $63,800. The previous auction record was set nearly a decade earlier in 1985, when the National Portrait Gallery paid $59,400 for a portrait of the photographer Matthew Brady.

Web Wise

The Puget Sound Photographic Collector's Society, dedicated to collecting and preserving historical photographic materials, is on the Web at www.geocities.com/ Eureka/Park/3740.

Better Safe Than Sorry

Thanks to my sage advice, you rushed out and assembled a fine collection of daguerreo-types. Like a new puppy, they require special care.

All early photographic processes are susceptible to oxidation because of the metal used in their processing. The effect is intensified if they were exposed to high levels of relative humidity—such as that found on a flea market field. Follow these guidelines for safe storage:

➤ Store your daguerreotypes upright in photo envelopes or archival plastic sleeves.

➤ Keep them away from undue levels of UV light.

➤ Keep daguerreotypes as clean as possible. Never attempt to clean them yourself.

So You Want to Put Together a Collection of Photos?

Almost every serious collector of photography has a story of a lucky find that turned out to be a treasure. In most cases, it happened to his brother's cousin's sister's third cousin. This section will show you how to make your dream come true without waiting for lightning to strike. You *can* put together a quality collection of photographs at a reasonable price without a bolt from the blue.

Please keep in mind that the following ideas are just that—ideas, not guaranteed investments. Trust your own tastes and instincts. And always remember the cardinal rule of collecting: Buy only what you love and can live with. With art, it will usually be pieces that make a strong emotional connection, that touch your soul in some private way.

A Few Grand for Photos

So you have a few thou to spend on photos. If that's the case, consider adding prints from some of the following photographers to your collection.

➤ **Retro chic.** One hot field is documentary photography, especially the realistic social photos of the 1960s or the conceptual photographs of the 1970s. Danny Lyon's photographs, fine examples of this genre, sell in the $3,000 to $5,000 range.

➤ **California dreaming.** Some of the West Coast photographers are being hyped as hot. These include John Divola, Joann Callis, Eileen Cowin, and Richard Misrach. The Los Angeles Center for Photographic Studies offered a David Levinthal print for $250, what one dealer termed a "real steal." Levinthal's Polaroids (20 by 24) usually fetch $4,000 a piece.

➤ **Hey, Abbott.** Berenice Abbott comes with impeccable credentials: She began her photographic career as an apprentice in Man Ray's studio. Born in 1898, Abbott is famous for her documentation of New York City life.

➤ **A big fuss.** Photographer Adam Fuss is making a big hoopla in collector circles. A lucky find is one of his prints in the $3,000 range; an average picture goes for about $8,000.

➤ **Trail blazers.** Cindy Sherman and Sherrie Levine put photography on the art map in the early 1980s. Can't get hotter than that.

➤ **Songs of self.** Nan Goldin, born in 1953, has been the art world's photographer of the hour for several years now. Her "warts and all" style is steeped in passion, immediacy, and rich color.

➤ **Batter up.** Take a look at Robert Riger's sports photos. Riger, who was an artist for *Sports Illustrated,* started by using his photos as reference materials for his illustrations.

➤ **A rose by any other name.** Among the most highly touted photographers is Aaron Rose. He works in the tradition of such masters as Alfred Stieglitz—but with a modern twist. Each of Rose's photographs goes for about $5,000. They are created with a special camera that Rose himself made.

➤ **Surf's up.** Hiroshi Sugimoto has attracted attention for his soothing photos of the ocean. They start around $2,500.

➤ **Movers and shakers.** Lee Friedlander, Helen Levitt, Robert Adams, Eadweard Muybridge, Nicholas Nixon, Neil Winokur, J. John Priola, Andres Serrano, McDermott & McGough, Germaine Krull, and Joel-Peter Witkin are all fabulous photographers; some offer prints that start around $1,000.

➤ **See the world.** In general, American masters of photography are hot right now. You can capitalize on this by collecting the photographs of European whiz kids. The images created by Patrick Faigenbaum, a French photographer, go for around $3,500. Another hot prospect is Roger Parry, a yet-to-be-discovered French photographer. His photos are in the same range as Faigenbaum's.

Champagne Tastes on a Beer Budget

Say you're just starting out. Or maybe you're busy tithing to the dentist, plumber, or auto mechanic. If that's the case, here are some recent photos advertised for sale at online auction sites. Do your homework, and you might be able to put together a portfolio that will give you pleasure for years to come.

➤ Richard Avedon photographs, 1947–1977, $118.61
➤ Civil War Abraham Lincoln photographs, $30.00
➤ Cecil Beaton war photographs, 1939–1945, $24.99
➤ 1958 L.A. Dodgers team pix photographs, $31.00
➤ Sotheby nineteenth- and twentieth-century photographs, $24.99
➤ Two original Kodak (round) photographs, 1899, $30.00
➤ Berenice Abbott photographs, $31.00
➤ Horace Nicholls Edwardian photographs, $17.00
➤ Three photographs by Walery, Gen. Pershing, Magnin, $28.89
➤ 1939 New York World's Fair actual photographs, $4.50

Shutterbugs of the World, Unite!

It's not only photographs that set collectors' pulses racing; cameras are also hot collectibles. Vintage cameras are especially popular with some collectors. These include certain types of Argus, Brownie, Ensign, Kodak, Leica, and Zeiss Ikon cameras. Newer cameras have their fans as well; Polaroid and Nikon send some pulses racing. Still other collectors go for unusual cameras, such as miniatures and subminiatures.

Here are some recent brands and prices offered for sale. Use this list to get a general idea of the various offerings and their prices. Consult specific guidebooks for further information.

➤ Alpa 6 lens and camera #25, $380.00

➤ #3 Kodak Junior roll film camera, 1890, $49.99

➤ Leica Ii C, ca. 1948, $175.00

➤ Polaroid "Highlander" 80a, includes presentation box, 1950s, $29.99

➤ Photosphere, Paris, ca. 1888, $1,525.00

➤ Voigtlander Ultramatic Outfit with Zoomar, mint, $510.00

The Least You Need to Know

➤ Some artists create highly desirable photographs.

➤ Those old daguerreotypes in your attic could be worth a lot of money. If you buy them, store them properly.

➤ Documentary photographs, certain West Coast photographers, and others (Berenice Abbott, Adam Fuss, Cindy Sherman, Sherrie Levine, Nan Goldin, Robert Riger, and Aaron Rose) are prized at present.

➤ You can build an enviable collection of photos for far less money, however, if you do your homework and shop carefully.

➤ Display and store your photographs properly.

➤ Cameras are also highly prized by collectors.

Chapter 20

Some Day My Prints Will Come: Prints and Lithographs

In This Chapter

➤ How prints are made

➤ Different types of prints

➤ Collectible prints

➤ Authenticity, condition, rarity, provenance, subject matter, importance, skill, and special considerations

---

Any original work of art worth its paint, clay, or ink will tend to be pricey because it's unique. On the other hand, prints are not originals and thus are usually not as pricey. They are more likely to fall within the budgets of a larger group of collectors, since there are more of them (prints, not collectors). The price of a print tends to become inflated only when it is very rare or autographed. By collecting prints, you can display superb examples of many first-class artists in your home, for a surprisingly affordable outlay of cash.

In this chapter, you'll learn how prints are made. Exploring the different printing methods will help you understand the value, rarity, and pricing of this collectible. Along the way, you'll do some shopping to find the hidden values in the print market. Then I'll explain how you can avoid being ripped off in the print biz. Roll the presses!

Psst! Wanna Come to My Room and See My Etchings?

Let's make sure we're all on the same page: A *print* is a picture or design made by reproducing an image with a machine. Here are some print guidelines:

➤ Prints are issued in deliberately limited numbers, usually under the guiding hand of the artist who created the original picture. Such prints are often numbered and signed.

➤ If you buy a quality print from an etched plate, it will most likely be signed and numbered.

➤ Normally, the outside figure in the margin indicates the total number of prints produced in that edition. Preceding that figure is a stroke (or slash) and another figure. This figure is the number of that impression in order of printing. For example, a print numbered "5/500" is the fifth impression in a series of 500. The higher the second number, the more prints there are—and the less valuable each one potentially is when you're talking about a newly released series of prints as opposed to an older series of prints.

Learn the Lingo

A **print** is a picture or design made by reproducing an image by machine.

Before you start shelling out any serious bucks for prints, it's wise to learn a little about the different types of prints that are available. Some printing techniques are relatively modern, and others have a long and noble history. Let's take a look at each one in turn. Some methods are subcategories of others, but I've listed every term separately to make it easier for you.

Engraving

In the *engraving* method, an engraver uses a small tool to etch a metal (often copper or steel) plate. Lines are scribed, ink is applied, the plate is wiped clean, paper is pressed on top, and pressure is applied. The quality of the engraving is determined by the variety of the lines. The finest and rarest engravings (such as Hogarth's) are very expensive, but fortunately for collectors, modern and affordable examples abound.

Hand-colored engravings were intensely collected in the 1920s. Because they are largely ignored today, they're a rich field for modern print collectors. A great bargain is a framed print in the low $100s.

Intaglio Printing

In *intaglio printing,* recesses are made by etching or engraving the flat surface of a plate. The recessed portions are then filled with ink, and the rest of the plate is wiped clean.

The print is made by transferring the ink to damp paper or other material. Again, the process requires considerable pressure. This is not a process for sissies.

American intaglio prints tend to be less detailed than European examples. Simple prints by lesser artists can be had for the low $100s.

Etching

Etching is a subcategory of intaglio. Included are etchings on hard plates, soft grounds, drypoint, aquatint, and mezzotint. Each achieves a different effect; aquatint, for example, includes tones (degrees of lightness and darkness) as well as lines. The first dated etching is marked 1513.

Rembrandt's etchings, dated a century later, are most often associated with this technique. It doesn't take a rocket scientist to know that Rembrandt's etchings are going to cost a pretty penny, but if you yearn uncontrollably for an original Rembrandt, later prints from the same plates are affordable for the reasonably well-heeled.

Tricks of the Trade

Prints by Impressionists are generally very expensive (as is anything by the Impressionists), but etchings by the landscape artists of the Barbizon School can sometimes be found for decent prices.

Mezzotints were a very popular collectible in the 1930s, but interest later faded. As a result, these prints can often be picked up today for sensible prices.

Lino Cutting

Lino cutting is the printing technique you probably learned in school, when you attacked an innocent piece of linoleum with a sharp tool. You and I usually created cheesy prints of the Starship Enterprise and gouged all our fingers in the process, but in the hands of a skilled artist, lino cutting results in striking posters.

Lithography

Fortunately, oil and water don't mix. Otherwise, we wouldn't have salad dressing or lithography. *Lithography* is a process in which a greasy crayon is used to trace a design on a very porous stone. The stone is then soaked in water, and it absorbs the moisture in its clear areas. Ink is rolled onto the surface and it clings to the crayon areas but is repelled by the wet parts. A sheet of paper is then rolled on the stone, picking up the design from the remaining ink.

Caveat Emptor

Since Currier and Ives prints are so popular, they have been reproduced widely, especially on overpriced Christmas cards. If you plan to buy an original Currier and Ives print, check the paper stock carefully to make sure that you are getting a genuine original print, not a recycled Christmas card.

Want to collect lithography? Then read on!

1. **Color my world.** Around the turn of the century, color lithographs were hot stuff, but collector interest faded fast. To the modern eye, many of these colored lithographs seem fussy and stodgy, so there hasn't been terrific collector interest. But if you're the fussy and stodgy type, you're in luck. You can pick up original lithographs to your liking for reasonable prices.

2. **Pulling no punches.** In contrast to the out-of-favor picturesque views of the early nineteenth century, political lithographs from the same era are keenly collected today. Satirical lithos, especially those of Daumier and Gavarni, are popular now.

3. **I'm dreaming of a white Christmas.** Currier and Ives was the most famous nineteenth-century American lithography firm. Active from 1834 to 1906 under several names, this New York company recorded important social scenes, big ships, and sentimental glimpses of American life. Although the prints were originally priced from a few cents to a few dollars, they have been collected fervently for many years. As a result, some prices are steep. Here are some recent examples:

   ➤ "Franklin Pierce, 14th President of the United States," #2127, small folio, dated 1852, very good condition with ¾-inch margins, $155

   ➤ "Arkansas Traveler/Scene in the Backwoods," #270, small folio, dated 1870, very good condition with 1-inch margins, $280

   ➤ "Autumn in the Adirondacks/Lake Harrison," #323, small folio, in very good condition with 1½-inch margins, $350

   ➤ "Autumn Fruits," #317, medium folio, dated 1861, very good condition with 1-inch margins, $430

   ➤ "Chicago as It Was," #1026, small folio, very good condition, 1-inch margins, $675

   ➤ "American Farm Scenes," #2, large folio, dated 1853, very good condition, $3,600

4. **Poster child.** Lithography was also important to the world's poster makers. Color lithography techniques improved after the 1860s, so there's a marked increase in the poster output after that. Posters were made to announce just about any type of occasion and to advertise any product. Some have elements of folk

art, while others are more sophisticated. Art Nouveau styles and theater themes are especially popular with collectors. Check *Prints, Posters, and Photographs: Identification and Price Guide* (Susan Theran, Avon Books) to price litho prints and posters.

5. **Modern times.** Lithography is undergoing a revival today, and some fine artists are being recognized and their work collected. Check major city newspapers for announcements of important exhibits and sales. You may favor modern masters such as LeRoy Neiman and Andy Warhol, or go for more traditional styles. "Collecting Pepsi-Cola," a litho print 23 inches by 32 inches, will set you back $50, for example.

Relief Printing

In *relief printing* (also known as *letterpress*), a block of wood or metal is cut or carved away, leaving in raised relief the uncut parts of the original flat surface. These raised parts are coated with ink; the cutaway parts remain clean. The print is made by pressing paper to the inked surface and applying pressure to make a clear print.

Surface Printing

The modern process of surface printing is a kissing cousin to planographic printing and screen printing. *Surface printing* involves forcing ink through a fine mesh of silk or a silklike synthetic material.

Woodcut Printing

Woodcut printing, probably the most ancient form of relief printing, was used by the Chinese as early as the ninth century A.D. To create a woodcut print, an artist draws a design in reverse on a block of wood. The outlines are defined, and the extra wood is cut away. You can usually tell a woodcut print because of its bold, heavy, and plain lines, although some prints are characterized by more complex shadings.

Tricks of the Trade

If you like the Currier and Ives look but not their prices, check out the prints made by Sarony & Major and Kellogg, two contemporaries of Currier and Ives. They are very similar in style but much less costly.

Web Wise

The GS and Company Art Gallery (www.kinkade.net/gshome. html), Keens Fine Art Galleries (www.keen-art.demon.co.uk), and Rare-Prints.com (www. rare-prints.com) offer online galleries.

This Albrecht Dürer woodcut print, made in 1515, is an outstanding example of the art form.

18. A rhinoceros: from a woodcut by Albrecht Dürer, 1515

Masters of wood-cutting include Albrecht Dürer (1471–1528), Hans Holbein (1497–1543), and Hans Burgkmair (ca. 1473–1531). Among the most famous wood-block prints made during this time include the Dance of Death series and the Triumphal Arch and Car. Of course these prints are seriously collectible, but they very rarely come onto the market and command out-of-this-world prices when they do.

There are also colored woodcut prints. Here are two of the most common techniques:

➤ **In living color.** These color woodcuts were created with more than one block, each color requiring a separate printing.

➤ **Hand-colored.** Even more rarely, you may see woodcuts in which the colors have been applied by hand. These are most often found in Japanese wood-block prints.

Tricks of the Trade

Shopping for woodcut prints? Most eighteenth-century broadsides (advertisements, announcements, and poems) include woodcuts. Many nineteenth-century folk prints are also woodcuts.

It's not difficult to find simple eighteenth- and nineteenth-century woodcuts for less than $100.

Wood Engraving

This technique is similar to woodcuts except that differences in materials result in finer drawing and more detail. The most famous old masters of this art are the romantic visionary Edward Calvert (1799–1883) and the romantic visionary madman William Blake (1757–1827). Some more modern masters include Robert Gibbings, Eric Ravilious, and Joan Hassall.

False Profits

Now that you know how prints are made, it's time to study as many prints as you can and decide which ones appeal to you. Your personal taste is crucial when it comes to collecting prints (or any art, for that matter). That's because what's pricey today has the greatest potential for loss tomorrow. Instead of buying what everyone else is buying, it's more profitable and more fun to develop your own tastes and style. Remember: Today's personal tastes can become tomorrow's hot art.

Whatever prints you decide to collect, here are some ground rules:

1. **Authenticity.** Is it the real thing? Scholars sweat blood trying to authenticate all works of art. When it comes to authenticating a print, experts study the kinds of paper available to the artist, the watermarks, plate wear, and other factors to judge who actually made it. The creation of Japanese wood-block prints involved such a complex division of labor that tracing how they were actually produced can take more time than it took to produce them!

2. **Condition.** A torn, cropped, or sheared print is not going to be as valuable as one that is in mint condition. Also be on the lookout for prints that have been "backed" (stuck down on backing) or blurred by rubbing and handling. These are not good collectibles because their value is already diminished. Damaged prints sell for less than those in flawless condition.

Caveat Emptor

Try to avoid later prints made from early engravings. The color of the new paper may make the print look odd, the background may look overly fuzzy from wear, or the background may look overly sharp from a tool-time touchup.

Learn the Lingo

The **provenance** of an artwork is the record of any and all former owners. An impressive provenance can greatly increase the value of a print or other artwork.

However, some contemporary artists, reacting to the mandates about condition, are scratching, abrading, or creasing their work on purpose. In some cases, this is taken as an artistic statement and so increases the value of a print. For now, at least.

3. **Rarity.** The price of each print depends on the size of the edition. All other things being equal, prints from a limited edition are worth more than those from an unlimited edition.

Tricks of the Trade

Ideally, every print that you buy should look as if it has just come straight off the press.

Caveat Emptor

Prints without plate marks are not necessarily forged. The prints may have been commissioned for use as book illustrations and so were engraved on plates larger than the plates on which they were to appear. As a result, the margins were trimmed and the plate marks cut away.

4. **Provenance.** The *provenance* of a work of art is the history of who owned it. A print from a well-known museum or private collection is worth more than an otherwise equivalent print from an unknown source. There's also a healthy dose of snob appeal when it comes to provenance. Hence the enormous prices paid for trifles owned by the famous and infamous.

5. **Subject matter.** People buy what they know best. As a result, American prints are sold mainly in America, British prints in Britain, German prints in Germany, and so forth.

6. **Importance.** When it comes to prints, influence and technical innovation such as aquatint, chiaroscuro, and pointillism make a print seem important. Important = expensive.

7. **Skill.** Prints that are hard to make may be considered more valuable that those that are easier to produce.

8. **Special considerations.** Some collectors are willing to pay more for old prints that have clean, wide margins. This has resulted in some fakery—I bet you're shocked. In the hands of a skilled forger, a print can be trimmed back to the edge of the printed surface and carefully inlaid into a new (and obviously not original) mounting. The resulting print may be pretty, but it's worth less than an untouched original.

Stop the Presses!

So how can you avoid being ripped off in the print biz? Here are some tips:

1. **See the light.** Hold every print you want to buy up to the light. This will help you see repairs such as patches and redrawings.

2. **Check the paper.** Forgers often try to pass off modern prints as older ones, but the paper is a real tip-off that something isn't kosher. Old paper will feel silky; new paper has a harder, stiffer feel.

3. **Offsetting and upsetting.** Offset printing has made it possible to create faithful reproductions of old prints. If you're into old prints, be sure to carefully examine each one to see if it really is old.

4. **Who is number one?** Beware that some contemporary printmakers number their works in a short series and then sell complete sets in different parts of the country. Buyers are tricked into thinking they are buying limited edition originals when they're not.

5. **I've been framed!** Sometimes modern prints are tarted up in fancy frames to make them look like more than they are. Although the prints may cost only a few cents to make, the frames make them look like a million bucks.

Tricks of the Trade

Look for the obvious. If your picture is labeled a museum reproduction, it's valuable as a decoration, not as an investment.

Go West, Young Collector

Trigger may be dead and stuffed, but Roy Rogers and Dale Evans are still going strong. That's because the Old West is once again rip roarin'. Partly as a result of the renewed interest in anything Old West, the art of Frederic Remington is enjoying a comeback.

Remington was born in New York in 1861. As an adult, he moved to the West, capturing the excitement of the wide open spaces in his paintings, sketches, and bronzes. Remington is to the West as blondes are to Hollywood. In 1990 one of Remington's paintings sold for almost $4.5 million.

Tricks of the Trade

Look in boxes of papers at auctions, flea markets, old house sales, and country sales. Perhaps you'll find one of Remington's wood-block prints.

It's not likely that either of us can afford one of his paintings, but there is still a niche for you and me—Remington's woodblocks. Early in his career, Remington created a series of wood-block prints for *Harper's Weekly*. This is the only place such work appears, and the original woodblocks seem to have vanished. These prints date from 1886; in 1980, 119 of his prints appeared in the magazine. Some are signed; some aren't.

Go East, Too

Japanese wood-block prints are as collectible as Remington's prints. Because a far wider range of Japanese wood-block prints is available, they are much easier to amass. Some of the prints show beautiful scenery; others, portraits of citizens. There are wood-block prints that document important events in Japanese life, too.

The golden age of Japanese wood-block printing is generally accepted as the 1700s and 1800s. These prints were quite popular; in some cases, more than 100,000 impressions were made from the same scene. Some collectors seek woodcut prints from the Meiji period (1868–1912), for their lush color. If you like Asian art, this might be an area to examine in greater depth.

The Least You Need to Know

➤ Prints offer first-class art at affordable prices.

➤ Prints are issued in deliberately limited numbers, often numbered and signed.

➤ The figure in the margin indicates the total number of prints produced in that edition, separated by a stroke from the number of that impression in order of printing.

➤ The value of a print depends on its authenticity, condition, rarity, provenance, subject matter, importance, the artist's skill, and special considerations.

➤ Hot areas include Currier and Ives lithographs, Art Nouveau posters, Japanese woodcuts, and Frederic Remington prints.

➤ The Artist Formerly Known As "Prints" doesn't collect woodblocks.

Chapter 21

Pretty as a Picture: Drawings and Paintings

In This Chapter

➤ Drawings as collectibles

➤ The artist's tools: paper, ink, pens, and pencils

➤ *Fraktur*, silhouettes, paper cutting (also known as "Scherenschnitte"), and caricatures

➤ Art history

➤ Collecting paintings for pleasure and profit

➤ Top 10 ways *not* to buy paintings

➤ Damaged and fraudulent paintings

As G. K. Chesterton said, art, like morality, consists of drawing the line somewhere. In this chapter, I'm going to draw the line—and color in the spaces. When I'm done, you'll be ready to plunge into the exciting world of collecting drawings and paintings. We'll start with drawings.

Since oil paintings get all the press, novice art collectors are apt to think that drawings take a backseat in the art collecting world. Not so. To the right crowd, drawings are every bit as important as their more assertive cousins, paintings. Here, you'll first survey the different kinds of drawings, with special attention paid to those that you may not realize are trendy collectibles, such as *Fraktur*, silhouettes, paper cutting, and caricatures. I'll help you discover which types of pictures to collect to fit your taste and budget.

Then I'll teach you the steps you need to know to collect paintings. You'll learn where to shop—and where not to shop. You'll learn the importance of researching before purchasing and how to determine pricing. Along the way, you'll also learn about the major schools of highly collectible art. By the end of this chapter, you'll be an art expert (or at least feel that way!).

The Material Is the Message

Unless the artist is the newfangled sort who executes drawings on subways and sidewalks, a drawing will be made on paper of some kind, using ink of some kind. (That's why you have to be 18 to buy markers and spray paint, especially around Halloween.) To buy drawings with confidence, you have to know a little bit about how they are made. Let's start with paper.

Paper Trail

Paper was first produced in China nearly 2,000 years ago, but the process remained within the country. The Egyptians went their own way, stripping the thin membranes from papyrus reeds to use for a writing medium. In the days before animal rights, people made parchment from the skins of sheep and goats; the finer-grained vellum was made from the skins of calves and kids. Soon, papermaking techniques spread across the world, and animals breathed a collective sigh of relief.

During the Renaissance, all the paper used for drawings in Western Europe was made from cotton or linen rags. In the early 1800s, economical papermakers realized that wood pulp would make an equally nice—and far cheaper—paper. Paper used for watercolors was still made with cloth, however. While paper is the most common drawing medium, there are also drawings on cloth, wood, bone, ivory, and other materials.

Big Deals

Drawing in charcoal was especially popular during the Victorian period. Most of the pictures were done on regular paper, but some were executed on sandpaper, called "marble," giving strange results. On the low end of the scale, these sell for $150 to $350; upper-end pieces can go for as much as $2,000. Most of these pictures are landscapes, often copied from earlier European oil paintings. They're attracting a wide following, so now is the time to snap them up.

What does all this paper stuff mean to you as a collector of drawings? It means that experts can examine a drawing under a microscope and tell by the paper when it was made. We give them a few years in either direction, but they're still remarkably accurate.

Of course, this doesn't stop forgers from trying to artificially age paper to trick the unwary collector. Some efforts are as blatant as dipping drawings in tea to make the paper look aged. Sophisticated forgers, on the other hand, use chemicals to produce convincing age marks, and even acid to simulate the appearance of a watermark.

Inky Dinky Bottle of Inky

The earliest inks were likely made from charred bones that had been ground to a powder and mixed with a binder. In the Middle Ages, ink was made from salts mixed with fluids produced by cuttlefish. In the second half of the nineteenth century, aniline inks were introduced. An expert can sometimes date a drawing and determine whether it is authentic by examining the ink.

Get the Point: Pens and Pencils

The style of a drawing will be influenced by the type of drawing implement the artist uses, the range of choices being limited by what was available at the time the drawing was made. Dürer, da Vinci, and Michelangelo didn't have easy access to an OfficeMax or Staples, so they often used chalks to make their rough drawings. Here are some other common drawing implements:

Caveat Emptor

If you add pastel drawings to your collection, be sure that they are correctly framed under glass to prevent smudging. Also, hang pastel drawings in a place where they won't be disturbed. Vibrations can cause smudging.

➤ **Pens.** Medieval scribes and illustrators often used pens cut from the quills of large birds, such as swans and geese. Metal pens didn't appear until late in the 1700s. The invention of steel pen nibs at the end of the eighteenth century led to a new interest in pen-and-ink drawings. Today, artists have fountain pens, ballpoint pens, and felt-tipped markers available.

➤ **Pencils.** The pencils available in the early eighteenth century were rough affairs, made from lead and tin. Graphite was discovered early in the century, but it wasn't until the very end of the 1700s that it was refined and made into drawing implements. In 1795 N. J. Conte devised a way to make graphite leads into sticks. These were fired in a kiln and voilâ! Pencils were born. The process whereby pencils are made is still based on this method.

➤ **Pastels.** Pastel drawings are admired for the purity of their color. Unfortunately, pastel drawings are fragile and especially prone to damage.

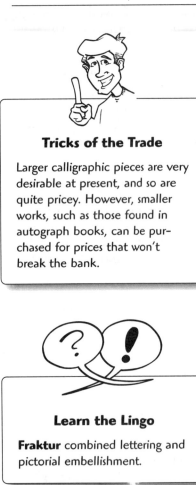

Tricks of the Trade

Larger calligraphic pieces are very desirable at present, and so are quite pricey. However, smaller works, such as those found in autograph books, can be purchased for prices that won't break the bank.

Learn the Lingo

Fraktur combined lettering and pictorial embellishment.

Tricks of the Trade

Never pass up an old autograph book without looking through it. Good calligraphy is often discovered this way.

Jest Plain Folk

Many attempts have been made to formulate a precise definition of American folk art, with mixed success. According to the curator at the folk art museum in Williamsburg, Virginia, one of the defining criteria is that the artist has no formal art training. But everyone has an opinion, so let's just say it's like the judge's famous definition of pornography: You can't put it into words, but you know it when you see it.

The pioneer collectors of folk art, in the early decades of the twentieth century, swooped down first on oil paintings, followed by watercolors. However, under the twin pressures of decreasing supply and increasing demand, interest has swelled in collectible drawings, silhouettes, and cut paper.

Quick-Draw McGraw: Drawings

Folk artists didn't start making pencil drawings until oil painting was a well-established art form. There are a few pencil portraits, mainly from the 1870s and 1880s, but much of the work consists of sketches done as studies for oil paintings or watercolors. Ink drawings, however, are a different matter.

Fraktur

When they weren't busy milking the cow or birthing the lambs, Pennsylvania calligraphers of the eighteenth and nineteenth centuries wrote certificates—birth, baptismal, wedding—whatever needed to be attested. Many are written in German, but others clearly show the influence of the Mother Country in style and subject.

At the beginning of the twentieth century, these certificates came to be called *Fraktur,* reviving a term from the sixteenth century. Fraktur combined lettering and pictorial embellishment.

The area where calligraphy and drawings overlap is of considerable interest to collectors today. The work of Pennsylvania German calligraphers is especially prized by American collectors of this art form. Good Fraktur cost thousands of dollars, but smaller pieces can go for considerably less than $1,000. European versions, still not a major collectible, are very affordable. Consult Currier's *Price Guide to American and European Prints at Auction,* by William P. Carl (Currier Publications), for specific pricing information.

The Shadow Knows: Silhouettes

A *silhouette* is a profile portrait cut out of black paper, a shadow outline. The contrast between the black and the white and the precision of the cutting combine to produce a very dramatic effect. Since silhouettes were cut quickly by an expert, they were inexpensive. Until the camera preempted the field, silhouettes served as the most accessible form of a family portrait. Many were enhanced with chalk, ink, or watercolor details.

Silhouettes were at the height of their popularity from 1800 to 1850. Many silhouettes are signed by their makers. Today, portraits are the most popular collectibles, but landscapes and pictures of people in action are also eagerly sought after. A silhouette from the mid-nineteenth century sells on the average for about $250. An unusual family record illustrated with silhouettes, made in 1830, went for $1,250. Since silhouettes are easily faked, I recommend that you buy them from a reputable dealer.

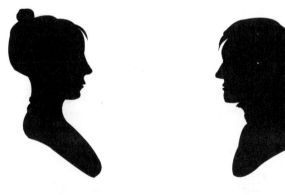

Silhouettes provided an inexpensive, fast type of portraiture.

Cut and Paste

Another collectible offshoot of drawing is *paper cutting,* a folk art form. The technical term for this art form is "Scherenschitte." In addition to cut paper, watercolor was also used in many instances. Cut-paper pictures from Pennsylvania, made in the late 1880s, sell for anywhere from $275 to $450. An elaborate cut-paper picture from the same time and place recently fetched more than $1,000 at an auction.

You can also find cut-paper tinsel pictures. The tinsel creates a beautiful shimmering effect. Tinsel work is found mainly in the latter half of the nineteenth century. A neglected art form, tinsel cuttings are still underpriced. A tinsel painting from the mid-nineteenth century sells for $250 to $550.

The Line Kings

Caricatures are another type of highly collectible drawing. For our purposes, a *caricature* is a drawing that exaggerates a particular physical or facial feature of a person, including the person's clothing, dress, or manners, to produce a ludicrous effect. "Caricature" comes from an Italian word that means to "exaggerate" or "overload," and so these drawings do. They may also poke fun at political, social, or religious situations.

The work of the following caricaturists is highly collectible:

Tricks of the Trade

The art world perpetuates the belief that the rarity of a work of art merits a rare price. Here's the truth: The artistic value of a work of art has nothing to do with its rarity. The real value of visual art lies in its ability to move you and satisfy your sense of beauty.

Eighteenth century:

➤ George Townshend
➤ William Hogarth
➤ Thomas Rowlandson
➤ James Gillray
➤ George Cruikshank

Nineteenth century:

➤ Sir Max Beerbohm
➤ Sir Leslie Ward
➤ Sir David Low
➤ Charles Philipon
➤ Honoré Daumier
➤ Gustave Doré
➤ Henri Toulouse-Lautrec
➤ George Grosz
➤ Thomas Nast

Big Deals

Thomas Nast is credited with creating such diverse characters as the Republican elephant, Democratic donkey, and the modern-day image of Santa Claus.

Twentieth century:

➤ Bill Maudlin
➤ Herbert Lawrence Block ("Herblock")

➤ Pat Oliphant

➤ Jules Fieffer

➤ Walt Kelly

➤ Al Hirschfeld

Hirschfeld's caricatures of theater and movie stars are especially popular now; he has been dubbed the "line king" for his expressive use of line. His caricatures, especially those that contain "Ninas" (the name of his daughter) hidden in the folds, command top collector dollars.

Be Art Smart

"I'll have the BLT on white with mayo." If only buying paintings was as easy as ordering lunch! Unfortunately, it's not. For one thing, lunch is cheap and art is expensive. Prices for investment-grade paintings start in the low hundreds and spiral rapidly upward.

How much is an American painting worth? As this book goes to press, the record is $27.5 million for George Bellows' 1910 oil painting *Polo Crowd* (December 1999). This price smashed the $11.1 million paid in 1996 for John Singer Sargent's *Cashmere*.

Tricks of the Trade

An art treasure can appear at any time and in almost any place. If you think you've unearthed a masterpiece, study photographs of the artist's other works. If you find your painting there, you know you have a copy. If not, there is a slim chance that you're on to something. In that case, have an art appraiser look at the picture to determine whether it merits appraising. If so, determine the fee in advance and get it in writing.

The market for American art of every kind is rising. In fact, the best portraits and landscapes of the eighteenth and nineteenth centuries are rising in value faster than Donald Trump's ego. What should you do if you want to collect paintings? Read on to find out!

Art 101

Start by brushing up on your art history. Here's a crib sheet for the most-often talked about modern art:

➤ **Barbizon.** These landscape paintings are characterized by dark foregrounds that frame a lighter middle ground, the central theme. A three-dimensional effect is created by the lighting.

➤ **Impressionism.** Pioneered by Monet, Renoir, and Cézanne, Impressionist paintings are marked by fabulous lighting and atmosphere.

Caveat Emptor

Family portraits are rarely valuable, almost never as much as the owner anticipates. Unless painted by a recognized master, portraits usually have only sentimental or family value. Don't count on selling a family portrait to finance a cruise or college education.

Tricks of the Trade

Countless portraits of nameless English and European worthies painted by equally nameless English and European artists populate the walls of antique shops. If you're looking for a painted ancestor to match your eighteenth-century furniture, consider buying one of these anonymous—and affordable—portraits.

➤ **Cubism.** Look for a geometric quality that re-shapes known forms. Aside from Pablo Picasso, the major Cubists are George Braque, Juan Gris, and Fernand Léger.

➤ **Ashcan School.** This is a realistic slice of city life produced in the 1920s.

➤ **Surrealism.** Like abstract art, surrealism uses shapes, forms, and colors that have no natural counterpart. The Big Man on Campus was Salvador Dalí.

➤ **Expressionism.** Headquartered in Germany from 1905 to the 1920s, Expressionist art is marked by a revelation of the artist's personal emotions. The major players were George Grosz, Otto Dix, Max Beckmann, Wassily (or Vasili) Kandinsky, and Paul Klee.

Know Thyself

When you feel the urge to collect paintings, start by identifying the kinds of art you like. Remember, you have to live with the painting, and it can be easier to get rid of a recalcitrant spouse than a mediocre painting. With the first, you're usually willing to take a loss; with the second, you'll likely want to recoup your initial investment.

Say you're looking for a painting with a little green and some peach to fit over the mantel, something light or floral like the one you saw in the model house down the street. Or perhaps you want a hunting scene to go in the den or a portrait of some ritzy-looking old guy for the dining room. Ritzy portraits always give a dining room some class.

If these scenarios fit your interest in art, then your goal is to locate decorative art. In that case, you find a picture you like that fits your budget, and everyone is happy. And don't let anyone tell you differently. Remember—*you* have to live with the painting, not your arrogant neighbor, contemptuous in-laws, or conceited boss.

Collecting for Cash

But let's say that you want to collect paintings that will appreciate in value, art that might someday finance that vacation—or your retirement. If that's the case, you're on the right page.

But first, a stern warning: People who invest in art solely for speculative purposes often wind up losing the most. During the 1980s run-up in stock and real estate prices in Japan, for example, a whole bunch of investors with more sawbucks than savvy happily exchanged piles of cash for Renoirs, van Goghs, and other icons of Western art. From 1987 through 1991, Japanese buyers spent more than $8.7 billion on art. A van Gogh and a Renoir bought for $161 million by Ryoei Saito, then president of Daishowa Paper, were later quietly disposed of by his creditors, Fuji Bank, at a loss of more than one third.

So, how can you avoid these same blunders when you invest in art? Whether you have a lot of money to spend or a little, these tips will work for you:

1. **Learn the ropes.** Get a working knowledge of the art world by becoming familiar with art personalities, art dealers, art galleries, and the art community.

2. **Research.** Go to art museums. Study the paintings and see what appeals to you. Then read up on your favorite art in art museum libraries. Try a private or state museum, college, or university that has a strong art history department. Kiss up to the research librarian; he or she can be of invaluable assistance.

3. **Consult price guides.** Find out how much the paintings you like cost by looking in various price guides. For example, you may wish to check out *The Official Price Guide to Fine Art,* by Susan Theran (House of Collectibles). You'll find other price guides listed in Appendix B, "Further Reading."

4. **Comparison shop.** To select the best art for your taste and budget, stifle the impulse to buy immediately. Instead, shop around.

5. **Shop smart.** Stick to well-known galleries and dealers. This offers you protection that you can't get with fly-by-night vendors.

6. **Deal with dealers.** Get to know the dealers who sell the paintings you like. An art dealer who knows you mean business will scour the market to help you get the paintings you want at a fair price. Buying from a dealer can also help you avoid damaged art, which you may find in secondhand shops, frame shops, and resale outlets.

Caveat Emptor

Don't fall prey to the "one-of-a-kind" myth—that no two paintings are exactly alike. You can *always* find another painting that looks virtually identical to the first one. I promise.

Paying the Piper

Paintings and drawings don't start out as just something else to buy and sell, but once they leave the artist's studio, they become a commodity like guns and butter. This brings us to the realities of the art economy: value and pricing.

Tricks of the Trade

A great pencil drawing is usually more valuable than a lousy oil painting, but as a rule of thumb, an oil painting will be more valuable than other media (such as watercolors or drawings) by the same artist.

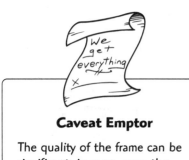

Caveat Emptor

The quality of the frame can be significant; in some cases, the frame can be worth more than the painting itself. This is a serious tip-off that the painting isn't a rare masterpiece.

Value

The art world is not a democracy: Some paintings are worth more than others. Collectors pay more for paintings that are judged to be of greater depth, significance, and quality than those judged to be haphazard, lightweight, and weak.

Pricing

Art prices can change over time because of shifts in public taste or fashion. You won't find any Art Police to control pricing or quality. A fluctuation in the overall economic climate is also a factor in what a painting will cost. Take the case of the Impressionists.

After having their art derided during their lifetimes, several of the pioneer Impressionists got their revenge: They lived long enough to see their work accepted and even embraced. Nonetheless, even the most far-seeing of these painters could not have anticipated the outrageous prices their works fetch today. Around 1900, it was still possible to buy a painting by Vincent van Gogh for about $190, a Cezanne for $1,000, a Manet for $2,000, a Monet for less than $5,000, and a Renoir for $10,000.

Prices rose slowly but inexorably as the century marched to its close. In 1958, for instance, van Gogh's *Public Gardens in Arles* set a new record for a painting when it sold for $370,000; less than 12 years later, paintings by van Gogh, Monet, and Renoir were selling for nearly $1,500,000 each. The upward trend continued: In 1980 van Gogh's *Le Jardin de Poete, Arles* was sold for $5,200,000; five years later, his *Paysage au Soleil Levant* fetched $9,000,000. With this kind of investment potential, who needs to follow the Dow Jones?

Top Ten Ways *Not* to Buy Paintings

You've learned how to buy paintings. Now find out how *not* to buy paintings:

1. Don't buy any painting when you're under the influence. No "morning after" art, please.

2. Don't buy paintings at night. You tend to be more impulsive at night. Not a good time to spend big bucks.

3. Don't buy serious paintings on vacation. Buy fun art as a souvenir of your trip, but not serious art. You might forget how the couple next to you danced with the lampshades on their head, but you'll never forget the dreadful overpriced painting you bought—because you're still paying off the charge card.

4. Don't buy a painting because you're enchanted by the seller. Good sales people are charmers; that's why they're in sales and not dentistry. To help you resist the glib sales pitch, bring a cranky friend along.

5. Don't buy paintings from trucks, street vendors, one-shot auctions, and other quickies. Hot dogs, ice cream, and Danish are all fine from trucks. No art or shellfish, please.

6. Don't buy paintings over the phone. Even though paintings are a visual medium, unscrupulous people sell them over the phone—and innocent people buy them.

7. Don't buy any painting because it's "hot." A hot painting can cool off faster than a hot pretzel.

8. Don't buy any painting just because the gallery is posh. The appearance of the gallery is not a reliable indicator of its quality. Some of the best dealers operate out of modest quarters (and vice-versa, of course).

9. Don't buy any painting under pressure. What works for fire drills works for art sales: Stop, drop, and roll. Stop and think. If your credit is good, the picture will be there tomorrow or a week from tomorrow.

10. Don't buy art based on predictions. Past performance is no indication of future earnings. If it was, my stock portfolio would be worth a whole lot more than it is.

Damaged Goods

Experienced art dealers and collectors generally avoid paintings that are damaged beyond a certain point. The most serious investors/collectors won't touch a painting that's damaged in *any* way. But depending on the type of art, some collectors will accept certain amounts and types of damage.

The precise amount varies according to the usual suspects: age of the art, rarity, importance of the artist, and so on. For example, people who collect Gothic panel paintings from the 1600s will accept more damage on their paintings than those people who collect contemporary acrylic landscapes.

Here are three guidelines to follow when assessing the relationship of damage to value:

1. **The greater the damage, the less the value.** Under 5 percent, damage is considered minor. Over that, things get a little dicey. Ten percent is generally the upper limit of "acceptable" damage.

2. **The location of the damage is as important as the extent.** Even the smallest amount of damage in the wrong place can destroy the value of a painting.

3. **Restorers will downplay the effect of the damage.** Restorers like to restore and are often justly proud of their work. There are many reputable, honest restorers, but some just want to get their brushes and rags on your painting. These restorers are apt to tell you that the damage isn't a problem. It usually is.

Tricks of the Trade

Some restorers will downplay the effect of the damage. Restorers like to restore and are often justly proud of their work. Since they want to get their brushes and rags on your painting, they are apt to tell you that the damage isn't a problem. It often *is*.

Caveat Emptor

Art fraud is one of the IRS's favorite targets.

Liar, Liar, Pants on Fire: Fakes and Frauds

Take this quick quiz. How many of the following statements are true?

1. Every kind of art can be faked.
2. Forged art sells in every price range.
3. Forgeries are everywhere.

Unfortunately, they're all true. Great painters of every period have been imitated and faked. Many artists were even copied while they were still active because their work was so popular. While those paintings might have been sold as copies during the artist's lifetime, once the artist's work fades from the public eye, the line between real and reproduced is blurred. If the original artist is resurrected from obscurity, even art experts may be hard pressed to distinguish the original from the copy.

And what happens if no one knows that an artist's works have been copied? Even greater confusion results. In such a case, it's likely that many pictures with the artist's signature—all fakes, of course—will be sold as authentic.

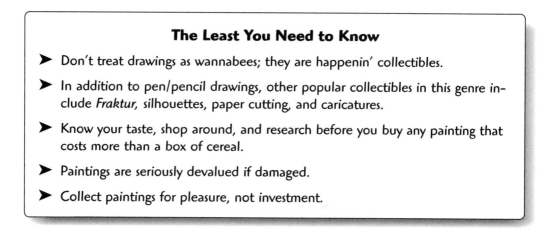

The Least You Need to Know

➤ Don't treat drawings as wannabees; they are happenin' collectibles.

➤ In addition to pen/pencil drawings, other popular collectibles in this genre include *Fraktur*, silhouettes, paper cutting, and caricatures.

➤ Know your taste, shop around, and research before you buy any painting that costs more than a box of cereal.

➤ Paintings are seriously devalued if damaged.

➤ Collect paintings for pleasure, not investment.

Part 6

All That Glitters Isn't Gold— but It's Probably Collectible

In 1903 a Canadian blacksmith, Fred La Rose, threw his hammer at a marauding fox, missed—and struck silver. The hammer landed on what turned out to be the world's richest vein of silver. La Rose sold his claim for $30,000. By 1913 the vein had yielded silver worth more than $300 million.

Today, throwing a hammer is more likely to land you a stay in the county jail than a fortune. But there is another way that you might amass a fortune, or at least have a whole lot of fun. How? By collecting precious metals, jewelry, and gems.

For thousands of years, people have collected and worn precious stones and metals for decoration and as talismans to protect them from ill health and misfortune. The stones are treasured for their color, translucence, durability, and monetary value. Gold has been prized by human beings since the Stone Age. The Egyptians were probably the first to cut and polish gems to increase their beauty.

There's a wealth of precious metals, jewelry, and gemstones for every collector's taste and budget. Costume jewelry is equally desirable. In Part 6, you'll discover collectibles that you can wear as well as display.

Chapter 22

Putting on the Glitz: Collecting Jewelry

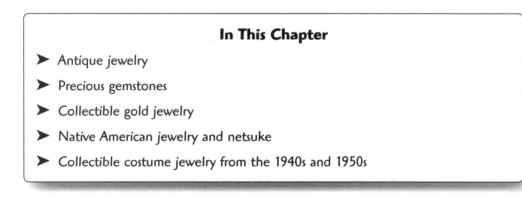

In This Chapter

➤ Antique jewelry

➤ Precious gemstones

➤ Collectible gold jewelry

➤ Native American jewelry and netsuke

➤ Collectible costume jewelry from the 1940s and 1950s

If diamonds are a girl's best friend, then collectible jewelry is *everyone's* buddy! In this chapter, you'll learn that you don't need a million bucks to put together a beautiful—and valuable—jewelry collection.

The chapter kicks off with the generally accepted definition of antique jewelry and a survey of some of the most collectible types. Then I'll explain the characteristics of the jewelry produced in each era to help you identify when a piece of antique jewelry was made. You'll learn about gemstones, too, from amethysts to zirconium. Along the way, I'll show you how to decode gemstone labels so you'll understand what you're being sold.

Next comes a discussion of the different types of gold and how the purity of gold is measured. Collectible Native American jewelry is covered, along with *netsuke*, the highly collectible button-size Japanese toggles.

Happy days come again with a survey of the collectible costume jewelry of the 1940s and 1950s, pieces made from enamel, metal, glass, plastic, sterling silver, and wood. So let's put on the glitz as we explore collectible jewelry and gemstones.

Oldies but Goodies: Antique Jewelry

Rare platinum sapphire and diamond ring, circa 1920 ... $4,500.

Ever drool over an ad like this? People who collect antique jewelry like to explain their extravagance by claiming they are buying a piece of history. They have a point, but let's tell it like it is: A lot of antique jewelry is just plain gorgeous. Here's my proof:

This 1930s beauty is platinum with diamonds and sapphires. It even has the original band. I paid $1,200.

But not to worry—you can buy gorgeous antique jewelry for far less. Here are some recently advertised pieces:

➤ Victorian collar pin with very old amethyst glass stones. Center oval stone has unusual cut and is set in a bezel surrounded by tiny glass pearls. Brass with gold overlay. Measures 1⅝ inches by 1¼ inches. $79.

➤ 1890s sash pin, stamped brass with gold plating. Large red glass stone in center is bezel set. Stone slightly scratched. Measures 2¼ inches wide by 1⅜ inches high. $65.

➤ Art Nouveau sash pin, stamped brass with gold overlay. Beautiful design of calla lilies and intricate scrollwork. Three small sapphires set into center of each lily. About 2¾ inches wide by 2 inches high. $175.

➤ Portrait pin of a handsome man from the 1920s. Rolled edge, celluloid cover, and "C" clasp closure. Measures 1⅛ inches in diameter. $29.

➤ Late 1920s silver and blue stone sash pin. Heavy and sturdy, this pin measures 2⅝ inches by 2¼ inches. Large stones are prong set. $40.

According to law, antique jewelry isn't antique until it can make a birthday appearance with Willard Scott because it's a hundred years old. However, this definition has been broadened to include any jewelry that looks old and wasn't made yesterday. The following chart can help you place "antique" jewelry into manageable periods.

Jewelry Periods

Name	Dates
Georgian	1790–1837
Early Victorian	1837–1860
Mid-Victorian	1860–1880
Late Victorian	1880–1901
Art Nouveau	1880–1914
Arts and Crafts	1890–1914
Edwardian	1901–1910
Art Deco	1920–1940

Shop 'Till You Drop

First stop: stores that sell antique jewelry. Study as many pieces of antique jewelry as you can. Discover which periods, styles, artists, and materials appeal to you. Buy a jeweler's loupe so you can examine each piece carefully.

Dating

Next, how can you figure out when a piece of antique jewelry was made? Here's a rundown of the characteristics of the jewelry produced in each era:

➤ **Georgian.** Brooches tend to be square or rectangular and chunky. Pearls are often used as borders, and black-and-white enamel is common. Most pieces are 18K gold. The Georgians were a mournful lot, so expect a lot of memorial jewelry.

This Georgian ring has a characteristic rectangular stone.

➤ **Early Victorian.** Pieces are lighter in feeling and construction: Rings have flat sides and often incorporate enamel in the design. Some mourning pins include snippets of hair from the deceased. Necklaces often sport garnets, pearls, and swirls of gold. An early Victorian 14K gold locket brooch with pearl and blue enamel motif in mint condition costs about $1,000.

The gold swirls clearly mark this as an early Victorian necklace.

➤ **Mid-Victorian.** Elaborate lockets and chains suit mid-Victorian taste; silver makes a bold stand. You'll find the influence of ancient Greece and Rome; pieces once again get as large as Queen Victoria's considerable brood. A mid-Victorian gold and opal cluster brooch with a butterfly and sword sells for about $900.

This large brooch is from the mid-Victorian period.

➤ **Late Victorian.** Engraved patterns combine an interest in naturalism and a fascination with the crescent motif. There's already a whiff of Art Nouveau. Lots of simple and delicate pendants called *lavalieres*.

➤ **Art Nouveau.** Look for lush enamels and exotic forms. The iris and the idealized female form were especially popular. This style of jewelry is currently a very hot collectible.

➤ **Arts and Crafts.** Soft-colored enamels, mother-of-pearl, silver, twisted braid trim, ornate clasps. For example, a silver brooch embellished with Russian amber cabochons made of silver, measuring 2⅝ inches by 2¼ inches, in excellent condition sells for $150.

➤ **Edwardian.** These pieces are light and delicate. Look for diamonds and white metals such as platinum. Settings are airy and pierced. Pins start at about $150 for silver; $500 for platinum and diamonds.

➤ **Art Deco.** Art Deco jewelry captures the flashiness of the 1920s. Onyx, carnelian, and marcasite are popular stones. These pieces are eagerly sought by collectors.

Big Deals

Carol McFadden of Oil City, Pennsylvania, had collected 18,750 different pairs of earrings as of January 1995. Her collection earned her a place in the *1996 Guinness Book of World Records*.

Material Girl

Don't overlook the costume jewelry of the 1800s. Much of it is beautiful—and quite valuable today. Its value derives from the odd materials from which it was made as much as from its age and appearance. Here are some of the materials you may encounter in antique costume jewelry:

➤ Aluminum, a rare and costly metal in the 1850s, was very popular for jewelry until the 1880s.

➤ Bog oak from the Irish bogs or swamps was carved with various designs and made into jewelry.

➤ Cut steel was often faceted to mimic more expensive metals. This is called *marcasite*.

➤ German silver, also called *nickel silver*, is an alloy made from copper, zinc, and nickel.

➤ Gutta-percha, a brown-to-black mixture of resin, sawdust, and latex, was molded into beads and brooches.

➤ Hair jewelry is just what it sounds like, locks cut from the head of the beloved, who was usually deceased. Ornaments made from hair were very popular in the Victorian era.

Gemstones: Gravel with an Attitude

Gemstones are uptown versions of the gravel on your driveway. A *gemstone* can be cut and polished into a *gem*. When it's set, it becomes a *jewel*. The market is flooded with inferior versions of every possible gemstone—nothing more than gravel with an attitude.

Truth or Dare

How can you tell a noble gemstone from a common chunk of glass? Here are some tests:

1. **First, take its temperature.** Touch it with your tongue. (Yes, you heard right.) Gemstones (with the exception of an opal) will remain cool; glass warms up fast. This is not to say that you don't want glass; you just want to make sure you're paying the right price for it.

2. **Try a little water torture.** A drop of water will hold its shape on a real gemstone; on glass, it spreads out like a couch potato's rear end.

3. **Look at the setting.** Glued stones are likely worth a lot less than those held in place with prongs. You will have to look at the stone under a loop or microscope.

4. **As a very last resort, try the scratch test.** If you can etch glass with the stone, it's probably genuine. Unfortunately, you've probably damaged the gem—unless it's a diamond—in the process, which is why this is your last resort.

Amethyst to Zirconium

Let's survey the most collectible gemstones, so you can better recognize what people are collecting—and why.

Caveat Emptor

Beware of imitation amber; true amber is warm to the touch. To test a piece, heat the end of a pin and apply it to a hidden surface of the amber. If the piece is really amber, it will smoke and emit a pine smell.

1. **Amber.** Amber is petrified pitch. It often contains bits of insects and bark, which most collectors feel enhance its value. They look for rich amber brown pieces filled with relics from ages long gone. Some collectors seek out rosaries made of amber, which date back to the 1400s.

2. **Amethyst.** According to myth, these stones protect the wearer against intoxication. A variety of quartz, the rich purple is the most desired color.

3. **Aquamarine.** This gem shades from a light bluish green to deep blue, which is the rarest. The deeper the blue, the more collectible the gem.

4. **Coral.** No one knows whether coral is a plant or an animal, but we do know that the most prized coral is the dark red variety found off the coast of Tunisia and Algeria. Black coral is next in value; pink coral trails behind.

5. **Diamonds.** Diamonds are the hardest and brightest of the gems. When collecting diamonds, look for the 4C's: cut, color, clarity, and carat. The clearest, largest, best-cut stones are the most valuable. It is rare for any diamond under a carat to be purchased for investment. Further, investment-grade diamonds are rarely mounted and worn, Liz Taylor's habits notwithstanding.

6. **Emeralds.** An emerald is one of the easiest gemstones to identify because of its *occlusions* or flaws; a totally flawless genuine emerald is almost impossible to acquire. Be wary of the numerous synthetic emeralds. A true emerald will not change color under the light. Emeralds are one of the most highly prized of all gems.

Tricks of the Trade

Early diamonds were cut in as few as 24 facets, which accounts for their lack of brilliance when compared with modern diamonds cut in 58 facets.

7. **Garnets.** Garnets are found in several colors, including pink, brown, and black, although the ruby red shade is the most common. A violet garnet is called a "rhodolite." The stones will change color under the light. Most garnets are considered costume jewelry.

8. **Ivory.** Ivory from Asian elephants cannot be legally imported into the United States because the Asian elephant is protected as an endangered species. The African elephant, however, is just "threatened," so its tusks *can* be imported. Nonetheless, I could make a good case that we're splitting (elephant) hairs here, so you shouldn't collect *any* ivory. If you do decide to buy ivory, make sure that you are buying from a first-class dealer who gives you clear documentation of the ivory's source. That's because ivory has look-alikes, like bone. Today, most affordable synthetic is plastic.

9. **Jade.** The jade you're most likely familiar with comes in greens that range from lettuce to spinach, but it also occurs in brown, yellow, black, blue, and an off-white. Jade has long been revered by the Chinese; it is still used in China as a symbol of high rank and authority. Warning: Soapstone can fool the novice.

10. **Jet.** A variety of coal that's dense and glossy, jet is making a strong comeback on the collector trail. It's hard to tell jet from black plastic, so beware. The real thing is heavy, feels warm when touched, and like amber, will take an electrical charge when rubbed.

11. **Lapis Lazuli.** The most valuable varieties of this soft, deep blue gemstone are uniform in color, although lapis often has flecks of iron pyrite (fool's gold) and occasionally real gold. If it is streaked with white, it is considered of lesser quality.

Caveat Emptor

Most colored stones on the market today have had more dye-jobs than even *my* hair. Heat, chemicals, and radiation are used to improve the color and smooth out imperfections. Because some color enhancements are not permanent, ask what's been done to the stone *before* you buy it.

12. **Opals.** Look for a fiery stone. Some are milky white and tinted with flashes of color; so-called "black opals" have a dark color. Opals are easily cracked, so carefully check that they are perfect. Also, some opals have been synthetically treated or backed with a black material to enhance color. Obviously, these are of lesser value.

13. **Pearls.** *Natural pearls* form in oysters all by their lonesome. *Cultured pearls* are seeded and returned to their ocean homes to grow. *Mikimoto pearls* are a brand name for a company that started culturing pearls in 1908. *Biwa pearls* are cultured freshwater pearls. The majority of modern pearls are cultured.

14. **Ruby.** Rubies were said to preserve the body and health of the wearer and to remove evil thoughts. The rubies with an orange-yellow color are the most desired. Star rubies reveal a star when they are cut.

15. **Sapphire.** Although the word *sapphire* comes from a Greek word that means "blue," these stones come in yellow and green as well as blue and violet.

16. **Topaz.** According to an ancient superstition, topaz can cure insomnia and avert sudden death. These stones commonly range in color from gold to deep brown, but blue topaz are not uncommon. Citrine is a less-expensive variation.

Big Deals

Topaz, tourmaline, garnet, and other semiprecious stones have become very popular with collectors, especially Brazilians. Rio is the center of this hype.

17. **Zircon.** Zircon is a real gemstone but considerably more common and thus less valuable than its first cousin, diamonds. Don't confuse a zircon with a *cubic zirconia,* which is an artificial diamond.

Truth in Advertising

Beware of how a gemstone is labeled. Here are some examples of deceptive labeling:

➤ Cape May diamonds, Bohemian diamonds, and Herkimer diamonds are *quartz*— the stuff on your sidewalk.

➤ Gilson opal and Slocum opal are *plastic*—the stuff used to make your food storage containers.

➤ Girasol pearls, Laguna pearls, simulated pearls, and Majoica pearls—fake, fake, fake. Even confirmed landlubbers have been closer to oysters than these "pearls" have ever been.

To avoid problems later, ask these five questions when you buy a colored gemstone:

1. Is this a genuine stone or a synthetic stone?
2. Is the color natural?
3. Is the color permanent?
4. What is the gem called and what does its name mean?
5. Is the clarity acceptable, or are there too many flaws?

When you're buying valuable stones such as diamonds, get a receipt with the description, color, weight, carats, and so on. Reputable dealers always give such receipts.

All That Glitters Isn't 14K

What's the allure of gold? First of all, it doesn't tarnish, rust, corrode, or fade. It can withstand thousands of years in a Pharaoh's tomb; it is impervious to salt and water. It's *malleable* (able to be molded) and *ductile* (flexible). One ounce of gold can be formed into a wire 50 miles long. It also looks really neat around your neck, wrist, or dangling from any port.

At the End of the Rainbow

To make gold sturdier, it's usually mixed with another metal, such as copper, silver, nickel, or platinum. How many of these golds do you collect?

➤ Yellow gold is an alloy of gold, copper, and silver.

➤ White gold is an alloy of gold, copper, and nickel or platinum.

➤ Pink gold has gold, copper, and silver. The pink color comes from greater amounts of copper.

➤ Red gold has even more copper.

➤ Green gold has silver as its main component, along with gold, zinc, and copper.

➤ Purple gold is an alloy of gold and aluminum.

What's Up, Doc?

The purity, or fineness, of gold is measured in *karats*. ("Carat" is used for gemstones.) The word probably comes from ancient times, when the seeds of the carob plant were used to measure the weight of gemstones.

Tricks of the Trade

How can you tell real gold from fake? Phony gold will dissolve in nitric acid, whereas real gold won't. A jeweler can perform this test for you.

Caveat Emptor

The Federal Trade Commission requires that all gold jewelry sold in America be labeled with karats. Therefore, a 14K piece of gold jewelry cannot be advertised solely as "gold"; it must also be stamped "14K."

The scale goes from 1 to 24, with 24 karats (abbreviated as 24K) being the purest form of the metal. A standard alloy sold in America is 18K gold (18 parts out of 24 are gold), which would be 75 percent pure gold. You will also find 14K, 12K, and 10K. Antique rings are sometimes 22K; the high amount of gold makes them soft and helps explain why they are often very thin and worn.

Imported gold jewelry will often have the amount of gold expressed in a fraction or decimal rather than the K format. For example, 750/1000 and .750 are the same as 18K. To make your life more complex, there is no international gold scale. Japan, for instance, recognizes nine grades of gold between 24K and 9K, while Italy has five (from 18K to 8K).

Anything less than 14K gold is generally considered costume jewelry; anything less than 10K is definitely the jewelry equivalent of a fun fur. There are a number of ways to cover base metal with gold; all are considered costume jewelry. Here are some terms used in the jewelry industry to describe these methods:

➤ **Vermeil** is gold-coated silver or other metals.

➤ **Gold-filled** pieces have a gold coating ¹⁄₂₀ or *more* of the total weight of the piece.

➤ **Gold-plated** pieces have a gold coating ¹⁄₂₀ or *less* of the total weight of the piece.

➤ **Gold electroplate** is a coating no less than 7 millionths of an inch.

➤ **Gold wash** is anything thinner than electroplate.

Big Deals

In contrast to gold, which has been the stuff of jewelry forever, platinum didn't become the stuff of jewelry until the dawn of the twentieth century. Its rise in popularity was followed by other platinum favorites such as Marilyn and Jayne. "Platinum" refers both to a specific metal and to a group of six related metals whose names suggest they would be equally at home on the periodic table: *platinum, palladium, rhodium, ruthenium, iridium,* and *osmium.*

Native American Jewelry

The days when a tourist could buy an exquisite squash-blossom necklace in a teepee are as long past as the buffalo. During the past few decades, every Native American art form has zoomed up faster than a harried executive's blood pressure. The finest examples of American Indian art are already in museums or noted private collections.

A few years ago, there was a real rush of interest in Native American jewelry, but the interest has slacked off somewhat. Buyers have become disillusioned because of imitations and lack of knowledge about what they were buying. "Turquoise" may be plastic. Unwary collectors have bought pieces from gift shops in Arizona and New Mexico, returned home, and found their prizes stamped "Taiwan" on the back. If you're planning to buy collectible-grade Native American jewelry, make sure you receive a valid bill of sale guaranteeing what you got.

Tricks of the Trade

Some collectors of American Indian art have turned to Eskimo items in an attempt to get in on the bottom floor. Soapstone figures, bone masks, jewelry, and scrimshaw pieces are affordable and popular. Average scrimshaw prices range between $200 and $800 but can soar into the thousands—not affordable to most of us!

Netsuke

Some of the smallest items valued by jewelry collectors are *netsuke* (pronounced *net-ski*). These button-size toggles were used by the Japanese to attach their purses to their sashes as part of their traditional dress.

Netsuke were made for hundreds of years and reached their peak as an art form between the 1600s and 1800s. Usually made of wood or ivory, they were carved in a great many shapes, the one proviso being that they should not have any sharp points to catch on clothing.

More than 2,000 artists made signed netsuke, and there are many more unsigned ones. Since the 1850s, fake netsuke have been made. The price of the genuine article reached a peak in 1980 and 1981, when one collector reputedly paid $250,000 for a single netsuke. Since then, prices have come down.

Happy Days Are Here Again: Jewelry of the 1940s and 1950s

The 1940s and 1950s boasted big cars, big families, and some big jewelry. *Costume jewelry*—inexpensive funky pieces—from this era is in great demand among collectors. With costume jewelry, the design is often more important than the material content.

Big Deals

The outbreak of World War II was marked by a new fashion for women: brooches with the insignia of various army regiments, the Royal Air Force, and the Royal Navy. To cater to all pocketbooks, these were made in diamonds and gold as well as rhinestones and base metals. Both varieties are hot collectibles today.

Jewelry from half a century ago varies greatly in materials and look. Some rings and bracelets were made from wood, glass, inexpensive metal, and plastic; the inexpensive materials thus make them very reasonable collectibles. Here are some of the most highly collected pieces, arranged by materials:

1. **Enamel.** Enameled silver jewelry is very much in demand by collectors. Pieces start around $30. For example:

   ➤ Delicate blue enameled clip-back earrings with pavé trim. Clips have an open backed design. $28.

   ➤ Enamel and copper necklace set. Enamel is robin's-egg blue with copper open-work overlay. Each link on the necklace measures 1½ inches by ½ inch. Necklace measures 17½ inches. Ear clips measure 1 inch by ½ inch. Excellent condition. $125.

➤ 1940s signed Coro owl clip earrings. Gold plated with enamel paint. Owls have large faux blue-sapphire eyes. Clear small rhinestones on the top of the head, wings, and tail feathers. Clips can be worn separately or together as a brooch. Measures 2 inches by 2 inches. $150.

2. **Metal and glass.** These materials were often combined to simulate the look of diamonds and silver. Many of the pieces have a Victorian look, but there are some hideously gaudy pieces that Liberace would have loved. Actually, I collect them, too. Rhinestone expansion bracelets run between $50 and $100; plastic and rhinestone specimens cost less than $50 on average. Here are some actual ads:

➤ Round, clear rhinestone, cushioned ear clips in gold tone. Clips have design patent number but no signature. Measures $15/16$ inch in diameter and original price tag from the early 60s is still attached. $28.

➤ Sapphire blue and clear rhinestone clip earrings measure 2¼ inches long with a pear-shaped stone at the bottom. Prong set in rhodium. $30.

➤ Large oval clips with two rows of clear rhinestones. Two stones are graying. Earrings measure 1¼ inches long by ⅞ inch wide. $30.

3. **Plastic.** Collectors seek out Bakelite bracelets, rings, brooches, pins, and hair clips in bright orange, green, red, yellow, and blue. These usually sell for under $50 each. Character pins featuring Mickey Mouse, Donald Duck, Goofy, and other Disney characters are also highly collectible but still reasonably priced. Here are some recently advertised pieces:

➤ Three Bakelite spacer bangles in butterscotch, tan swirl, and chocolate. $18.

➤ Tube-shaped root beer Bakelite bangle embedded with brass pins with floral tops. $28.

➤ Set of seven Bakelite bangles, five butterscotch and two orange. $46.

➤ Pair of tomato red Bakelite bangles. $48.

➤ Cherry red Bakelite domed bangle bracelet measures 2⅝ inches inside diameter, $11/16$ inch wide and ½ inch thick. $52.

4. **Sterling silver.** Geometric necklaces, pendants, and earrings are sought-after by sophisticated collectors. George Jensen pieces command prices starting around $100. Big, clunky charm bracelets have enjoyed a rebirth in popularity and the trend shows no signs of abating.

5. **Wood.** Wooden pins and earrings, often boasting large jungle plants and animals, are very popular. They go for about $5 to $10 each.

Caveat Emptor

Broken costume jewelry is very difficult to get repaired. Only the rarest pieces are worth the trouble and expense of repair. In nearly all instances, you're better off waiting for a piece in good or excellent condition to come to market.

Fortunately for collectors of this type of jewelry, it's relatively easy to find great pieces. I've hit up all my aged aunts as well as the aged relatives of friends and co-workers. For example, my nifty ice-blue sequined clip-on earrings came from Betsy Sullivan's 90-year-old aunt.

Yard sales, charity bazaars, online auctions, and estate auctions are also great sources. Better-quality examples such as those by Jensen are offered at auctions specializing in 1940s and 1950s memorabilia. Other collectible signatures to look for are Miriam Haskell, Weiss, and Trifari. Try to get complete sets—they're worth much more that way. Earrings and necklaces, for example, often came with bangles. Compare all pieces in a set to make sure that they match.

The Least You Need to Know

➤ Technically, antique jewelry must be 100 years old, but now anything two or three generations old is considered an antique.

➤ Gold must be labeled in karats to indicate its purity.

➤ It is very tricky to find authentic Native American jewelry.

➤ Be wary of how gemstones are labeled and colored.

➤ If you want as many rings as a frat house coffee table, consider collecting twentieth-century costume jewelry. It's affordable, fun, and appreciating in value.

Heavy Metal

In This Chapter

➤ Silver, the siren of metals

➤ Pewter, copper, brass, bronze, iron, and steel collectibles

➤ Bottle tickets, brass beds, and lithographed tins

History remembers Paul Revere for his midnight ride in 1775 from Boston to Lexington to warn the armed American patriots, the Minutemen, that the British troops were on the march. But Revere had already assured himself of a lasting reputation among discerning collectors for his skill as a silversmith. Today, Revere's finely engraved silver pieces still generate high bids in the world's auction rooms.

Silversmiths and other metalworkers have always had a place in history, from the ancient Egyptians on. In this chapter, you'll learn how to evaluate the different types of silver, from sterling to plate. Then you'll find out about the base metals used to make collectible items: pewter, copper, brass, bronze, iron, and steel. Finally, I'll clue you in on some other important metal collectibles, including bottle tickets, brass beds, and lithographed tin cans.

The Silver Standard

Collecting silver poses both problems and opportunities. The main problem is that pieces from the 1700s that are clearly marked with their maker are out of the reach for the average collector—that's you and me, kiddo. But in the plus column, a lot of beautiful, collectible silver is still available. Most of it was made between 1840 and 1930, and there's more than enough to go around.

In its pure state, silver is too soft to be made into anything but mush. Add a dash of copper, however, and you get a shiny, strong alloy known as "sterling silver." Let's look at some of the different types of silver that collectors seek.

American Sterling

Sterling silver is .925 pure silver. "Sterling" is the most frequently found mark on American sterling silver, but you may also find the notations "925," "925/1000," and "Sterling. Weighted" on pure silver pieces. "Sterling. Weighted" means that the piece is sterling silver but a dark, powdery leadlike substance has been added to the base to provide additional balance and weight to the piece. Almost any piece that is marked "sterling" will be more valuable than one marked "Sterling. Weighted."

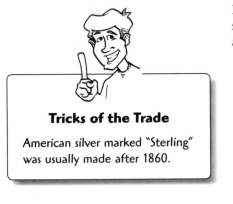

Tricks of the Trade

American silver marked "Sterling" was usually made after 1860.

Looking for some interesting and affordable sterling silver to collect? Art Nouveau may fit your bill. For example:

➤ A small sterling silver dish from the late 1800s goes for under $100.

➤ You can find a sterling silver magnifying glass or a letter knife for about $100 each.

➤ A sterling silver dressing table set from the turn of the century runs over $300. Add some cut crystal to the set and you add about $100.

Dresser sets featuring ornate silver-backed hairbrushes like this one are an affordable and graceful addition to a silver collection.

American Coin Silver

Before 1850 "solid" silver pieces contained only 900/1000 parts of pure silver (or less), with 100/1000 parts other metals. Known as "coin silver," it was often marked *coin, pure coin, standards, premium,* or *dollar.* Sometimes the letter *C* or *D* was used; other times, coin silver was marked with the maker's name. Just to make your collecting life a little more difficult, sometimes it wasn't marked at all.

To add insult to injury, the silver could be marked with pseudo hallmarks. American silversmiths slapped these faux silver hallmarks on their products to suggest that their silver was as fine as British silver, which had clear hallmarks. The American hallmarks included profiles, animals, and stars. Since American coin silver can be marked in so many ways, it is often overlooked and is even shunned as (horrors!) plated silver.

Here are some prices to give you an idea of the market for coin silver collectibles:

➤ Small coin silver spoons from the early 1800s sell for between $10 and $25 each; large spoons, $250 for a set of six.

➤ A coin silver serving dish from the late 1700s might fetch as much as $300.

English Sterling Silver

Early Americans may have cornered the market on freedom, wide open spaces, and bears, but the Brits had it all over us in silver. Collectors of antique silver drool at the very hint of English sterling silver because to many people it epitomizes the silversmith's art.

Antique English sterling silver can be marked in several ways:

1. A full lion, facing left.

2. A letter. These changed over the years, so consult an English silver book for the full alphabet.

3. The silversmith's hallmark, usually his initials. The most valuable antique English silver was produced by Hester Bateman, Paul Storr, Paul de Lamerie, and Matthew Boulton. Beware: Their marks have been remade as many times as Michael Jackson's face.

4. A "guild" mark, telling where the silver was made. The most frequently seen ones are the anchor (Birmingham), crown (Sheffield), castle (Edinburgh), and harp (Dublin).

5. The head of a monarch. It may or may not appear.

Caveat Emptor

Collector alert: Avoid silver plate produced in the East, especially India. It is not high quality.

Tricks of the Trade

Old silver pieces not marked are often worth more than those that are marked.

Continental Silver

The Yanks and Brits didn't have the silver market cornered; the silver centers in Europe also produced high-quality sterling. Unfortunately, it's very difficult to identify Continental silver. Here's some general information so that you can tell whether you have stumbled upon a find of genuine Continental silver:

➤ Antique French silver sometimes carried an ornate capital letter with a crown or a fleur-de-lis.

➤ Antique German silver often sports a half-moon or crescent and a crown, along with the number "800."

➤ Eastern European countries marked their silver with a castle or shaped center design encircled with numbers.

➤ Old Italian silver can have a Roman or classical portrait with other hallmarks.

Sterling Silver from the Former Soviet Union

Russian artisans are noted for their skill with silver. In the main, Russian silver is quite valuable and certainly an important part of many a silver collection. In addition, Polish and Hungarian silversmiths created (and continue to create) magnificent pieces. Collectors prize the religious artifacts made from silver in these countries.

This sterling silver piece is a fine example of Hungarian silver.

Danish Silver

In addition to great butter cookies and the Little Mermaid, the Danish people produced some highly collectible silver. George Jensen (1866–1935) heads the list for his beautiful Art Nouveau and Art Deco styles. Other top-notch Danish silver designers include Johan Rohde, Harold Nielsen, Sigvard Bernadotte, Kay Bojesen, Evald Nielson, Frantz Hingelberg, Holger Kyster, Hans Hansen, Mogins Ballin, Peter Hertz, and Henning Koppel.

Fortunately for collectors, Danish silver is easy to authenticate because the maker's mark appears on all the silver the Danes produced between 1490 and 1893. Since then, retailers have added their names to the maker's mark as well.

Victorian and Modern Silver Plate

Once shunned by serious collectors of silver, many silver-plated pieces from those stuffy Victorians are now hot. The rising prices of sterling silver, the dearth of fine examples, and the general lust for collectibles has fueled this fire. How can you tell which silver-plate pieces to collect? Try these guidelines:

1. Look for pieces with copper bases; they're often the best-quality silver plate.

2. Examine the piece for smoothly finished surfaces, crisp designs, and the depth of the raised work.

3. Among the hottest silver-plate collectibles are pieces that are no longer made, such as Victorian pickle castors, epergnes, baskets, and lemonade pitchers.

Not to make your life any more difficult than it already is, but silver plate can have nearly as many marks as a Dalmatian. Well, at least silver plate doesn't shed or drool.

Look for these marks to identify silver plate:

➤ A1

➤ Alaska silver

➤ Argentine silver

➤ Craig silver

➤ EPBM (Electroplate on Britannia metal)

➤ EPC (Electroplate on copper)

➤ EPNS (Electroplate silver on a nickel base)

➤ EPWM (Electroplate on nickel, white metal mounts)

➤ German silver

➤ Inlaid silver

➤ Nevada silver

➤ NS (nickel silver)

➤ Plate

➤ Quadruple

➤ Sheffield Reproduction

➤ Silver on copper

➤ Silver plate

➤ Triple plate

Tricks of the Trade

How can you tell if unmarked silver is really silver and not silver plate? Look at the place of greatest wear, such as the back of a spoon. If you see a different color showing through, usually brass-looking, you will know that you've got silver plate, not solid sterling or coin silver.

Price check:

➤ A silver-plate creamer, sugar bowl, and tray made by F.B. Rogers in the early twentieth century runs about $100.

➤ Commemorative spoons your bag? One from the 1893 Columbia Exposition can join your collection for a mere $50.

➤ A silver-plate brush and mirror set from the turn of the century runs under $250 and is a good investment.

When you're trying to determine a fair price for a collectible piece of silver, always consult a reliable price guide, such as *The Official Identification and Price Guide to Silver and Silverplate,* by Jeri Schwartz (House of Collectibles). Remember, however, that prices quoted are not guarantees of value.

The Baser Metals: Pewter, Copper, Brass, Bronze, Iron, Steel

Silver gets a lot of good press because it's shiny and sexy. But that's not to say that other collectible metals don't have their day in the sun. For every collector who covets silver, there's one who lusts after pewter, copper, brass, bronze, iron, or steel.

Collectors don't seek out these metals because they can't afford silver, either. True collectors are attracted to these base metals because of their unique qualities. Like children in a large family, each one of these metals is special in its own way and valued for its unique qualities. Let me introduce you to the pleasures of pewter, copper, brass, bronze, iron, and steel.

The Poor Man's Silver: Pewter

As you'll learn in Chapter 25, "Spit and Polish," pewter is an alloy of tin. For nearly 500 years, it was one of the most important metals found in any home; even a pauper owned a pewter plate. Since it is a soft alloy, pewter had a relatively short working life. As a result, there are few survivors from the zillions of pewter items that were in daily use.

The earliest pieces found date from the 1600s. The most commonly found antique pewter objects are plates and dishes from the 1700s and mugs from the 1800s. American pewter from the 1700s is harder to find than a parking spot in Manhattan during rush hour.

It was not until the twentieth century that pewter became a collectible. Almost at once, fakes were created. Unfortunately, old pewter is easy to fake. In France, clever scam artists place modern reproductions of valuable old pewter in grass cuttings to give the new pewter a convincingly old patina. Acid is also used to make new pewter look old. Some of these methods are so convincing that even sophisticated auctioneers have had the pewter pulled over their eyes, so to speak.

So how can you tell a valuable old pewter piece from a fake? Fakers are savvy enough to stamp "genuine" marks on their work, so cross out this method. But even if they leave the marks off, genuine old pewter was not always marked, so it's a wash. Instead of searching for marks, examine the surface of the piece carefully. Ask yourself these questions:

➤ How did the piece get its bruises?

➤ Do the bruises match real wear? Fakers tend to bang away at a piece in a pattern to make it look old.

➤ Is the piece oxidized where you would expect it to be? It takes at least 50 years for a real oxide to develop. Look for bubbles—these are very hard to fake.

Interested in prices? Here are some benchmarks:

➤ A porringer with open-work handles from the 1700s recently sold for $400.

➤ A teapot made in Connecticut in the early 1800s fetched $350.

➤ A pewter coffeepot made before 1850 sells for $150 to $300, depending on condition and style.

➤ A pewter bowl made in New York around 1850 should set you back less than $200; a very large plate (16 inches), about $350.

Tricks of the Trade

Victorian factory–made pewter is a good investment. In general, it's much cheaper than earlier pewter, and it comes in a wide variety of forms. Best of all, most metal collectors haven't cornered the market yet.

The Alloy Kids: Copper, Bronze, Brass

Since copper is too soft to be used on its own, it became an alloy. The most common alloys of copper are *bronze* and *brass*. Bronze is made by adding tin to copper; brass is an alloy of zinc and copper.

It wasn't until 1945 that brass and bronze pieces were widely collected; as a result, few fakes were produced then. Today, the market is flooded with excellent reproductions of wall sconces, alms dishes, ladles, candle molds, and other popular and valuable forms.

Copper alloys present special difficulties to connoisseurs because these pieces are difficult to date and authenticate. But, hey, that doesn't stop determined collectors like you and me. As a result, prices for brass and copper are high and have been so for many years. Pieces in great demand—marked andirons, kettles, and early buttons—command princely sums. Are you of more modest means? Consider focusing on smaller utensils and later spun-brass kettles.

Check out these prices before you go shopping:

➤ Copper saucepans with brass handles from the mid-1800s sell for $100 and up.

➤ Copper cooking pots with wrought-iron handles, dating from the 1800s, cost about $100.

➤ Turn-of-the-century copper funnels? About $25 to $75. Mugs or oilcans? Around $50 each.

Tricks of the Trade

Hand-cut screws are a tip-off that an object was made before or during the Industrial Revolution. Machine-made modern screws date from after 1850.

➤ Brass Pennsylvania-Dutch punch-decorated bed warmers from the 1800s go from $150 up to $400.

➤ A brass cattle bell fetches cattle if rung and about $80 if sold; a brass spoon, about $60.

Bronze figures are an extremely popular collectible. The signed statues, most of which were made in France and Russia, are among the most eagerly sought. Bronze statues produced today command astronomical prices—if the artist is famous. Some collectors are happier buying the work of known contemporary artists than investing in older pieces that have no history.

Steel Yourself

Until the 1800s, steel was difficult to make, so it was used chiefly for tools, weapons, and some jewelry. Improved manufacturing techniques led to better combinations of carbon and iron, and so steel became a major player from the early Victorian period on.

Iron, in contrast, has been used since earliest times. Until the Industrial Revolution, wrought iron was by far the most common use of this metal. Iron tends to oxidize fast, so it is easy to make reproductions look old. But wear isn't so easy to fake, which makes this a good way to separate the real from the fake. Look for wear at the points where an object would have been put to the hardest use.

Here are some sample prices:

➤ A cast-iron tea kettle from 1860 sells for about $250.

➤ Large wrought-iron serving tools from 1830 cost about $200 each; a hanging griddle from 1850, about $150.

➤ Wrought-iron New England trivets dating from the 1800s should cost you under $100 each; a wrought-iron candy mold from the turn of the century, about $150.

Collectors' Darlings

Bottle tickets, brass beds, and lithographed tins are a few of the metal items that hold a special place in collectors' hearts and wallets. Here's the scoop:

1. **Ring around the bottle: bottle tickets.** Bottle tickets are silver beverage labels used in eighteenth- and nineteenth-century England and America before modern packaging techniques. They are labeled with the names of the liquor, such as *whiskey, port,* and *brandy.* Important manufacturers include Tiffany and Gorham.

2. **A good night's sleep: brass beds.** In the 1950s, most brass beds were tossed on the trash heap. No doubt the tossers kicked themselves soon after when brass beds became a highly popular collectible. Contrary to public opinion, most brass beds are not made entirely of brass, since the posts would be too soft to support the weight of the mattress. On good-quality brass beds, the ornaments will be solid brass.

   With brass beds, more is better. The fancier the bed, the better. The more decorations, the more collectible. Condition is also crucial. Worn brass beds are a bad deal because replating is expensive.

Tricks of the Trade

How brassy is your bed? Check it with a magnet. The magnet will cling to the steel, but not to solid brass.

3. **Try to contain your excitement: lithographed tins.** In the 1870s, new machinery made it possible to print in color. In the resulting avalanche of printed items, one stands out to collectors of metal items: tin containers. These containers held everything from coffee to cookies, grease to gunpowder. What matters to collectors of these tins?

   ➤ Age, color, and condition are the touchstones.

   ➤ Avoid repainted tins.

   ➤ Rust harms value.

   ➤ Oddly shaped tins and those holding unusual products command high prices.

The Least You Need to Know

➤ Silver comes in different grades. From most to least silver content, these are sterling silver, coin silver, and silver plate.

➤ Many objects made of pewter, copper, brass, bronze, iron, and steel are also hot collectibles.

➤ Bottle tickets, brass beds, and color lithographed tins are popular metal-based collectibles.

Part 7

Taking Care of Business

Two men tried to pull the front off a cash machine by running a chain from the machine to the bumper of their truck. Instead of pulling the front panel off the machine, however, they pulled the bumper off their truck. Scared, they left the scene and drove home ... with the chain still attached to the machine ... with their bumper still attached to the chain ... with their vehicle's license plate still attached to the bumper.

This just goes to show that it pays to plan ahead—especially when you're trying to rob a cash machine or creating a collection of prized objects.

In Part 7, you'll learn how to protect your purchases. I'll teach you how to inventory and insure your beautiful and valuable things. And what about keeping your collection in tip-top condition? Not to worry; you'll learn how to display, store, and clean the items in your collection.

Chapter 24

Inventory and Insure

In This Chapter

➤ It's inventory time!

➤ Worksheet wonders

➤ Protecting your assets

➤ Insurance 101

The average collection represents a considerable emotional and financial investment. You've put a lot of *yourself*—as well as time and money—into gathering your treasured items. A growing collection tends to establish a presence of its own, like a beloved family pet. All collectors are concerned about taking the best possible care of their collections, but relatively few know what to do. As a result, they do not take full advantage of what's easily available to them. Not you.

In this chapter, you will learn how to inventory your collection. You will discover how to find out what you really have in your collection—and why it's vitally important to know. Then I'll give you a quick course in insuring your pretty things to make sure they're fully protected.

Cataloging: Do You Know What You Own?

Quick—how many radios do you have? What's the serial number on your camera—you know, the one from the 1950s? Where did you put cousin Ethel's pearls and Uncle Eric's coin collection? How many Paul buttons do you have in your Beatles' memorabilia collection?

Tricks of the Trade

Why not get the whole family involved? Every year when I inventory my collections, I lasso the kids to help tote that barge and lift that bale. This is also a great way to keep them up to speed on what they're inheriting.

Most people put things away carelessly, often cramming things in closets just before the in-laws arrive. Maybe you reassure yourself with a brave, "I'll sort the closet/drawer/attic and under the bed in a few weeks," but weeks stretch into months and years. By then, you might be too frightened to reach under the bed. Lord knows what's living there.

Bite the bullet, plunge in, and take the chest test. Complete the following Household Inventory to start sorting all your possessions. Describe each object in as much detail as possible. Here are some details to include:

➤ Size (height, weight, depth, length)
➤ Color
➤ Condition
➤ Number of items (for example, 12 sterling silver soup spoons)
➤ Brand name (for example, International Sterling Silver)
➤ Pattern (for example, Wild Rose)
➤ Age
➤ Serial numbers and other identification marks
➤ Cost
➤ Source

Household Inventory Worksheet

Take a complete inventory of your possessions by completing this worksheet. If you need more space, add additional sheets of paper.

Kitchen

Collectible ceramics _____

_____

_____

Collectible furniture _____

_____

_____

Collectible glass _____

_____

_____

Collectible household tools _____

_____

Collectible metalware _____
_____

Collectible wine _____
_____
_____

Other collectibles _____
_____

Dining Room

Art _____
_____

Collectible candlesticks _____
_____
_____

Collectible ceramics _____
_____
_____

Collectible china _____
_____
_____

Collectible furniture _____
_____
_____

Collectible crystal _____
_____
_____

Collectible linen _____
_____

Collectible silver _____
_____
_____

Other collectibles _____
_____
_____

Family Room/Living Room

Cameras (make and model) _____
_____

Collectible books _____
_____

continues

continued

Collectible clocks _____

_____

_____

Collectible dolls, games, toys _____

_____

Collectible furniture _____

_____

_____

Collectible lamps _____

_____

_____

Collectible records _____

_____

_____

Collectible textiles, such as carpets _____

_____

Collectible tools _____

_____

Computers (make and model) _____

Collectible paintings _____

Collectible prints _____

Collectible statues _____

Televisions (make and model) _____

VCR (make and model) _____

Collectible radios _____

Stereo (make and model) _____

Other collectibles _____

_____

Bedroom #1

Art _____

_____

_____

Collectible furniture _____

_____

_____

Collectible jewelry _____

_____

_____

Collectible quilts _____

_____

_____

Collectible lamps_____

_____

Other collectibles _____

_____

_____

Bedroom #2

Collectible furniture _____

_____

_____

Other collectibles _____

_____

_____

Bedroom #3

Collectible furniture _____

_____

_____

Other collectibles _____

_____

_____

Attics, Basements, and Other Storage Areas

Collectible baseball and other cards _____

_____

Collectible comics _____

_____

continues

continued

Collectible books _____

_____

Collectible plastic toys _____

_____

Collectible plush toys _____

_____

_____

Collectible records and tapes _____

_____

_____

Other collectibles _____

_____

_____

Bank Vault

Collectible jewelry _____

_____

_____

Collectible coins _____

_____

Collectible stamps _____

_____

Stock certificates _____

_____

Tricks of the Trade

There are several easy-to-use home inventory computer programs available. If you go this route, be sure to print out a hard copy of the inventory and store it in your bank safe deposit box or a fireproof filing cabinet.

Do You Know What's in Your Collection?

Can you accurately describe every item in your collection if something happened to it? Quickly now, how many of the pens in your collection have black barrels? How many of your prints have wooden frames? How many have metal frames? How many of your candlesticks have fluted bottoms—and how many don't? When you buy pieces one at a time, it's easy to forget the specific details of pieces purchased years ago.

Now that you've spent a weekend figuring out what you own, you are ready to really look at your collection. In this exercise, you are going to separate the collector from the pack rat, the connoisseur from the Collier brother.

Collection Inventory Worksheet

Catalog your collection by filling out this chart. If necessary, add additional sheets of paper.

Name of collection _____

Title of Piece/Current Description	Source	Date of Purchase	Cost	Value
1.				
2.				
3.				
4.				
5.				
6.				
7.				
8.				
9.				
10.				
11.				
12.				
13.				
14.				
15.				
16.				
17.				
18.				
19.				
20.				
21.				
22.				
23.				
24.				
25.				

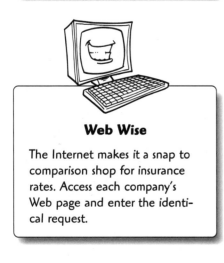

Now that you know exactly what's in your collection, where you've stored it, and what it's worth, you can begin learning the best way to take care of it all.

An Ounce of Prevention ...

Some collectors aren't aware of the true value of their collections because they can't believe that prices have risen as fast as they have. Even some insurance experts and museum curators may not be sure what a collectible is worth. Rest assured that there is one class of people who know exactly what specific collectibles go for—thieves. That's why insurance was invented. And that's why you should have as much of it as you need or want.

No matter what Ed MacMahon assures you when you're staring bleary-eyed at the television at 3 A.M., you're the only person who can decide what kind of insurance you want and how much you are willing to buy. Insuring collectibles is complex because agents deal most often with life insurance, homeowner's insurance, and car insurance—not collectibles insurance. Even so-called insurance experts may not be sufficiently versed in policies for collectibles. I've cut through the sales spiel to give you a crash course in Insurance 101. Start here:

Cover Yourself

These hints can make it easier for you to get the insurance coverage you need—no more, no less.

➤ Standard homeowners' policies or tenants' policies insure the contents of your home, apartment, or place of residence.

➤ Standard homeowners' policies have limits on the amount of loss you can claim for specific items. For example, even if your coin collection is worth $10,000, you're limited to a clearly specified amount under a standard homeowners' policy. Here are some examples:

$200 limit on coins and gold

$1,000 limit on jewelry

$2,000 limit on firearms

$2,500 limit on silver flatware

➤ Depending on your policy, you will be paid for complete replacement of the item or for the replacement cost minus wear-and-tear (called *depreciation*).

➤ Your insurance claim cannot exceed the amount of your coverage under your basic homeowner's policy. If you have $100,000 of insurance coverage, you can't claim a $150,000 loss. (Actually, you can *claim* anything you want, but you'll get zip.)

➤ Most standard homeowners' policies cover only those hazards listed in the policy, such as fire, lightning, windstorm, riots, vandalism, and theft. Check your policy: You are probably covered for a car running into your house or a blimp landing on your roof—but not for a flood. Your collection might survive blimp pressure, but not water damage.

➤ Many easily available homeowners' insurance policies will not insure especially valuable or irreplaceable collectibles. For this reason, collectors often buy special insurance policies in addition to their regular homeowners' policies.

➤ The easier the collectible is to lose, the more it will cost to insure it. A grand piano sitting in your living room will cost less to insure than the antique pin on your lapel, even if both are worth $50,000. Why? The likelihood of a quick-fingered thief stealing the pin is greater than the chance of a refugee from the World Wrestling Federation carrying away your piano.

Learn the Lingo

Depreciation is the insurance term for replacement cost minus a deduction for damage. For example, an antique pearl necklace appraised at $500 in perfect condition might be depreciated 25 percent for three missing pearls.

Tricks of the Trade

Whether you have insurance or not, get a professional photographer to take high-quality pictures of your items of value. On the back of each picture, describe the item. If possible, attach the bill of sale. Save the photos in a secure place. They will prove that you did indeed own the items, if something happens to them.

➤ The cost of the insurance policy for a valuable collection can exceed the cost of the entire collection. If this happens to you, consider insuring only the most valuable pieces in your collection.

➤ Most insurance companies offer special collectibles policies for the following items: fine arts, jewelry, cameras, china, crystal, silver, musical instruments, stamps, coins.

Learn the Lingo

Replacement cost means the cost, at the time of the loss, of a new article identical to the one damaged, destroyed, or stolen.

Walk This Way

So how can you make sure you get exactly the insurance you need for your collection? Follow these five steps:

1. Take the time to find a broker who knows the ropes about collectibles insurance.
2. Shop around for the best insurance rates.
3. Talk to other collectors in your geographic area.
4. Don't sign anything you don't understand.
5. Review your policy every year.

The following chart shows some of the most-often-used insurance policies available for collectibles:

The Inside Scoop on the Insurance Biz

What It's Called ...	What You Get ...
1. Actual cash value	1. Replacement cost of the item or an item of like kind—minus depreciation
2. Replacement cost guarantee	2. The lost article replaced with something of the same value by today's standards. The item is not depreciated.
3. Scheduled	3. An add-on to your policy. endorsement In case of loss, you get the appraised value for your collectibles. The collection must be appraised beforehand.
4. Valuable	4. The amount that you and the items policy company agree upon. Since this negotiation may degenerate into the Hundred Years' War, the amount may have to be established by an expert who serves as a mediator. The collection must be appraised beforehand.

If your collectibles have been stolen, you can place a free recovery ad with the Antiques & Collectibles Dealer Association and the *Antique Week* Newspapers Web site. Entries will appear on the site for two months, unless they are notified before that time that the items have been recovered. Listings may be resubmitted for an additional period. Their Web site is www.thefinfo@collectors.org.

The Least You Need to Know

➤ You should catalog all your possessions, especially the items in your collection.

➤ Include information on the object's size, color, condition, brand, age, cost, and source. Note any serial numbers, too.

➤ Insuring collectibles is complex. Make sure that you get the coverage that you need to protect your specific collection.

➤ Always keep all receipts. It's not a bad idea to take pictures of your valuables, too.

Chapter 25

Spit and Polish

In This Chapter

➤ Displaying your pretty things

➤ Storing the good stuff

➤ Spring cleaning for your collection

➤ Enjoying your collection

"Oh, I'd never display my plush toys," an acquaintance once told me. "They might fade or get dusty," she said. Each to his own taste, I always say, but if this collector knew how to display and clean her valuables correctly, she might think differently. That's what this chapter is all about.

First, I'll suggest different ways to display your various collections to their advantage. You'll discover how to get the maximum pleasure from your desirables, collectibles, and antiques—while minimizing chances for damage. You'll learn how an effective display can enhance your appreciation many times over. Then we'll explore safe and easy ways to clean the items in your collections. No muss, no fuss: just lots of clean things!

A Place for Everything and Everything in Its Place: Displaying and Storing

Why own something beautiful if you can't display it—or at least some of it? But in order to preserve and safeguard your collectibles, you must restrict their exposure to harmful elements. Harmful or inadequate displaying and storage methods can speed up the deterioration of your collectibles or result in damage occurring. This is not to

Web Wise

For further information, why not contact the Ephemera Society of America, Inc. It's a nonprofit organization devoted to furthering the collection, study, and preservation of ephemera (paper items). They can be found on the Web at www.ephemerasociety.org.

Caveat Emptor

Beware of cabinet lighting. A too-bright light or one that is left on too long can crack certain types of porcelain, especially pieces that are already damaged. Glass shelving is a good idea because it helps you keep the wattage to a minimum but still get light into all corners of the cabinet.

say that you can't enjoy your collection, but some pieces are best chuckled over in the dark. First, let's look at two popular storage methods: albums and cabinets.

Albums and Scrapbooks

Ephemera such as cigarette cards, playing cards, bookmarks, and stamps should never be stuck into a scrapbook. Even the small translucent stamp hinges are unsuitable. One of the neatest ways to display such items is to cut a diagonal nick in the paper of the album leaf and insert the ephemera in place—the same way that photographs in albums are held in place with stick-on corners.

You can also buy the stick-on corners or make them yourself by cutting diagonally across the corners of envelopes.

Cabinets

Nothing sets off your small collectibles like a fine cabinet—and it also serves to protect your collection. Match the type of cabinet to the type of collectible.

➤ Use cabinets with simple rectangular shelves for books.

➤ Use cabinets with ornate back paneling for china, crystal, and the like.

➤ Use cabinets with elaborate glass shelves for china, crystal, and so on.

➤ Use cabinets with glazed side panels to display objects.

Now, let's look at specific ways to display and store the most popular types of collectibles.

Glass

You know these eternal truths: Whichever line *you* are standing in will be the one that moves the slowest, anything that tastes good is bad for you, and glass breaks. The rule of thumb in my house: The more I treasure a piece of glass, the more likely I am to break it. As a result, I strongly recommend that you store glass collectibles in a locked cabinet, under a dome, or in a Lucite box, and don't invite me over to handle your glass. Here are some other suggestions:

➤ Handle only one glass collectible at a time. Two-handed glass handling is so tricky that it should be an Olympic event.

➤ Glass expands when heated and shrinks when cooled. For this reason, don't store glass near sources of very cold or very hot air, such as air conditioners or heating vents.

➤ Some types of glass can be damaged by sunlight. Discoloration can occur, so keep glass away from the sun's direct rays.

Paper Collectibles

Even the finest paper is fragile—that's why it's paper and not prestressed concrete. Paper can be easily damaged by soiled hands—or even by moisture from clean hands. Corners snap off, sheets tear, edges break. To prevent this kind of damage, frame prints immediately, or store them in special sleeves or drawers designed for that purpose. Also:

Tricks of the Trade

When it comes to storing paper collectibles, ultraviolet light is the baddest of the bad light boys because it serves as a catalyst for many chemical reactions. This includes the formation of acid compounds that can make paper brittle and weak.

➤ **Keep light levels low.** Some people cannot so much as look at a pastry without gaining weight. Paper has the same problem with light: Every time a paper product is exposed to light, damage occurs. Ideally, paper collectibles should be stored in the dark, exposed only to light when needed. If you must use lights, avoid fluorescence.

➤ **Keep the temperature low and constant.** Keep the room temperature between 68° and 72°F, with as little variation as possible. For every 10° drop in temperature, the life of your paper is doubled. High temperatures also support the growth of mold and fungus.

➤ **Keep humidity low and constant.** Relative humidity levels should be no more than 50 percent, no matter what the season. Paper is *hygroscopic,* which means that it gives off and absorbs humidity from its surroundings. Bouncing between high and low levels of humidity accelerates this process. In addition, high humidity allows mold and bacteria to grow, which can lead to a paper breakdown called *foxing.*

➤ **Keep items off floors and walls.** It is tempting to display that rare print or bold magazine cover on the wall. Resist the temptation; your heirs will be glad that you did. Elevate stored paper collectibles 6 to 10 inches off the floor to protect

Caveat Emptor

Little critters love to munch on paper collectibles. Check for unwanted visitors when you sort and store your ephemera.

Tricks of the Trade

To test the quality of pewter, draw it across a sheet of clean white paper. Fine pewter should leave almost no trace; lower-grade pewter, in contrast, leaves a pencil-like mark.

Modern pewter is sprayed with a sealant. Pewter that has turned dark is either an authentic and valuable antique or a cheap pewter imitation. If you suspect the former, take it to an expert. If you suspect the latter, don't buy the piece.

against floods. Never place printed material directly against a wall, especially an outside wall. Condensation can form. Toss in poor air circulation. The result? Mold and mildew.

➤ **Use proper storage containers.** Store books and paper items carefully. Polypropylene and polyethylene bags are fine for short-term storage of comics and books. Over time, however, the bags will break down. Place your printed material on enameled metal or sealed wooden shelves. In the presence of moisture, woods send off vapors. This forms an acidic compound that can eat away at paper.

➤ **Handle with care.** All printed materials should be handled carefully. Wash your hands before you touch these collectibles to prevent potentially corrosive oils from being deposited on the paper. Then lay the book or magazine on a flat surface. Turn the pages slowly to prevent damage to the spine, staples, or stitches.

➤ **Frame paper collectibles properly.** Frame shops can provide acidfree mats and special UV-filtering glass, both of which can help prevent damage.

Pewter

The term *pewter* refers to metal that is created by combining different amounts of white alloys, tin, lead, and antimony. The tin content determines the grade of the pewter. According to standards established by the British and American Pewter Guilds, "fine pewter" must contain at least 92 percent tin. Since tin is expensive and lead is not, low-grade pewter can contain as much as 50 percent lead; "pewterlike" collectibles may contain as much as 75 percent lead. As a result, many different grades of pewter are available to collectors.

Since pewter is a relatively soft metal, keep it away from extreme sources of heat, such as radiators. It's not a great idea to bake it in the sun, either.

Photographs

Who are we kidding? You finally got that gorgeous photograph you've been coveting, so of course you're going to frame it and enjoy it. And so you should, says our hedonistic side. Let the neighbors drool, and the picture fade. But our obsessive side says: No, no, no! Don't display your collectible photos that way! Here's what you should do and why.

Web Wise

The Chicago Photographic Collectors Society promotes the history of photography and photo equipment. It's on the Web at www.chicagophotographic.org.

1. **Be good.** The American National Standards Institute recommends that you store black-and-white prints and negatives in non-buffered materials. They really want you to store *all* your photos in the dark and under cover in the driest possible environment. What works for prudes works for photos.

2. **Here's why.** Color photographs are less stable than black-and-white photographs because their dyes fade erratically. For example, blues may fade out before yellows. It's because color transparencies use organic dyes, which are not durable. Color photos are especially sensitive to UV light. They can be kept more stable if they are stored at cool temperatures.

Stuffed Toys

Keep stuffed toys away from direct sunlight; they will fade. In this context, "stuffed toys" is an oxymoron, because these "toys" are collectibles that are meant to be displayed, not handled. Consider displaying them on shelves high enough to discourage handling.

Wood

Since wood is a living material, it will change with increases and decreases in moisture. When the air is very humid, wood will swell; when it is very dry, wood can shrink and crack. Normal changes in temperature and humidity will not affect properly dried and seasoned wood—but quick and drastic changes will. Follow these suggestions to correctly store wooden collectibles such as furniture and statues.

➤ Don't place valuable wooden collectibles such as antique furniture near air conditioners, air ducts, or radiators.

➤ Don't expose collectible wood to direct sunlight. The light will bleach the wood and lighten its color.

Big Deals

As of May 31, 1993, George E. Terren of Southboro, Massachusetts, has the world's largest collection of miniature liquor bottles—31,804.

Is Cleanliness Really Next to Godliness?

It's spring and the urge to clean has stolen upon you, like your four-year-old's desire to play at 5 A.M. on the only day all week that you can sleep late. The house smells damp and musty; the closets are sour and stale. A perfect excuse to clean your collectibles, you think. But time is short. Why not toss the lot into the dishwasher? The washing machine?

Caveat Emptor

The first rule of cleaning a collectible is **conservation:** Do nothing that cannot be undone. When in doubt, keep your hands to yourself and consult an expert in cleaning fine collectibles.

Stop. Take a deep breath. When the urge to clean collectibles comes upon you, arrange the Band-aids in size order or alphabetize your canned goods. When you have calmed down, turn back to your collection. Then start with these general guidelines. Follow the steps for each specific type of collectible.

Don't clean any collectible ...

➤ If you are tired or feeling under the weather.
➤ Unless you have sufficient time to complete the task from start to finish.
➤ If you are not sure of the process.
➤ Unless you have all the right tools.
➤ Unless you have clearly identified the material from which the item is made.

Some collectibles are exceptionally durable. For example, museums are filled with porcelain vases that have survived foreign wars, domestic battles, and maniacal cleaning fits. It's pretty hard to destroy a coin, and nails are as hard as, well, nails.

But other collectibles are very fragile. Paper, such as books, stamps, prints, postcards, playing cards, baseball cards, paper money, and comics, can deteriorate very quickly in adverse conditions. Antique textiles can be very fragile, too. Depending on their material and construction, some collectibles require considerably more care than others.

Furthermore, what's good for one collectible could be devastating to another. Too much care can be as damaging as too little—and sometimes more so. Certain cleaning processes could bleach antique light colors as white as rice—or leave the fabric in tatters. That said, let the cleaning begin.

Ceramics

Because porcelain is the hardest of all the ceramics, it requires the least care. Since it is completely impervious to water, it's easiest to clean. Don't take this as carte blanche to put your Ming vase in the dishwasher, however. Many porcelain items are extremely fragile. The greatest threat to these items is breakage. Follow these steps when cleaning ceramic products:

Tricks of the Trade

Office-supply stores offer compressed air in a can, used for removing dust from delicate computer parts. You might be able to use this product to clean certain collectibles, too.

➤ You can easily clean slightly dusty items by brushing gently with a small, soft brush.

➤ Don't use feather dusters and cleaning cloths on porcelain figurines and statues. A piece of the statue can catch on the cloth and break off.

➤ There's nothing wrong with using your lungs and simply blowing off a light coating of dust. No windstorms here, though. Don't go for the first-place ribbon in the hog-calling contest. You're not auditioning for the Italian opera. Nice short, gentle, even puffs.

➤ When the porcelain is more soiled, it's bath time. You will need two sinks or basins. Follow these steps:

Tricks of the Trade

Use baby shampoo to clean your china. It's gentle and doesn't leave a thick film. (In a pinch, it's also a great cleaning agent for hard and gas-permeable contact lenses, as well as a great eye-makeup remover.)

1. Line each basin with a thick layer of soft towels.

2. Fill the first basin with a dash of gentle detergent and warm water.

3. Fill the second basin with $\frac{1}{4}$ to $\frac{1}{2}$ cup of white vinegar and warm water.

4. Immerse the collectible in the first basin and then rinse in the second.

5. Let the piece air dry.

6. Never wash more than piece at a time.

Here are two neat cleaning suggestions:

1. To make a crack seem to disappear, first soak the object for a few hours in distilled water. Then mix one part hydrogen peroxide to three parts water. Add a drop of ammonia. Give it a nice soak again.

2. To get rid of food stains on china, try a foaming denture cleaner. Test a small, unobtrusive part first. Fruit and ink stains respond well to a paste of household salt. Rust remover works on ... you guessed it, rust!

Copper

Unlike silver, copper likes it a little tougher. You can remove small scratches with jeweler's rouge, but something grossly discolored with verdigris needs a harder approach. Start with copper cleaner. If that doesn't work, you can try bleach in boiling water. In extreme cases, a powder cleaner will remove stubborn stains.

Glass and Crystal

The cleaner your glass is, the more it will sparkle. Sparkle is what **glass** does best. Therefore, you should dust your glass collectible daily with a light brush. You should also floss twice a day and get at least 60 minutes of moderate exercise three times a week. So for those of you, like me, who are too busy flossing and jogging to clean your glass collectibles every day, try these cleaning hints:

➤ Experts are divided on recommended methods for cleaning fine crystal. One crystal-cleaning camp suggests this method: Soak large pieces in a basin of warm **water to** which ½ cup of clear ammonia has been added. Rinse in another basin that contains warm water and a dash of clear vinegar.

➤ Another school of thought inveighs against ammonia and water. They recommend washing crystal in isopropyl alcohol because it evaporates completely, leaving no film. I favor this method, but the smell always knocks me for a loop.

➤ Don't soak crystal figurines.

➤ Wear white cotton gloves when you clean your crystal to prevent smudges and fingerprints.

"Sick glass" has a permanently frosted look. You can have the piece professionally polished to remove outside marks, but inside the bottle is much harder to clean. Gloss over the problem by attaching a piece of cotton to the end of a stick. Soak the cotton in mineral oil and rub it over the marks until they disappear. Cork the bottle to prevent the oil from evaporating.

Iron

Cast iron is brittle and so must be handled carefully. Unfortunately, it is also a magnet for rust. I prefer to leave the rust because it marks the item as authentic, but if you tend toward compulsive, you can use fine steel wool and oil to work off the rust. Be careful: The item will cease to look antique if you get carried away.

Paper Collectibles

Dust your framed prints quickly and lightly with a lintfree cloth or feather duster. If the print is very dirty, remove it from the wall to clean. Don't try to clean it while it's still hanging; it could fall and the glass shatter. More serious for a collector, the dust could work its way behind the glass and damage the print. Here's how to do it:

➤ Hold the print on an angle so the dust falls away.

➤ Never spray any glass cleaner directly on the surface. The liquid could seep into the frame and damage the print. Instead, gently clean the glass with a cloth that has been lightly dampened with a mild glass-cleaning solution.

➤ Water damages wood. Clean the frame with a dry cloth.

Caveat Emptor

The Professional Picture Framers Association warns that framed art is not protected forever—regardless of the method used to frame the art. Check the print or picture often for signs of discoloration or insects. You may need to take the print to a framer for evaluation and, if necessary, repair.

Pewter

Like most metal collectibles, pewter is easy to clean. But the quality of the pewter dictates how much cleaning it can take. In the past, pewter was kept gleaming by scrubbing it with oil or sand and rushes. Today, tastes have changed.

➤ Remove surface dirt from pewter with a soft brush. Work downward and blow away the dust.

➤ If necessary, pewter can be washed. Soak the object in water. Keep it relatively cool; pewter melts easily.

➤ Use a mild soap and rinse completely.

➤ If this doesn't restore your pewter to its original tone, you need the services of a professional pewter cleaner.

Silver

Clean large silver items with a soft cloth or sponge and the highest-quality plate powder you can find. Be sure that the cleaning powder is soft enough not to scratch but strong enough to tackle tarnish and discoloration. Remember that silver is a soft metal, so be especially gentle on embossed (raised) surfaces. Wear plastic gloves; this stuff is nasty to hands. You can attack recalcitrant stains with a mixture of jeweler's rouge and water.

Stuffed Toys

Some older stuffed toys, especially bears, are filled with materials that may attract unwelcome visitors of the insect variety. If you suspect that your stuffed collectibles have unwanted houseguests, you can strip the doll or bear down and give it a chemical bath. First, remove any of the bear's leather or plastic detailing. If these accessories do not come off, stop. Take the collectible to a professional for debugging.

But if you *can* get the bear bare, place it in a container that you have lined with unbleached muslin. Fill two muslin bags with moth crystals, and place them next to the bear. Seal the container. Wait about a month. Decant and air out.

Vacuum your collectible stuffed toys. Follow these easy steps:

➤ Place cheesecloth over the toy first to protect eyes and other delicate parts that might be worked loose by too much suction.

➤ Clean the creature's eyes with dry cotton swabs.

➤ Use cornmeal to remove stains. Sprinkle a teaspoon directly on the stain. Allow 24 hours for it to set. Then vacuum.

➤ Be very, very careful about using chemical stain removers. I don't recommend them because they can discolor plush. If you feel utterly compelled to use a chemical stain remover on a stuffed collectible, be sure to first test it on a hidden part of the body.

Caveat Emptor

Many modern collectible bears and cloth dolls are touted as "washable." Don't believe it. You can wash these collectibles, but you're gambling big time. Washed bears can become stiff, limp, or even disintegrate. Dyes can bleed or mottle. Trims can become damaged; eyes and internal metal parts can rust.

Wood

Under no circumstances should wood be washed. In general, clean your wooden treasures with a soft, untreated cloth. I do not recommend any wax or cleaning compound because it could damage the surface.

Big Deals

Let's twist again, like we did last summer .... Starting in 1950, Helge Friholm of Soborg, Denmark, has amassed 73,832 different bottle caps from 179 countries. Her collection made the *Guiness Book of World Records*. Don't get any ideas from this, Gentle Reader.

The Least You Need to Know

➤ Sloppy storage can speed up the deterioration of your collectibles or even damage them, so store everything correctly.

➤ Match the method of storage to the specific collectible.

➤ Keep your collectibles clean.

➤ If you're not sure how to clean an object, leave it alone or hire an expert to do the job.

Future Collectibles

The forecast is good—collecting will continue be a pleasurable and lucrative hobby. Certainly collectors in the year 2096 will be willing to pay a fortune for today's ephemera. It's not too late to get in on the fun and profits. Here's how.

How do items become hot collectibles? Which pop-culture icons are going to rise in value—and which ones should be heaved into the trash compactor now?

Rule #1: When the demand for an item is greater than the supply, the market price will rise.

Rule #2: When enough people begin to collect an item that was previously only functional, the item will increase in price.

Okay, so how do you do it? To determine which things will become the sizzlin' collectibles of the future, figure out what people are *not* collecting today. I know, that's easier said than done. The collectors' explosion has called attention to the fact that virtually anything can become collectible. Items that people sneered at a decade ago—beer cans, magazines, bottle caps, toothpick holders, modern toys—have all become valuable today. As a result, people are saving everything—or so it seems. But there are still a few untouched areas to explore.

Here is my forecast. If you decide to squirrel away any of these items, make personal pleasure, rather than profit, your prime motive.

Ephemera

I think ephemera of all sorts is going to continue to be a much-desired collectible. I see all throwaway items growing in popularity. Today's hottest items are discussed in Chapter 9, "Pulp (Non)Fiction," so here's my prediction for future collectibles:

➤ **It's all in the packaging.** Advertising pieces, made of tin, glass, and wood, from the nineteenth and early twentieth centuries are already very collectible, but their counterparts from the present are often ignored. Consider looking more carefully at contemporary promotional items for cigarettes, drinks, and automobiles.

➤ **Trick or treat.** As the world becomes increasingly politically correct, we'll see fewer Halloween masks and costumes. Right now, witch masks are on the wane because they discriminate against those who practice the ancient religion called "Wicca"; hobo masks are a no-no because they mock the homeless. So stash those costumes in a safe place. And don't forget to keep the boxes!

Tricks of the Trade

Consider coffins as collectibles. People will still die in the future, but we may not have six feet in which to plant 'em. A choice coffin from today may command a hefty price in the next century.

Caveat Emptor

Collecting plastic is not without its perils. The Tupperware collection at the Museum of Modern Art is discoloring, and it smells terrible. A set of 1946 plastic nesting bowls in the collection is a molten mess—toxic as well as unsightly. Some plastics are so unstable and subject to uncharted chemical reactions that no one quite knows how to protect them. Let the collector beware.

➤ **A day at the races.** Anything associated with gambling has captured the public's imagination. Think about assembling a collection of ephemeral items associated with racetracks (both horses and dogs), the different state lotteries, and casinos.

➤ **A night at the opera.** Culture is a biggie, too. Go for contemporary theater posters, programs, and autographs. Menus are especially promising.

➤ **I'm all business.** Save personal business cards from famous people—especially if you can get the cards with autographs.

➤ **Hope on the horizon.** AIDS ephemera—posters, leaflets, and the like—are already being collected in anticipation of a cure.

➤ **Blast off.** Space-age toy models from the late 1950s and 1960s, inspired by *Sputnik* and the *Apollo* missions, are usually tin and sell for $50 to $250 now. The 1970s brought less desirable, but still collectible, plastic toys. These should cost you $5 to $25 at local flea markets.

Space-related items, such as postcards and pamphlets, can still be obtained for very little. Now is the time to look carefully at space-related items, especially ephemera such as stamps, photographs, and autographs of astronauts. Get on the shuttle before the race for spaceiana blasts off!

➤ **Hit the road, Mac.** If every car is going to be equipped with a computerized guidance system, drivers in the future won't include any Wrong-Way Corrigans. And there won't be any maps, either. As a result, gas station maps may be next century's antiquities. Pundits predict that the most valuable maps will be those of today's wide open spaces, which will become tomorrow's suburbs. Think Colorado, Idaho, and the Dakotas.

➤ **ET, phone home.** The ink is barely dry on phone cards, and already they're a hot collectible—in all forms. For example, there's a price guide devoted to phone cards that bear the images of cartoon characters. Called *Comics e Cartoons Phone Cards*, it's by Elizabetha Minella (Epierre; 1998). It's written in English and Italian.

The Future Is Plastic

Plastic is currently gaining great popularity among collectors. Because of this, I think that plastic items such as cereal bowls, banks, figurines, and novelty toys will become even more desirable. Buy plastic items that are special in some way. Look for a clever design, bright color, unusual action, and interesting purpose. Here are some specific ideas:

➤ **Opposites attract.** Refrigerator magnets have their fans. Since this collectible is still very low-profile, keep the ones you have clean and away from direct sunlight. Hey, you never know.

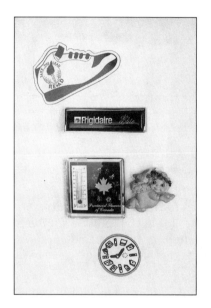

Stuck on you.

➤ **Snowglobes.** These globes are little plastic paperweights, filled with water and "snow," that depict a scene. When the globe is shaken, it looks like it is snowing. It's pretty … and no one has to shovel real snow. What could be better?

➤ **Live long and prosper.** You know that Disneyana is already an important collectible. I predict that in the future, many items that bear a famous cartoon or movie character will be hot. Peanuts, Garfield, Star-Trek, Star Wars—look for characters who made a great impact on the public's consciousness now.

Web Wise

The McDonald's Collectors Club is at www.mcdclub.com.

*May the (collectible) force
be with you.*

Bits and Bytes

Remember that most collectibles are items that are still being produced, albeit in a different form. We still collect china, which has been made for centuries; glassware, books, furniture, and paintings are all popular collectibles.

Computer memorabilia seems a likely bet for the future collectibles markets because it is changing very quickly yet will be around in the future. Pamphlets, books, advertising, hardware, software, postcards, computer watches, and hand-held calculators are all things to consider saving. Hand-held calculators, in fact, have already become established as a collectible.

When putting aside an item that you think will become a future collectible, remember to save the entire package: the box, instructions, and the item.

Gaze Into My Crystal Ball

Here are some other predictions from my (collectible) crystal ball. Take the ideas that appeal to you. Remember: Storage space is limited and you have to live with all this stuff.

➤ **The medium is the message.** The T-shirt craze took off about 40 years ago, when simple shirts became the canvas for advertising and personal expression. By the 1970s, young and old alike were sporting T-shirts hyping their favorite drink, band, state, political affiliation, drug, leisure-time activity, sport, movie, food, or belief. Hand-lettered, silk-screened T-shirts might just be the clothing collectibles of the future.

➤ **Royal nonsense.** If Chuck and Di's divorce is any indication, we may be seeing the end of the royal line in England. Devout Anglophiles have always cherished the likeness of their favorite royal on a *beaker* (mug), but if the royals go the way of the Edsel, royal family souvenirs may be worth more than the pound.

➤ **Get the scent.** For years, people have been collecting lovely perfume bottles. What about the contents? The scents of today are the memories of tomorrow. Ever since the late pop artist and cultural trendsetter Andy Warhol began collecting designer perfume, those in the know got on the scent. So think about stashing away today's best perfumes.

Caveat Emptor

Perfume is a very difficult collectible to store in mint condition. Like fine wine, exquisite perfumes lose their bouquet. They also evaporate.

VidKids

Video madness is upon us, as people line up outside their local movie store clamoring for the latest release. In just a few short years, video has become a way of life for most Americans. Consider saving material related to videos. Here are some ideas:

➤ Original releases, especially of movies that were released in two or more versions

➤ Posters

➤ Novelties

➤ Toys and games

➤ Stickers

➤ Video games and game systems

Web Wise

The Anime Toy Collections site includes information on Sailor Moon, Marmalade Boy, Magical Knight Rayearth, Samurai Pizza Cats, Gatchaman, Pokémon, and more. They're at www. webring.org/cgi-bin/webring?ring= innermoon;l.

A few final suggestions. First, look for items linked to big stories, such as national scandals, historical events, and national movements. Possibilities include Watergate, the first test-tube baby, and feminism. There is already a hot market for items linked to the Kennedy assassination; a market is developing for Watergate memorabilia.

Second, take a look at what children are playing with now. These toys and novelties are apt to be popular in 30 years—when those same children have grown up. They will create the demand for the items of their youth.

311

Chuckie's hot now. Will he chill tomorrow?

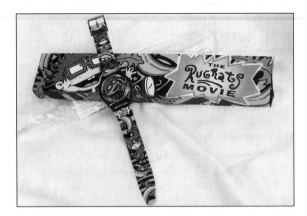

Vice

What are the hot symbols of vice? Cigarettes, condoms, playing cards, and booze. In the future, they may be the hot collectibles as well.

➤ **Cigarettes.** In the 1600s, the Puritans believed that tobacco was good for whatever ailed ya'. They even gave their horses a puff from the old cheroot to whisk away evil spirits. Today we know enough to keep the stogies away from Mr. Ed—see how much progress we've made in 300 years? Any century now, tobacco will be outlawed. When that happens, the smart cookies who have unopened packages of cigarettes, cigars, and chewing tobacco will command more than smoke. Remember how the invention of lighters made matches a collectible?

➤ **Sex.** Like chastity belts, the day will come when condoms will be a curiosity and collectible. In the future, people will have developed less cumbersome methods of birth control than condoms … or they will have figured out another way to pass the time when there's nothing on cable.

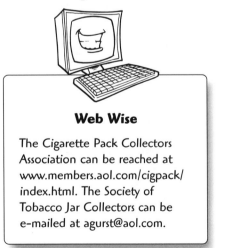

Web Wise

The Cigarette Pack Collectors Association can be reached at www.members.aol.com/cigpack/index.html. The Society of Tobacco Jar Collectors can be e-mailed at agurst@aol.com.

➤ **Gambling.** Remember Atari's Pong? It was the first of the video games. That little ball went boing, boing, boing across the screen until you were ready to scream. How prehistoric that video game seems now. But in the future, even today's glitzy videopoker will seem as old-fashioned as virginity. So stash away unopened packages of playing cards against the day when all games beep and buzz.

➤ **Booze.** You know that beer bottles and other alcoholic beverage bottles are popular collectibles. Consider related collectibles such as labels and corkscrews. But move fast; there's already an association of corkscrew collectors (CorkscrewNet at www.corkscrewnet.com).

Further Reading

Americana

Morykan, Dana, and Harry Rinker. *Warman's Country Antiques & Collectibles*. Iola, WI: Krause, 1999.

Schroy, Ellen T. *Warman's Americana & Collectibles*. Iola, WI: Krause, 1999.

Art

Andacht, Sandra. *Japanese Woodblock Prints*. Iola, WI: Krause, 1999.

Brown, Jay. *The Complete Guide to Art Prints: How to Identify, Invest & Care for Your Collection*. Iola, WI: Krause, 1999.

Naifeh, Steven. *The Bargain Hunter's Guide to Art Collecting*. New York: Morrow, 1982.

Autographs

Martin, Kevin. *The 1999 Official Autograph Collector Price Guide*. Odyssey Publications, 1999.

Banks, Mechanical

Rogers, Carole G. *Penny Banks: A History and Handbook*. New York: E. P. Dutton, 1977.

Baseball Cards

Baseball's Top 500: Card Checklist & Price Guide. Edited by Sports Collectors Digest. Iola, WI: Krause, 1999.

Beckett, James, ed. *Beckett Baseball Card Price Guide*. No. 21. Beckett, 1999.

Beckett, James, and Dennis Eckes. *The Sport Americana Baseball Card Price Guide*. Laurel, MD: Den's Collectors Den, 1999.

Erbe, Ron. *The American Premium Guide to Baseball Cards*. Florence, AL: Books Americana, 1982.

Fritsch, Jeff. *Baseball Card Team Checklist*. No. 7. Edgewater Book Co., 1995.

Beanie Babies

Brecka, Shawn. *The Bean Family Pocket Guide*. Iola, WI: Krause, 1999.

Phillips, Becky, and Becky Estenssoro. *Beanie Mania Guidebook: Your Guide to Collecting Beanie Babies*. Dinomates, Inc., 1998.

Stowe, Holly, and Carol A. Turkington. *The Pocket Idiot's Guide to Beanie Babies*. New York: Macmillan, 1998.

Ty Plush Animals: Secondary Market Price Guide & Collector Handbook. CheckerBee Publishing, 1999.

Bears

Brecka, Shawn. *Big Book of Little Bears*. Iola, WI: Krause, 1999.

Mandel, Margaret Fox. *Teddy Bears and Steiff Animals*. Collector Books, 1984.

——. *Teddy Bears and Steiff Animals: Second Series*. Collector Books, 1996.

——. *Teddy Bears, Annalee's and Steiff Animals: Third Series*. Collector Books, 1997.

Yenke, Ken. *Teddy Bear Treasury: Identification and Values*.

The Beatles

Stern, Michael, and Barbara Crawford. *The Beatles: A Reference & Value Guide*. Collector Books: 1998.

Beer Cans

Beer Can Collectors of America. *The Beer Can*. Fenton, MS: Beer Can Collectors of America. Ace Books, 1981.

Toepfer, Thomas. *American Beer Can Encyclopedia*. Paducah, KY: Collector Books, 1976.

Books

Bookman's Price Index: A Guide to the Value of Rare and Out of Print Books. Detroit, MI: Gale Research Company, 1999.

Bradley, Van Allen. *The Book Collector's Handbook of Values*. New York: G. P. Putnam.

Huxford, Bob, and Sharon Huxford. *Huxford's Old Book Value Guide: 25,000 Listings of Old Books with Current Values*. 11th edition. Collector Books, 1997.

Jacobs, Larry. *Big Little Books: A Collector's Reference & Value Guide*. Collector Books, 1996.

Mandeville, Mildred S. *The Used Book Price Guide*. Kenmore, WA: Price Guide Publishers, 1983.

McClure Jones, Diane, and Rosemary Jones. *Collector's Guide to Children's Books 1850 to 1950: Identification & Values*. Collector Books, 1996.

Bottles

Creswick, Alice. *Fruit Jars: The Collector's Guide to Old Fruit Jars*. Grand Rapids, MI: Alice Creswick.

Hastin, Bud. *Avon: Avon Bottle Encyclopedia*. Ft. Lauderdale, FL: Bud Hastin, Collector Books, 1998.

Kay, Robert E. *Miniature Bottles: Miniature Beer Bottles and Go-Withs*. Batavia, IL: K & K Publications, 1980.

Kovel, Ralph, and Terry Kovel. *The Kovels' Bottle Price List, 11th edition*. New York: Crown, 1999.

Montague, H. F. *Modern Bottle Identification and Price Guide*, Overland Park, KA: H. F. Montague Enterprises.

Polak, Michael. *Bottles: Identification and Price Guide, 2nd edition*. Avon Books, 1997.

Celluloid

Dunn, Shirley. *Celluloid Collectibles: Identification & Value Guide*. Collector Books, 1996.

Lauer, Keith, and Julie Robinson. *Celluloid Collectors Reference and Value Guide*. Collector Books, 1999.

China and Pottery

Bagdade, Susan, and Al Bagdade. *Warman's American Pottery and Porcelain*. Iola, WI: Krause, 1999.

——. *Warman's English & Continental Pottery & Porcelain*. Iola, WI: Krause, 1999.

Cox, Susan N. *20th Century American Ceramics*. Iola, WI: Krause. 1996.

Degenhardt, Richard K. *Belleek*. Wallace-Homestead Books, 1993.

Husfloen, Kyle. *American & European Pottery Price Guide*. Iola, WI: Krause. 1995.

Kamm, Dorothy. *Antique Trader's Guide to American Painted Porcelain*. Iola, WI: Krause, 1997.

Miller, Muriel. *Royal Winton Collector's Handbook*. Iola, WI: Krause, 1999.

Clocks

Swedberg, Robert W., and Harriett Swedberg. *American Clocks and Clockmakers*. Iola, WI: Krause, 1999.

——. *Price Guide to Antique Clocks*. Iola, WI: Krause, 1999.

Coca-Cola Memorabilia

Petretti, Alan. *Coca-Cola Calendars*. Iola, WI: Krause, 1999.

——. *Classic Coca-Cola Serving Trays*. Iola, WI: Krause, 1999.

——. *Coca-Cola Collectibles Price Guide*. Iola, WI: Krause, 1999.

Schaeffer, Randy. *Price Guide to New and Vintage Coca-Cola Memorabilia*. Courage Books, 1995.

Coins

Alexander, Davit T., et al. *Coin World Comprehensive Catalog & Encyclopedia of United States Coins*. New York: World Almanac, 1990.

Bowers, Q. David. *Adventures with Rare Coins*. Los Angeles: Bowers and Ruddy Galleries, 1980.

——. *A Buyer's Guide to the Rare Coin Market*. Wolfeboro: NH: Bowers and Merena Galleries, 1990.

——. *Coins and Collectors*. Wolfeboro, NH: Bowers and Merena Galleries, 1988.

——. *Commemorative Coins of the United States: A Complete Encyclopedia*. Wolfeboro, NH: Bowers and Merena Galleries, 1991.

——. *United States Coins by Design Types*. Wolfeboro, NH: Bowers and Merena Galleries, 1989.

Bressett, Ken. *Guide Book of United States Currency*.

Brown, Martin R., and John W. Dunn. *A Guide to the Grading of United States Coins, 5th edition*. Racine, WI: Western Publishing, 1969.

Erano, Paul. *Fountain Pens: Past & Present*. Collector Books, 1999.

Ganz, David L. *The World of Coins and Coin Collecting*. New York: Charles Scribner's Sons, 1985.

Gibbs, William T. *Coin World Guide to U.S. Coins, Prices & Value Trends: 2000, 11th edition*. Signet, 1999.

Handcock, Virgil, and Larry Spanbauer. *Standard Catalog of Counterfeit and Altered United States Coins*. New York: Sandford J. Durst, 1979.

Harper, David C., ed. *2000 North American Coins & Prices: A Guide to U.S., Canadian and Mexican Coins*. Iola, WI: Krause, 1999.

Hudgeons, Mark. *The Official Guide to Detecting Altered & Counterfeit U.S. Coins & Currency*. Orlando, FL: House of Collectibles, 1985.

Krause, Chester L. *2000 Standard Catalog of World Coins, 27th edition*. Iola, WI: Krause, 1999.

—. *2000 Standard Catalog of World Coins, 1701–1800, 2nd edition*. Iola, WI: Krause, 1999.

—. *2000 Standard Catalog of World Coins 1801–1900, 2nd edition*. Iola, WI: Krause, 1999.

Porteous, John. *Coins*. New York: G. P. Putnam's Sons, 1964.

Shafer, Neil. *A Guide to Modern United States Currency*. Racine, WI: Whitman Coin Products, Western Publishing, 1975.

Comic Books, Comic Art, Comic Strips

Overstreet, Robert. *The Overstreet Comic Book Price Guide*. New York: Avon Books, 1996.

Disneyana

Tumbusch, Tom. *Tomart's Disneyana Catalog and Price Guide*. Dayton, OH: Tomart Publications, 1989.

Dolls

Augustyniak, J. Michael. *The Barbie Doll Boom: Identification and Values*. Collector Books, 1996.

Cross, Carla Marie. *Modern Doll Rarities*. Iola, WI: Krause. Antique Trader, 1997.

Deutsch, Stefanie. *Barbie the First 30 Years, 1959 Through 1989: An Identification and Value Guide*. Collector Books, 1995.

Dolan, Maryanne. *The World of Dolls*. Iola, WI: Krause, 1998.

Eames, Sarah Sink. *Barbie Fashion, 1959–1967*. Collector Books, 1997.

Foulke, Jan, and Howard Foulke. *Blue Book of Dolls & Values, 13th edition*. Hobby House, 1997.

Herlocher, Dawn. *200 Years of Dolls*. Iola, WI: Krause, 1996.

—. *Doll Makers & Marks*. Iola, WI: Krause, 1999.

Herron, R. Lane. *Warman's Dolls*. Iola, WI: Krause, 1999.

Olds, Patrick C. *The Barbie Doll Years: A Comprehensive Listing & Value Guide of Dolls & Accessories, 3rd edition*. Collector Books, 1999.

Rana, Margo. *Barbie Doll Exclusively For Timeless Creations: Identification & Values, Book 3*. Hobby House, 1997.

Ephemera

Hake, Ted. *Hake's Guide to Advertising Collectibles: 100 Years of Advertising from 100 Famous Companies.* Dimensions, 1992.

Forgery and Fakes

The Chase, the Capture, Collecting at the Metropolitan. New York: The Metropolitan Museum, 1975.

Goodrich, D. L. *Art Fakes in America.* New York: Viking, 1973.

Grafton, Anthony. *Forgers and Critics: Creativity and Duplicity in Western Scholarship.* London: Collins & Brown, 1990.

Hebborn, Eric. *Drawn to Trouble: Confessions of a Master Forger.* New York: Random House, 1991.

Hoving, Thomas. *False Impressions: The Hunt for Big-Time Art Fakes.* New York: Simon & Schuster, 1996.

Jeppson, Lawrence. *The Fabulous Frauds: A Study of Great Art Forgeries.* London: Arlington Books, 1971.

Jones, Mark, ed. *Fake? The Art of Deception.* Berkeley and Los Angeles: University of California Press, 1990.

———. *Why Fakes Matter: Essays on Problems of Authenticity.* London: British Museum, 1992.

Kurz, Otto. *Fakes: A Handbook for Collectors and Students.* New Haven: Yale University Press, 1948.

Mendax, Fritz. *Art Fakes and Forgeries.* London: W. Laurie, 1955.

Savage, George. *Forgeries, Fakes and Reproductions.* London: Barrie and Rockcliff, 1963.

Furniture

Ketchum, William C. *The New and Revised Catalog of American Antiques.* New York: Gallery Books, 1980.

Smith, Nancy. *Old Furniture: Understanding the Craftsman's Art.* Boston: Little, Brown, 1976.

Williams, Henry L. *Country Furniture of Early America.* Cranbury, NJ: A. S. Barnes, 1963.

General Guides

Brecka, Shawn. *Collecting in Cyberspace.* Iola, WI: Krause, 1997.

Collector's Information Bureau. *Collectibles Market Guide & Price Index.* Iola, WI: Krause, 1999.

Husfloen, Kyle. *Antique Trader's Antiques & Collectibles Price Guide 2000.* Iola, WI: Krause, 2000.

Kovel, Ralph M. and Terry H. Kovel. *Kovels' Antiques & Collectibles Price List 2000: The Best-Selling Price Guide in America.* Three Rivers Press, 1999.

Maloney, David. *Maloney's Antiques and Collectibles Resource Directory.* Iola, WI: Krause, 1999.

Norfolk, Elizabeth, ed. *International Antiques Price Guide 2000.* Antique Collectors Club, 1999.

Plans, Miriam. *Antique Trader's Cashing in Your Collectibles.* Iola, WI: Krause, 1999.

Schroy, Ellen T. *Warman's Antiques & Collectibles Price Guide.* Iola, WI: Krause, 1999.

Vesely, Milan. *Antiques for Amateurs.* Iola, WI: Krause, 1999.

Warman's Today's Collector. *Today's Hottest Collectibles.* Iola, WI: Krause, 1998.

Willard, Joe. *Antique Secrets.* Iola, WI: Krause, 1999.

Glass

Bagdade, Susan, and Al Bagdade. *Warman's Pattern Glass.* Iola, WI: Krause, 1999.

Bredenhoft, Tom, and Neila Bredenhoft. *Fifty Years of Collectible Glass, 1920–1970.* Iola, WI: Krause, 1999.

Burns, Carl O. *Imperial Carnival Glass.* Collector Books, 1996.

Florence, Gene. *Kitchen Glassware of the Depression Years.*

——. *Collector's Encyclopedia of Depression Glass.* Collectors Books, 1999.

Husfloen, Karl. *Collector's Guide to American Pressed Glass.* Iola, WI: Krause, 1992.

Kovel, Ralph M., and Terry H. Kovel. *Kovels' Depression Glass & American Dinnerware Price List, 5th edition.* Three Rivers Press, 1998.

Luckey, Carl. *Depression Era Glassware Identification & Value Guide.* Books Americana, 1995.

Quentin-Baxendale, Marion. *Collecting Carnival Glass.* Wallace-Homestead, 1998.

Schroy, Ellen. *Warman's Depression Glass.* Iola, WI: Krause, 1999.

——. *Warman's Glass.* Iola, WI: Krause, 1999.

Shuman, John A. *The Collector's Encyclopedia of American Art Glass.* Collector Books, 1987.

Swan, Martha Louise. *American Cut and Engraved Glass: The Brilliant Period in Historical Perspective.* Wallace-Homestead, 1994.

Jewelry

Baker, Lillian. *Fifty Years of Collectible Fashion Jewelry 1925–1975*. (Values updated in 1992.) Paducah, KY: Collector Books, 1986.

Ball, Joanne Dubbs. *Costume Jewelers: The Golden Age of Design*. West Chester, PA: Schiffer, 1990.

Ball, Joanne Dubbs, and Dorothy Torem. *Masterpieces of Costume Jewelry*. Atglen, PA: Schiffer, 1996.

Becker, Vivienne. *Antique and 20th Century Jewelery*. London: N.A.G. Press, 1980.

——. *Fabulous Fakes: The History of Fantasy and Fashion Jewelry*. London: Grafton Books, 1988; reprint, Atglen, PA: Schiffer, 1993.

Bell, Jeanenne. *Answers to Questions About Old Jewelry*. Florence, AL: Books Americana, 1985.

Dolan, Maryanne. *Collecting Rhinestone and Colored Jewelry*. 3rd edition. Florence, AL: Books Americana, 1989; reprint 1993.

Ettinger, Roseann. *Forties and Fifties Popular Jewelry*. Atglen, PA: Schiffer, 1994.

Farneti Cera, Deanna, ed. *Jewels of Fantasy: Costume Jewelry of the 20th Century*. New York: Harry N. Abrams, 1992.

Farneti Cera, Deanna. *The Jewels of Miriam Haskell*. Wappinger Falls, New York: Antique Collectors' Club, 1997.

Goldemberg, Rose Leiman. *Antique Jewelry: A Practical and Passionate Guide*. New York: Crown Publishers, 1966.

Griendl, Gabriele. *Gems of Costume Jewelry*. New York: Abbeville, 1991.

Kelley, Lygerda, and Nancy Schiffer. *Costume Jewelry: The Great Pretenders*. Atglen, PA: Schiffer, 1987.

Lynnlee, J. L. *All That Glitters*. Atglen, PA: Schiffer, 1986.

Mariotti, Gabriella. *All My Baskets. American Costume Jewelry 1930–1960*. Milan: Franco Maria Ricci, 1996.

Miller, Harrice Simons. *Costume Jewelry Identification and Price Guide*. New York: Avon Books, 1994.

Moro, Ginger. *European Designer Jewelry*. Atglen, PA: Schiffer, 1995.

Simonds, Cherri. *Collectible Costume Jewelry: Identification & Values*. Paducah, KY: Collector Books, 1997.

Schiffer, Nancy. *The Best of Costume Jewelry*. Atglen, PA: Schiffer, 1990.

——. *Costume Jewelry, The Fun of Collecting*. Atglen, PA: Schiffer, 1992.

——. *Fun Jewelry*. (Values updated in 1996.) Atglen, PA: Schiffer, 1991.

Kitchen Collectibles

Bercovici, Ellen, et al. *Collectibles for the Kitchen, Bath, & Beyond*. Antique Trader, 1998.

Davern, Melva. *Collector's Encyclopedia of Salt and Pepper Shakers: Second Series*. Collector Books, 1990.

Franklin, Linda Campbell. *300 Years of Kitchen Collectibles*. Iola, WI: Krause, 1998.

McNerney, Kathryn. *Kitchen Antiques, 1790–1940*. Collector Books, 1991.

Roerig, Fred, and Joyce Herndon Roerig. *Collector's Encyclopedia of Cookie Jars, Book I*. Collector Books, 1994.

——. *Collector's Encyclopedia of Cookie Jars, Book II*. Collector Books, 1991.

Westfall, Ermagene. *An Illustrated Value Guide to Cookie Jars*. Collector Books, 1983.

Marbles

Baumann, Paul. *Antique Marbles*. Iola, WI: Krause, 1999.

Grist, Everett. *Antique and Collectible Marbles*. Collector Books, 1992.

Metals

Dodge, Fred. *Antique Tins: Identification & Values*. Collector Books, 1994.

Dolan, Maryanne. *American Sterling Silver Flatware 1830s–1990s: A Collector's Identification and Value Guide*. Books Americana, 1992.

Gaston, Mary Frank. *Antique Brass & Copper Identification & Value Guide*. Collector Books, 1991.

Grist, Everett. *Collectible Aluminum/An Identification and Value Guide Including: Hammered, Wrought, Forged, and Cast*. Collector Books, 1993.

McNereny, Kathryn. *Antique Iron: Identification and Values*. Collector Books, 1989.

Movie Memorabilia

Dietz, James S. Jr. *Price Guide and Introduction to Movie Posters and Movie Memorabilia*. San Diego, CA: Baja Press.

Gallo, Max. *The Poster in History*. New York: American Heritage Publishing, 1974.

Hake, Theodore, and Robert D. Cauler. *Six-Gun Heroes: A Price Guide to Movie Cowboy Collectibles*. Des Moines, IA: Wallace Homestead Books, 1976.

Kidder, Clark. *Marilyn Monroe: Cover to Cover*. Iola, WI: Krause, 1999.

Paper and Paper Collectibles

Reed, Robert. *Paper Advertising Collectibles*. Iola, WI: Krause, 1999.

Utz, Gene. *Collecting Paper: A Collector's Identification & Value Guide*. Iola, WI: Krause, 1999.

Paper Money

Berman, Allen. *Warman's Coins and Paper Money: A Value & Identification Guide*. Iola, WI: Krause, 1999.

Criswell, Grover C. Jr. *Colonel Grover Criswell's Compendium, a Guide to Confederate Money*. Brannon Publishing, 1991.

Friedberg, Robert. *Paper Money of the United States*. 12th edition. Clifton, NJ: Coin and Currency Institute, 1989.

Krause, Chester L., and Robert F. Lemke. *Standard Catalog of United States Paper Money, 18th edition*. Iola, WI: Krause, 1999.

Newman, Eric P. *Early Paper Money of America*. Iola, WI: Krause, 1999.

Nussbaum, Arthur. *A History of the Dollar*. New York: Columbia University Press, 1957.

Pick, Albert. *Standard Catalog of World Paper Money*. Iola, WI: Krause Publications, 1990.

Oakes, Dean, and John Schwartz. *Standard Guide to Small Size U.S. Paper Money*. Iola, WI: Krause, 1999.

Rochette, Edward. *Making Money*. Frederick, CO: Renaissance House Publishers, 1986.

Slabaugh, Arlie. *Confederate States Paper Money*. Iola, WI: Krause, 1999.

U.S. Secret Service, Department of the Treasury. *Know Your Money*. Washington, DC: U.S. Government Printing Office, 1991.

Photographs

Mace, O. Henry. *Collector's Guide to Early Photographs*. Iola, WI: Krause, 1999.

Postcards

Allmen, Diane. *The Official Price Guide to Postcards*. New York: House of Collectibles, 1990.

Mashburn, J. L. *The Postcard Price Guide, 3rd edition*. New York: Colonial House, 1997.

Menchene, Ron. *Propaganda Postcards of World War II*. Iola, WI: Krause, 1999.

Wood, Jane. *The Collector's Guide to Post Cards*. L-W Books, 1984 (value update 1997).

Records and Memorabilia

Docks, L. R. *1915–1965 American Premium Record Guide*. Florence, AL: Books Americana, 1982.

Guiheen, Anna Marie. *Sheet Music Reference and Price Guide*. Collector Books, 1995.

Heggeness, Fred, and Tim Neely. *Goldmine Promo Record & Cd Price Guide*. Krause Publications, 1999.

Koeningsberg, Allen. *Edison Cylinder Records 1889–1912*. Brooklyn, NY: Allen Koeningsberg, 1988.

Murray, R. Michael. *The Golden Age of Walt Disney Records 1933–1988*. Antique Trader Books, 1997.

Neely, Tim. *Goldmine Record Album Price Guide*. Krause Publications, 1999.

Neely, Tim, ed. *Goldmine Price Guide to 45 rpm Records, 2nd edition*. Krause Publications, 1999.

Osborne, Jerry. *The Official Price Guide to Compact Discs*. House of Collectibles, 1994.

——. *The Official Price Guide to Country Music Records*. House of Collectibles, 1996.

——. *The Official Price Guide to Movie/TV Soundtracks and Original Cast Albums*. House of Collectibles, 1997.

Sorderbergh, Peter A. *Olde Records 1900–1947: Popular and Classical 78 rpms*. Des Moines: Wallace Homestead, 1980.

Umphred, Neal. *Goldmine's Price Guide to Collectible Jazz Albums 1949–1969*. Krause Publications, 1994.

——. *Goldmine's Price Guide to Collectible Record Albums, 5th edition*. Krause Publications, 1999.

Stamps

Carlton, R. Scott. *The International Encyclopaedic Dictionary of Philately*. Iola, WI: Krause, 1999.

Dunair, Gary. *Stamps: The Beginning Collector*. New York: Mallard Press, 1992.

Furman, Robert. *The 1999 Comprehensive Catalogue of United States Stamp Booklets: Postage and Airmail*. Krause Publications, 1999.

MacDonald, Davis S., ed. *2000 Bookman United States, United Nations & Canada Stamps & Postal Collectibles*. Iola, WI: Krause, 1999.

Schwarz, Ted. *Beginner's Guide to Stamp Collecting*. New York: ARCO Publishers, 1983.

Scott Standard Postage Stamp Catalogue (five volumes). Sidney, Ohio: Scott Publishing Company: yearly.

Wozniak, Maurice. *2000 Krause-Minkis Standard Catalog of U.S. Stamps, 3rd edition.* Iola, WI: Krause, 1999.

Teapots

Carter, Tina. *Collectible Teapots.* Iola, WI: Krause, 1999.

Tools

McNerney, Kathryn. *Antique Tools … Our American Heritage.* Collector Books, 1983.

Toys and Games

Barber, Malcolm, and Dave Selby. *Miller's Collectors Cars Price Guide 2000. Mitchell Beazley, 2000.*

Cain, Dana. *Film & TV Animal Star Collectibles.* Antique Trader, 1998.

Gillam, James H. *Space Toys of the '60s.* Collectors Guide Publishing, 1999.

Hake, Ted. *Hake's Price Guide to Character Toy Premiums: Including Premiums, Comic, Cereal, TV, Movies, Radio & Related Store Bought Items.*

Huxford, Sharon. *Schroeder's Collectible Toys: Antique to Modern Price Guide, 6th edition.* 1999.

Huxford, Sharon, and Bob Huxford, eds. *Schroeder's Antiques Price Guide.* Paducah, KY: Collector Books, 1999.

Johnson, Dana. *Collectors Guide to Diecast Toys and Scale Models: Identification & Values.*

——. *Matchbox Toys 1947 to 1998: Identification & Value Guide, 3rd edition.*

Mackay, James. *Childhood Antiques.* New York: Taplinger Publishing, 1976.

Marsh, Hugo. *Toys and Games.* London: Miller's Antiques, 1995.

Rinker, Harry L. *The Official Price Guide to Collectibles.* New York: House of Collectibles, 2000.

Rinker Enterprises. *The Official Price Guide to Antiques and Collectibles.* New York, 2000.

Santelmo, Vincent. *GI Joe: Official Identification and Price Guide 1964–1999.*

Stephan, Elizabeth. *O'Brien's Collecting Toys: Identification and Value Guide, 9th edition.* Krause Publications, 1999.

Whitworth, Harry A., et al. *G-Men and F.B.I. Toys and Collectibles: Identification & Values.*

Index

333

337

339

X–Z